ECCE ROMANI

A LATIN READING PROGRAM

II·B

PASTIMES AND CEREMONIES

SECOND EDITION

ECCE ROMANI

A LATIN READING PROGRAM

II·B

PASTIMES AND CEREMONIES

SECOND EDITION

Longman

Ecce Romani Student Book II-B
Pastimes and Ceremonies, second edition

Longman, 10 Bank Street, White Plains, N.Y. 10606

Associated companies:
Longman Group Ltd., London
Longman Cheshire Pty., Melbourne
Longman Paul Pty., Auckland
Copp Clark Pitman, Toronto

This edition of *Ecce Romani* is based on *Ecce Romani: A Latin Reading Course*, originally prepared by The Scottish Classics Group © copyright The Scottish Classics Group 1971, 1982, and published in the United Kingdom by Oliver and Boyd, a division of Longman Group. It is also based on the 1988 North American edition. This edition has been prepared by a team of American educators.

Photo credits: Credits appear on page xi.

Acknowledgments: Reiterated thanks are due to the consultants who contributed to the 1988 North American edition of *ECCE ROMANI*: Dr. Rudolph Masciantonio, Ronald Palma, Dr. Edward Barnes, and Shirley Lowe. In addition to the authors and consultants who contributed to this new edition and who are listed separately, thanks are due to the following people: to Mary O. Minshall for providing original material for the Frontier Life essays; to Ursula Chen, Julia Gascoyne Fedoryk, and Franklin Kennedy for their help on the Teacher's Guides; and to Marjorie Dearworth Keeley for help with the preparation of the manuscript. Finally, thanks are due to Longman Publishing Group's production team: Janice Baillie and Helen Ambrosio; and its editorial team: Barbara Thayer and Lyn McLean, for all they did.

Executive editor: Lyn McLean
Development editor: Barbara Thayer
Production editor: Janice L. Baillie
Production-editorial and design director: Helen B. Ambrosio
Text design: Creatives NYC, Inc.
Cover design: Circa 86
Cover Illustration: Yao Zen Liu
Text art: Yao Zen Liu
Maps: Laszlo Kubinyi
Photo research: Barbara Thayer

ISBN: 0-8013-1207-8

12345678910-DOC-999897969594

REVISION EDITOR: GILBERT LAWALL
University of Massachusetts, Amherst, Massachusetts

AUTHORS AND CONSULTANTS

Peter C. Brush
Deerfield Academy
Deerfield, Massachusetts

Sally Davis
Arlington Public Schools
Arlington, Virginia

Pauline P. Demetri
Cambridge Rindge & Latin School
Cambridge, Massachusetts

Jane Hall
National Latin Exam
Alexandria, Virginia

Thalia Pantelidis Hocker
Old Dominion University
Norfolk, Virginia

Glenn M. Knudsvig
University of Michigan
Ann Arbor, Michigan

Maureen O'Donnell
W.T. Woodson High School
Fairfax, Virginia

Ronald Palma
Holland Hall School
Tulsa, Oklahoma

David J. Perry
Rye High School
Rye, New York

Deborah Pennell Ross
University of Michigan
Ann Arbor, Michigan

Andrew F. Schacht
Renbrook School
West Hartford, Connecticut

Judith Lynn Sebesta
University of South Dakota
Vermillion, South Dakota

The Scottish Classics Group
Edinburgh, Scotland

David Tafe
Rye Country Day School
Rye, New York

Rex Wallace
University of Massachusetts
Amherst, Massachusetts

Allen Ward
University of Connecticut
Storrs, Connecticut

Elizabeth Lyding Will
Amherst College
Amherst, Massachusetts

Philip K. Woodruff
Lake Forest High School
Lake Forest, Illinois

CONTENTS

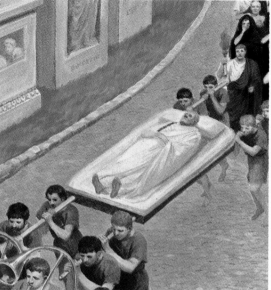

REFERENCE MATERIALS

MAPS

CREDITS

Special gratitude is extended to Jenny Page of The Bridgeman Art Library, London, for her invaluable assistance in locating illustrative materials sought for *ECCE ROMANI.*

The publisher gratefully acknowledges the contributions of the agencies, institutions, and photographers listed below:

Chapter 43
(p. 5) Photograph of a bronze oil flask and two strigils, reproduced by courtesy of The Trustees of the British Museum, London

(p. 9) Drawing of Hadrian's Baths at Lepcis Magna, reprinted by permission of the publisher George Braziller, Inc.

Chapter 44
(p. 17) "The Citharist from Stabia," scene from New Comedy, Pompeiian Wall Fresco, 1st Century A.D., Museo Nazionale di San Martino, Naples/ Bridgeman Art Library, London

Chapter 45
(p. 19) Art by Mahmoud Sayah in *The Rubaiyat of Omar Khayyam*, Random House, New York, 1947

(p. 25) "Ovid Among the Scythians" by Eugene Delacroix (1798–1863) National Gallery, London/Bridgeman Art Library, London

Chapter 46
(p. 35) Photograph courtesy Alinari/Art Resource, New York

(p. 43) "Girls Playing Knucklebones," photograph courtesy Scala/Art Resource, New York

(p. 47) Claudius, marble head, A.D. 41–54, Louvre, Paris/Bridgeman Art Library, London

(p. 48) Bust of Trajan, marble, A.D. 53–117, Ephesus Museum, Turkey/ Bridgeman Art Library, London

(p. 49) Marcus Aurelius (A.D. 121–180), Emperor A.D. 161–180: Gold aureus, private collection/Bridgeman Art Library, London

Chapter 47
(p. 55) Photograph by Peter Clayton

(p. 58) Model reconstruction of the Colosseum, Rome, private collection/ Bridgeman Art Library, London

Chapter 48
(p. 61) "Ave Caesar! Morituri te Salutant" by Jean Leon Gerome (1824–1904), Yale University Art Gallery, New Haven, Connecticut, gift of C. Ruxton Love, Jr., B.A. 1925

(p. 70) Fragment of gilded glass showing a gladiator, Rome, circa A.D. 400, British Museum, London/ Bridgeman Art Library, London

(p. 72) Drawing photograph courtesy The Mansell Collection

Chapter 49
(p. 80) The nymph Cyrene overpowering a lion is crowned by Libya, British Museum, London/Bridgeman Art Library, London

Chapter 50
(p. 97) Photograph of Roman betrothal ring, courtesy The Trustees of the British Museum, London

(p. 100) "In a Courtyard in Pompeii" by Luigi Bazzani (1836–1927), Waterhouse and Dodd, London/ Bridgeman Art Library, London

Chapter 51
(p. 103) Gold bulla from the House of Menander, Pompeii, A.D. 79, Museo e Gallerie Nazionali di Capodimonte, Naples/Bridgeman Art Library, London

(p. 110) Caracalla, Roman marble cuirassed bust A.D. 212–217, Louvre, Paris/ Bridgeman Art Library, London

Carved amethyst cameo of Emperor Constantine II (Emperor A.D. 337–340) British Museum, London/ Bridgeman Art Library, London

Chapter 52
(p. 119) Melitene, priestess of the Mother of the Gods, Roman marble bust, consecrated A.D. 162, Louvre, Paris/Bridgeman Art Library, London

(p. 120) Detail of "Landscape with the Father of Psyche Sacrificing to Apollo" by Claude Lorrain (1600–1682), National Trust, Fairhaven/ Bridgeman Art Library, London

(p. 122) "Tarquin the Elder Consulting Attus Nevius the Augur," by Sebastiano Ricci (1658–1734), Sotheby's, London/Bridgeman Art Library, London

Chapter 53
(p. 129) Drawing of Aurelius Hermia and his wife by Claudia Karabaic Sargent

Chapter 54
(p. 136) "Scene in a Classical Temple: Funeral Procession of a Warrior" by Joseph Charles Barrow by courtesy of the Board of Trustees of the Victoria and Albert/Bridgeman Art Library, London

Epilogue
(p. 147) Drawing of Roman soldiers destroying a German camp, courtesy Barnaby's

(p. 151) Marble statue of Socrates, British Museum, London

(p. 152) Roman Emperor as a Pharoah, Egyptian marble bust, 1st Century A.D., Louvre, Paris/Bridgeman Art Library, London

(p. 155) "Visit of a Sick Child to the Temple of Asclepius," oil on canvas by John William Waterhouse (1849–1917), The Fine Art Society, London/Bridgeman Art Library, London

(p. 158) Harl 4425, "Seneca Bleeding in Bath," Roman de la Rosa (c. 1487–1495), British Library, London/Bridgeman Art Library, London

(p. 160) "Philosophy," woodcut by Albrecht Dürer, in *The Complete Woodcuts of Albrecht Dürer*, ed.: Willi Kurth, Dover Publications, New York, 1961

Italy

The Roman Empire, A.D. 80

CALĒDONĪ
BRITANNIA
Londinium
GERMĀNĪ
Rhēnus
CALĒDONĪ
GALLIA
HISPĀNIA
Gādēs
Dānuvius
ILLYRICUM
Brundisium
Rōma
Neāpolis
Carthāgō
ĀFRICA
MACEDONIA
Athēnae
ACHAEA
ASIA
MARE MEDITERRĀNEUM
NUMIDIA
Tigris
Euphrātēs
IŪDAEA
AEGYPTUS
Nīlus

N

SCALE of MILES
0   250   500

AT THE BATHS

One of the main entertainments of the Romans was their daily visit to the baths — either to the public **thermae** or to the smaller, private **balneae**. They would expect to find three basic rooms: a warm room (**tepidārium**), which one would enter after undressing in the changing-room (**apodytērium**); a hot room (**caldārium**), where hot water would be provided in a specially heated room, which might also incorporate a steam bath; and a cold room (**frīgidārium**), where one could plunge into a cold bath after the heat of the **caldārium**.

In the big public bathing establishments one would also expect to find an exercise ground (**palaestra**), often in the open air, with a covered portico around it, where one might engage in a variety of exercises. There were various types of ball games, including a game involving the "snatching" (**rapere**) of a heavy ball (**harpastum**) and **trigōn**, a throwing and catching game played by three people with a ball also called **trigōn** from the name of the game. Men might engage in wrestling (**lūctārī**), fencing at a post (**pālus**), or weightlifting. After exercising, the Roman would be rubbed down with oil (**unguentum**), which cleansed and refreshed the skin. The excess oil was then removed with a special metal instrument (**strigilis**). Then the skin would be rubbed down with a towel (**linteum**).

In Rome the baths opened at noon and remained open till dusk. The opening and closing times were indicated by the striking of a gong.

Many establishments had separate facilities for men and women bathers; others fixed different hours for the two sexes.

The baths were regarded as social clubs, and people went there to exercise, play games, meet each other, and share gossip and news, as well as to bathe.

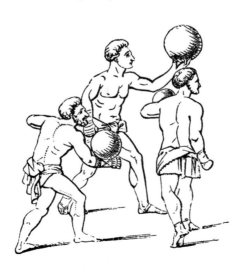

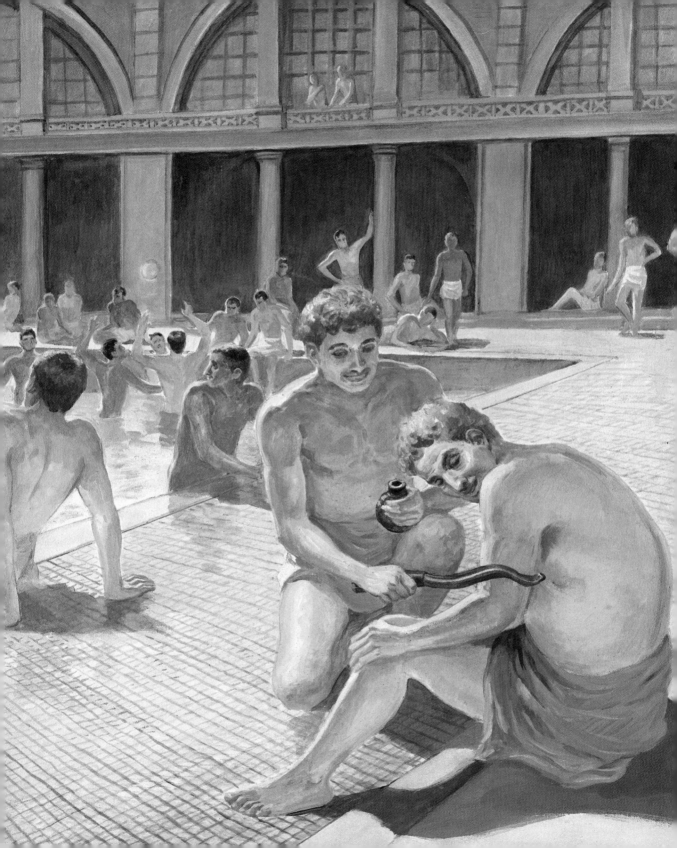

Iam hōra sexta erat. Titus Cornēlius, ut cōtīdiē solēbat, domō ēgressus, in Campum Mārtium ad Thermās Nerōnēās dēscendit, nam eō amīcī eius conveniēbant et dē rēbus urbānīs colloquēbantur.

Quō cum Titus pervēnisset, pecūniā datā, in vestibulum ingressus est. Ibi complūrēs ex amīcīs eum salūtāvērunt atque ūnā in apodytērium iniērunt. Vestīmenta exūta 5 trādidērunt servīs suīs, quī unguenta et strigilēs portābant.

Iam ūnctī in palaestram exiērunt ubi multī cīvēs variīs modīs sē exercēbant. Aliī harpastum rapiēbant, aliī trigōne lūdēbant, aliī lūctābantur, aliī pālum gladiō petēbant. Titus cum duōbus amīcīs trigōne lūdēbat. Cum satis sē ita exercuissent, ā servīs plūs unguentī poposcērunt et strigilibus dēfrictī sunt. Mox tepidārium, deinde caldārium 10 iniērunt. Hīc, cum calōrem et vapōrem vix patī possent, haud multum morābantur. Cum in tepidārium regressī essent, statim inde frīgidārium intrāvērunt et in aquam frīgidam dēsiluērunt. Posteā linteīs tersī, vestīmenta rūrsus induērunt.

Nē tum quidem domum discessērunt sed, vīnō sūmptō, inter sē colloquī coepērunt. Titum, cum ille semper vidērētur omnia audīvisse et vīdisse, dē rēbus urbānīs omnēs 15 rogābant. Maximē enim cupiēbant cognōscere quid in senātū agerētur, quid ā prīncipe contrā incendia factum esset, quī hominēs praeclārī iam in urbe adessent.

(continued)

1 **Campus Mārtius, -ī,** m., *the Plain of Mars on the outskirts of Rome*	7 **exerceō, -ēre, -uī, -itus,** *to exercise, train*
2 **Nerōnēus, -a, -um,** *of Nero*	11 **calor, calōris,** m., *heat*
4 **quō,** adv., *there, to that place*	**haud,** adv., *not*
Quō cum, *When…there*	14 **vīnō sūmptō,** *with wine having been taken, after a drink of wine*
pecūniā datā, *with his money having been given, after paying his entrance fee*	17 **contrā,** prep. + acc., *against*
vestibulum, -ī, n., *entrance passage*	

    7 **unguō, unguere, ūnxī, ūnctus,** *to anoint, smear with oil*
  10 **dēfricō, dēfricāre, dēfricuī, dēfrictus,** *to rub down*
  13 **tergeō, tergēre, tersī, tersus,** *to dry, wipe*
  16 **cognōscō, cognōscere, cognōvī, cognitus,** *to find out, learn*

Exercise 43a
Respondē Latīnē:

1. Quō Titus cōtīdiē ībat?
2. Quid Titus prīmum in thermīs fēcit?
3. Quibus trādidit vestīmenta sua?
4. Quid cīvēs in palaestrā faciēbant?
5. Quid Titus cum duōbus amīcīs faciēbat?
6. Cum satis sē exercuissent, quō iniērunt?
7. Cūr in caldāriō haud multum morābantur?
8. Postquam vestīmenta induērunt, quid sūmpsērunt?
9. Cūr omnēs Titum dē rēbus urbānīs rogābant?

"Nīl magnī," respondit Titus, "sed heri in Balneīs Palātīnīs rem rīdiculam vīdī; senex calvus, tunicā russātā indūtus, inter puerōs capillātōs pilā lūdēbat. Eās pilās quae ad terram ceciderant nōn repetēbat, nam servus follem habēbat plēnum pilārum, quās 20 lūdentibus dabat. Tandem hic senex digitōs concrepuit et aquam poposcit. Tum, cum manūs lāvisset, in capite ūnīus ē puerīs tersit!"

18	**senex, senis,** m., *old man*		**capillātus, -a, -um,** *with long hair*
19	**calvus, -a, -um,** *bald*	20	**follis, follis,** gen. pl., **follium,** m., *bag*
	indūtus, -a, -um, *clothed*	21	**digitus, -ī,** m., *finger*

20 **repetō, repetere, repetīvī, repetītus,** *to pick up, recover*
21 **concrepō, concrepāre, concrepuī,** *to snap (the fingers)*

Respondē Latīnē:

1. Quālem fābulam Titus nārrāvit?
2. Quid faciēbat senex quem Titus in Balneīs Palātīnīs vīdit?
3. Cūr servus pilās lūdentibus dabat?
4. Quid senex in capite puerī capillātī fēcit?

BUILDING THE MEANING
Subordinate Clauses with the Subjunctive (Review)

In Chapter 42 you learned about three kinds of subordinate clauses that have their verbs in the subjunctive. Here are examples from the story at the beginning of the present chapter:

1. **Cum** Causal Clauses:

   Hīc, **cum** calōrem et vapōrem vix patī **possent,** haud multum morābantur. (43:11)
   *Here, **since they were** scarcely **able** to endure the heat and the steam, they did not stay a long time.*

2. **Cum** Circumstantial Clauses:

   Quō **cum** Titus **pervēnisset,** in vestibulum ingressus est. (43:4)
   ***When Titus had arrived* there,** *he entered the entrance passage.*

3. Indirect Questions:

   Maximē enim cupiēbant cognōscere **quī** hominēs praeclārī iam in urbe **adessent.** (43:16–17)
   *They especially wanted to learn **what** famous men **were** now **present** in the city.*

		Active Voice	Passive Voice		Deponent Verb	
S	1	audīvíssem	audítus, -a	éssem	cōnátus, -a	éssem
	2	audīvíssēs	audítus, -a	éssēs	cōnátus, -a	éssēs
	3	audīvísset	audítus, -a, -um	ésset	cōnátus, -a, -um	ésset
P	1	audīvissémus	audítī, -ae	essémus	cōnátī, -ae	essémus
	2	audīvissétis	audítī, -ae	essétis	cōnátī, -ae	essétis
	3	audīvíssent	audítī, -ae, -a	éssent	cōnátī, -ae, -a	éssent

Exercise 43b

In story 43, locate five verbs in the imperfect or pluperfect subjunctive active and locate four passive subjunctive forms. Identify the tense, person, and number of each form.

Exercise 43c

Here are sample forms of the imperfect and pluperfect subjunctives, active and passive, of a regular verb and sample forms of the imperfect and pluperfect subjunctives of a deponent verb:

Regular Verb:

Imperfect Active
parārem

Imperfect Passive
parārer

Pluperfect Active
parāvissem

Pluperfect Passive
parātus essem

Deponent Verb:

Imperfect
cōnārer

Pluperfect
cōnātus essem

Give imperfect and pluperfect subjunctive forms of the following verbs in the designated person and number, following the pattern above. For deponent verbs give only passive forms:

1. dēfricō, dēfricāre, dēfricuī, dēfrictus: 3rd sing.
2. tergeō, tergēre, tersī, tersus: 1st pl.
3. repetō, repetere, repetīvī, repetītus: 1st pl.
4. colloquor, colloquī, collocūtus sum: 3rd pl.
5. regredior, regredī, regressus sum: 2nd pl.

Exercise 43d

Read aloud and translate each sentence, and then identify each subordinate clause by type (**cum** causal, **cum** circumstantial, or indirect question). Tell if the action in the subordinate clause was happening at the same time as the action of the main clause or had been completed before the action of the main clause:

1. Cum prīmā lūce profectī essēmus, iam dēfessī erāmus.
2. Ego nesciēbam cūr Rōmam proficīscerēmur.
3. Hodiē cum Titus domō ēgressus esset, ad thermās dēscendit.
4. Cum pecūnia data esset, Titus in vestibulum ingressus est.
5. Cum caldārium calidissimum esset, Titus ibi nōn diū morātus est.
6. Amīcī Titum rogāvērunt quid māne fēcisset.
7. Nēmō cognōvit quid herī in senātū āctum esset.
8. Cum senex calvus pilā lūderet, nūllam pilam ā terrā repetēbat.
9. Cum servus follem plēnum pilārum habēret, necesse nōn erat pilās ā terrā repetere.
10. Titus nārrāvit quōmodo digitī senis in capite puerī tersī essent.

Excercise 43e

Using story 43 and the sets of forms of the imperfect and pluperfect subjunctive as guides, give the Latin for:

1. When Titus had descended to the Campus Martius, he entered the Baths of Nero.
2. There his friends asked him what had been done in the Senate today.
3. Since he had been present in the Senate, he was able to tell everything.
4. When Titus was in the Palatine Baths yesterday, he saw a bald old man.
5. He did not know who the old man was.

THE BATHS

In addition to the many references to baths in Roman literature, much information about the **balneae** and **thermae** can be deduced from the archaeological remains of bathing establishments still evident today. In Rome, the great Thermae of Diocletian now house the National Museum, its extensive grounds having been laid out by Michelangelo centuries after the baths were built. Grand opera is performed during the summer months in the Baths of Caracalla.

At Pompeii, both public and private bathing establishments have been found, and even in many of the houses there are full suites of bathrooms—warm, hot, and cold rooms—which were apparently used only by the family. On country estates and in town houses, in addition to the suites of baths for the owner, there were bath houses for slaves.

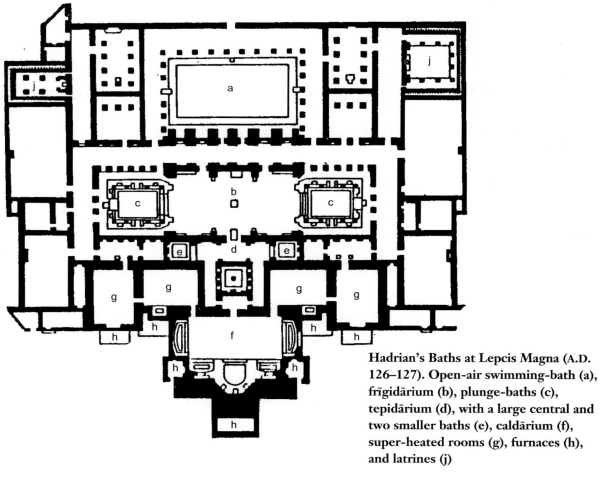

Hadrian's Baths at Lepcis Magna (A.D. 126–127). Open-air swimming-bath (a), frīgidārium (b), plunge-baths (c), tepidārium (d), with a large central and two smaller baths (e), caldārium (f), super-heated rooms (g), furnaces (h), and latrines (j)

The first public baths in Rome were built in the second century B.C.; they were small, practical wash-houses for men only. Later, bathing establishments called **balneae** began to be built at private expense and run for profit by individuals or a consortium. As the practice of bathing became more and more popular, huge baths (**thermae**) were built by the state. These were increased in size and splendor under the emperors, e.g., the Thermae of Caracalla (A.D. 217) and of Diocletian (A.D. 303).

Romans of all social classes could spend an hour or more in the luxury of such complexes for only a **quadrans**, the smallest Roman coin. Children were admitted free. The management of the state **thermae** was awarded for a fixed sum to a contractor. Sometimes a rich citizen or magistrate undertook to pay him the equivalent of the total entrance fees for a certain period, during which entry to the baths was entirely free.

So attached were the Romans to their daily hot steam-bath that they built baths in most communities throughout their Empire. Where there were hot springs, as in Bath, England, they used these and built gymnasia and dressing-rooms around them. Where there were no hot springs, they heated the air by a hypocaust (**hypocauston,** a Greek term meaning literally, "burning underneath"), a system whereby hot air from a furnace circulated under the raised floor and through ducts and vents in the walls. The fuel for the furnace, which was stoked by slaves, was wood and charcoal. Huge reservoirs were built near the baths to provide a constant and plentiful supply of water.

Bathers would take various articles with them to the baths, including towels, bottles of oil, and strigils. All but the poor would bring their own slaves to attend them, but it was possible to hire the services of others at the baths (e.g., masseur, barber). Attendants would guard clothes for a small fee.

Roman baths varied considerably in size and layout, but in all of them the following series of rooms was to be found:

1. **apodytērium:** a changing room with stone benches and rows of deep holes in the walls for holding clothes.

2. **frīgidārium:** cold room, with cold plunge bath at one side.

3. **tepidārium:** warm room, to acclimatize bathers to the difference in temperature between the cold and hot rooms.

4. **caldārium:** hot room, with hot bath and hot air like the modern Turkish bath. It was the best-lit room and was equipped with basins and tubs. Its ceiling was usually domed to allow condensation to run off.

The bathers could take the three stages of bathing in any order, but it was usual to end up with a cold plunge. Medicinal and perfumed baths were also available.

The baths became a suitable place for taking exercise. A large complex would have a court for ball games and an area for gymnastics and wrestling, in addition to the swimming pool. There were various ball games, each using a different type of ball and sometimes a racquet as well. Hoops or a dumbbell were also used for exercising.

The Roman baths were centers for recreation and relaxation in the fullest sense, and in the largest establishments the amenities could include gardens, reading rooms, and even libraries. "Snack-bars" (**popīnae**) were numerous inside the building or nearby, while vendors of every type advertised their wares on all sides.

A GRAFFITO FROM THE BATHS AT ROME

Balnea, vīna, Venus corrumpunt corpora nostra;
      at vītam faciunt—balnea, vīna, Venus.

    balnea = balneae   **Venus = amor**

      corrumpō, corrumpere, corrūpī, corruptus, *to spoil, harm, ruin*

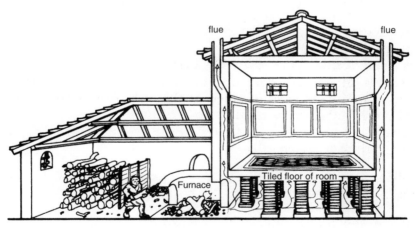

Diagram of a Hypocaust

ADDITIONAL READING:
The Romans Speak for Themselves: Book II: "An Unexpected Bath at Trimalchio's," pages 51–61.

STOP THIEF!

Marcus et Sextus ē lūdō ēgressī ūnā cum Eucleide et alterō servō domum ībant. Subitō Eucleidēs puerīs, "Vultisne ad thermās īre?" inquit.

Quibus verbīs audītīs, puerī maximē gaudēbant. Mox ad thermās advēnērunt et in apodytērium intrāvērunt, quod iam erat plēnum puerōrum quī ē lūdō ēgressī eō cum paedagōgīs vēnerant. Ibi vestīmenta exuēbant. 5

Marcus, vestīmentīs exūtīs, "Nunc in palaestram exeāmus," inquit. At Eucleidēs, "Minimē!" inquit. "Pater tuus mē iussit vōs ante nōnam hōram redūcere." Deinde alterī servō, cui nōmen erat Asellus, "Hīc manē!" inquit. "Vestīmenta dīligenter custōdī! Hīc enim solent esse multī fūrēs quī vestīmenta surrepta in urbe vēndunt."

Cui Asellus respondit, "Ego semper vestīmenta dīligenter custōdiō. Nēmō 10 vestīmenta, mē custōde, surripere potest."

Tum puerī, vestīmentīs trāditīs, in tepidārium intrāvērunt et inde in caldārium, ubi erat magna turba hominum. Subitō tamen exclāmāvit Sextus, "Aeger sum. Hunc calōrem patī nōn possum. Exībō et ad apodytērium regrediar."

Dum ē tepidāriō exit, Asellum prope vestīmenta sedentem cōnspexit. Dormiēbat 15 Asellus. Eō ipsō tempore vestīmenta ā servō quōdam surripiēbantur. Quod ubi vīdit Sextus, "Prehende fūrem!" exclāmāvit. Simul fūr clāmōrem Sextī audīvit, simul Asellus ē sellā exsiluit, simul Sextus ad iānuam cucurrit. Fūr in palaestram cōnfūgit, nam sē in turbā cēlāre in animō habēbat. Cum tamen inde in viam ēvādere nōn posset, in frīgidārium fūgit. 20

(continued)

3 **quibus verbīs audītīs,** *with which words having been heard, when they had heard this*	9 **fūr, fūris,** m., *thief*
6 **exeāmus,** *let us go out*	11 **mē custōde,** *with me on guard, while I am on guard*
	18 **sella, -ae,** f., *sedan-chair, seat, chair*

9 **surripiō, surripere, surripuī, surreptus,** *to steal*
17 **prehendō, prehendere, prehendī, prehēnsus,** *to seize*
18 **exsiliō, exsilīre, exsiluī,** *to leap out*
 cōnfugiō, cōnfugere, cōnfūgī, *to flee for refuge*

Exercise 44a
Respondē Latīnē:

1. Cūr puerī maximē gaudēbant?
2. Ubi vestīmenta exuēbant?
3. Cūr vestīmenta dīligenter custōdīrī dēbent?
4. Quid Sextus patī nōn potest?
5. Ubi sedēbat Asellus et quid faciēbat?
6. Cūr fūr in frīgidārium fūgit?

Sextus tamen fūrem cōnspectum subsequēbātur. Fūr, Sextō vīsō, iam valdē timēbat. In pavīmentō lāpsus in aquam frīgidam cecidit. Statim in aquam dēsiluit Sextus. Fūrem ex aquā trahere cōnābātur; sed frūstrā. Cum tamen adiūvissent adstantēs, fūr ā Sextō captus ex aquā extractus est. Quem captum Sextus dominō trādidit.

22 **pavīmentum, -ī,** n., *tiled floor*

21 **subsequor, subsequī, subsecūtus sum,** *to follow (up)*
22 **lābor, lābī, lāpsus sum,** *to slip, fall*

Respondē Latīnē:

1. Quī fūrem ā Sextō captum ex aquā extrāxērunt?
2. Cui trāditus est fūr?

BUILDING THE MEANING
Verbs: Perfect Passive Participles II

In Chapter 33 you saw the following sentence with a perfect passive participle:

Coquus **vocātus** ab omnibus laudātus est. (33:26)
*The cook, **having been summoned,** was praised by everyone.*
After being summoned, the cook was praised by everyone.
When summoned, the cook was praised by everyone.
When the cook had been summoned, he was praised by everyone.
The cook was summoned and praised by everyone.

Here the perfect passive participle modifies the subject of the sentence.
A perfect passive participle may also modify the direct or indirect object:

Coquum **vocātum** omnēs laudāvērunt.
*They all praised the cook **having been summoned.***
They all praised the cook who had been summoned.
When the cook had been summoned, they all praised him.

Coquō **vocātō** omnēs grātiās ēgērunt.
*They all gave thanks to the cook **having been summoned.***
They all gave thanks to the cook who had been summoned.
When the cook had been summoned, they all gave thanks to him.

Exercise 44b
Read aloud and translate the following sentences. Identify the case of all perfect passive participles and tell what they modify:

1. Amīcī Titum cōnspectum salūtāvērunt.
2. Titus rogātus quid in senātū agerētur, "Nīl magnī," respondit.
3. Vestīmenta exūta Marcus servō trādidit.
4. Strigilibus dēfrictī tepidārium ingressī sunt.
5. Vestīmenta dominō vocātō trādita sunt.

Ablatives Absolute

Another arrangement is also possible:

> <u>Coquō</u> **vocātō,** omnēs cēnam laudāvērunt.
> *<u>The cook</u> **having been summoned**, they all praised the dinner.*
> *<u>When the cook</u> **had been summoned**, they all praised the dinner.*

Here the participle does not agree with the subject of the sentence or with a direct or indirect object but rather with another word, **coquō,** which is in the ablative case. The two words taken together, **coquō vocātō,** make a construction known as the *ablative absolute*, in which a noun (or pronoun) and a participle are in the ablative case and make up a phrase that is separate from the rest of the sentence (Latin **absolūtus,** *complete in itself, self-contained*) and is usually set off by commas.

In addition to the translations given above, the ablative absolute **coquō vocātō** could be translated *after the cook had been summoned.* Some ablatives absolute may best be translated with *because, since, although,* or *if,* depending on the context.

The participle of an ablative absolute may also be in the present tense:

> <u>Fūre vestīmenta</u> **surripiente,** Sextus in apodytērium ingreditur.
> *<u>While the thief</u> **is stealing** the clothes, Sextus enters the changing room.*

Note that the ablative singular ending of present participles used in ablatives absolute is *-e,* not *-ī* (see Chapter 40, page 135).

The present active participle is used for an action going on at the same time as the action of the main verb of the sentence; the perfect passive participle is used for an action that was completed before the action of the main verb.

Often the present participle will be translated with a past tense in English because it describes an action going on in the past at the same time as the action of the main verb in a past tense:

> <u>Fūre vestīmenta</u> **surripiente,** Sextus in apodytērium ingrediēbātur.
> *<u>While the thief</u> **was stealing** the clothes, Sextus was entering the changing room.*

Since classical Latin has no present participle for the verb **esse,** ablatives absolute sometimes consist only of two nouns in the ablative case, e.g., **mē custōde,** *with me (being) a guard, as long as I'm on guard* (44:11), or of a noun and an adjective, e.g., **Sextō aegrō**, *since Sextus is (was) sick.*

Exercise 44c
Locate five examples of ablatives absolute in story 44. Translate the sentences in which they occur.

—— —— ——

Iūs et fūrī dīcitur. *Justice is granted even to the thief.* (Seneca, *On Benefits* IV.28)
lapsus calami *a slip of the pen*
lapsus linguae *a slip of the tongue*

—— —— ——

Exercise 44d

Read aloud and translate each sentence, and then identify the ablatives absolute. Comment on the temporal relationship between the participle of the ablative absolute and the action of the verb in the main clause:

1. Puerīs in lūdō clāmantibus, magister īrātus fit.
2. Magistrō īrātō, puerī ē lūdō missī sunt.
3. Lūdō relictō, puerī ad thermās iērunt.
4. Titō salūtātō, puerī in apodytērium iniērunt.
5. Vestīmentīs Asellō trāditīs, in palaestram iniērunt.
6. Lūdīs in palaestrā cōnfectīs, in tepidārium intrāvērunt.
7. Marcō in caldāriō morante, Sextus ad apodytērium regressus est.
8. Asellō custōde, fūr vestīmenta surripuit.
9. Fūre cōnspectō, Sextus magnā vōce clāmāvit.
10. Vestīmentīs ā fūre trāditīs, puerī domum iērunt.

Exercise 44e

Using story 44 and the information on ablatives absolute as guides, give the Latin for the following. Use ablatives absolute to translate subordinate clauses:

1. When they had taken off their clothes, they entered the warm room.
2. While Asellus was sleeping, a certain slave was stealing the clothes.
3. The thief, when he had seen Sextus, was very afraid.
4. While Sextus was trying to drag the thief out of the water, the bystanders were doing nothing.
5. When the thief had been handed over to his master, Sextus was happy.

BUILDING THE MEANING
Linking *quī*

In story 44 you met the following:

Quibus verbīs audītīs.... (3)	*When they heard* **these** *words*....
Cui Asellus respondit.... (10)	*Asellus replied* **to him**....
Quod ubi vīdit.... (16)	*When he saw* **this**....
Quem captum.... (24)	*Now that he had caught* **him**....

A linking **quī** is translated in English as either a demonstrative pronoun (*these, this,* etc.) or a personal pronoun (*him,* etc.), not as a relative pronoun (*which, whom,* etc.).

The relative pronoun at the beginning of a sentence provides a link with a person, thing, or action in the previous sentence:

Quibus verbīs refers to what Eucleides said in the previous sentence.
Cui refers to Eucleides, who had just finished speaking.
Quod refers to the theft Sextus had just seen.
Quem refers to the thief mentioned in the previous sentence.

THIEVES AT THE BATHS

Even as early as the time of the comic playwright Plautus (ca. 254–184 B.C.), Romans knew how difficult it was to guard their clothes at the baths:

> Even one who goes to the baths to bathe and watches his clothes carefully there has them stolen all the same, since he's confused as to which of the crowd to watch. The thief easily sees the one who's watching; the guard doesn't know who the thief is.

—Plautus, *Rudens* 382–385 (adapted)

Scene from a Roman comedy
Fresco, Museo Nazionale di San Martino, Naples, Italy

The following story was told by a guest at Trimalchio's dinner party:

We were just about to step into the dining room when a slave, utterly naked, landed on the floor in front of us and implored us to save him from a whipping. He was about to be flogged, he explained, for a trifling offense. He had let someone steal the steward's clothing, worthless stuff really, in the baths. Well, we pulled back our right feet, faced about and returned to the entry where we found the steward counting a stack of gold coins. We begged him to let the servant off. "Really, it's not the money I mind," he replied with enormous condescension, "so much as the idiot's carelessness. It was my dinner-suit he lost, a birthday present from one of my dependents. Expensive too, but then I've already had it washed. Well, it's a trifle. Do what you want with him." We thanked him for his gracious kindness, but when we entered the dining room up ran the same slave whom we'd just begged off. He overwhelmed us with his thanks and then, to our consternation, began to plaster us with kisses. "You'll soon see whom you've helped," he said. "The master's wine will prove the servant's gratitude."

—Petronius, *Satyricon* 30–31

PYRAMUS AND THISBE

In ancient Rome, the first contact the public was likely to have with a new poem or a completed section of a longer poem would be not through reading it in a book but through listening to it at a public reading (**recitātiō**) given by the poet in a private house or theater or recital room. Some enterprising poets even tried to gather an audience in the Forum, at the Circus, or in the public baths. The large public baths often contained, in fact, libraries and reading rooms and thus catered to the minds as well as the bodies of their patrons. Martial complained of a boorish poet who pursued him wherever he went, reciting his verses: "I flee to the baths; you echo in my ear. I seek the swimming pool; you don't allow me to swim."

After the adventure with the thief, Marcus, Sextus, and Eucleides relax in the library at the baths and enjoy listening to a recitation of one of the most famous love stories of the ancient world. The story of Pyramus and Thisbe, set in ancient Babylon and made familiar to English readers by Shakespeare's *Romeo and Juliet* and *A Midsummer Night's Dream*, was originally part of a long narrative poem, the *Metamorphoses*, by the Latin poet Ovid (43 B.C.–A.D. 17).

Legendary lovers of antiquity
Illustration by Mahmoud Sayah

Ōlim Babylōne habitābat adulēscēns quīdam pulcherrimus, nōmine Pȳramus. In vīcīnā domō habitābat virgō cui nōmen erat Thisbē. Pȳramus hanc virginem in viā forte cōnspectam statim amāvit. Et Thisbē, Pȳramō vīsō, amōre capta est. Sed ēheu! Parentēs et virginis et adulēscentis, quoniam multōs iam annōs inter sē rixābantur, eōs convenīre vetuērunt. Pȳramō Thisbēn nē vidēre quidem licēbat. Valdē dolēbant et adulēscēns et 5 virgō.

Erat pariēs domuī utrīque commūnis. Parva tamen rīma, ā nūllō anteā vīsa, ab amantibus inventa est. (Quid nōn sentit amor?) Quam ad rīmam sedentēs inter sē sēcrētō colloquēbantur, alter alterī amōrem exprimēns. Sed mox, ōsculīs parietī datīs, valedīcēbant invītī. 10

Tandem novum cōnsilium cēpērunt. Cōnstituērunt enim, parentibus īnsciīs, domō nocte exīre, in silvam convenīre, sub arbore quādam cōnsīdere. Itaque Thisbē silentiō noctis, cum vultum vēlāmine cēlāvisset, fūrtim ēgressa ad silvam festīnāvit. Quō cum advēnisset, sub illā arbore cōnsēdit. Ecce tamen vēnit leō saevus, ōre sanguine bovis aspersō. Quō cōnspectō, Thisbē perterrita in spēluncam, quae prope erat, cōnfūgit. Et 15 dum fugit, vēlāmen relīquit. Quod vēlāmen leō ōre sanguineō rapuit, sed mox dēposuit.

Haud multō post Pȳramus ex urbe ēgressus, dum ad arborem eandem prōgreditur, vēstīgia leōnis vīdit. Subitō puellae vēlāmen sanguine aspersum cōnspexit. Timōre tremēns, "Quid accidit?" clāmāvit.

(continued)

1 **Babylōn, Babylōnis**, f., *Babylon*
 Pȳramus, -ī, m., *Pyramus*
2 **virgō, virginis**, f., *maiden*
 Thisbē, Thisbēs, f., *Thisbe*
4 **rixor, -ārī, -ātus sum**, to *quarrel*
7 **uterque, utraque, utrumque**, *each*
  (of two), *both*
 rīma, -ae, f., *crack*
9 **ōsculum, -ī**, n., *kiss*

11 **cōnsilium, -ī**, n., *plan*
 cōnsilium capere, *to adopt a plan*
 īnscius, -a, -um, *not knowing*
13 **vultus, -ūs**, m., *face*
 vēlāmen, vēlāminis, n., *veil, shawl*
14 **ōre sanguine aspersō**, *his mouth spattered with blood*
15 **spēlunca, -ae**, f., *cave*

8 **sentiō, sentīre, sēnsī, sēnsus**, *to feel, notice*
9 **exprimō, exprimere, expressī, expressus**, *to press out, express*
 valedīcō, valedīcere, valedīxī, valedictūrus, *to say goodbye*
15 **aspergō, aspergere, aspersī, aspersus**, *to sprinkle, splash, spatter*
17 **prōgredior, prōgredī, prōgressus sum**, *to go forward, advance*

Exercise 45a
Respondē Latīnē:

1. Ubi habitābant Pȳramus et Thisbē?
2. Quandō Pȳramus Thisbēn amāvit?
3. Placuitne amor Pȳramī et Thisbēs parentibus?
4. Quid erat inter duās domūs?
5. Quid faciēbant amantēs ad rīmam parietis sedentēs?
6. Quid fēcerat Thisbē antequam ad silvam festīnāvit?
7. Quid Thisbē in silvā vīdit?
8. Quid vīdit Pȳramus ex urbe ēgressus?

"Ēheu! Ego tē occīdī, mea Thisbē, quod tē iussī in silvam noctū sōlam venīre, nec 20
prior vēnī. Sine tē vīvere nōlō." Gladiō igitur strictō, sē vulnerāvit atque ad terram
cecidit moriēns.

Ecce! Metū nōndum dēpositō, Thisbē ē spēluncā timidē exit, Pȳramum quaerit.
Subitō corpus eius humī iacēns cōnspicit; multīs cum lacrimīs, "Pȳrame," clāmat, "quis
hoc fēcit?" Deinde, suō vēlāmine cōnspectō, iam moritūra, "Ō mē miseram!" clāmat. 25
"Vēlāmen meum tē perdidit. Sine tē vīvere nōlō." Et gladiō Pȳramī ipsa sē occīdit.

Parentēs, dolōre commōtī, eōs in eōdem sepulcrō sepelīvērunt.

20 **nec,** conj., *and...not*
21 **prior, prior, prius,** gen., **priōris,** *first
     (of two), previous*

25 **moritūra,** *intending to die, determined
     to die*

     20 **occīdō, occīdere, occīdī, occīsus,** *to kill*
     26 **perdō, perdere, perdidī, perditus,** *to destroy*

Respondē Latīnē:

1. Cūr Pȳramus sē occīdit? Cūr Thisbē?
2. Cūr parentēs Pȳramum Thisbēnque in eōdem sepulcrō sepelīvērunt?

FORMS
Verbs: Future Active Participles

Since Chapter 20 you have seen the future active participle as the fourth principal
part of intransitive verbs, e.g., **veniō, venīre, vēnī, ventūrus.**

Transitive verbs form their future active participles by adding *-ūrus, -a, -um* to the
perfect passive participial stem, e.g., **portātus;** stem, **portāt-;** future active participle,
portātūrus, -a, -um.

Deponent verbs form their future active participles by adding *-ūrus, -a, -um* to the
perfect participial stem, e.g., perfect participle, **cōnātus;** stem **cōnāt-;** future active participle, **cōnātūrus, -a -um.**

The future active participle of some verbs ends instead in *-itūrus, -a, -um*, e.g.,
moritūrus, -a, -um (from **morior, morī, mortuus sum**):

> Thisbē...iam **moritūra,** "Ō mē miseram!" clāmat. (45:23–25)
> *Thisbe...now **about to die,** cries, "Poor me!"*

The following is a tabulation of the participles of non-deponent verbs in
conjugations 1–4:

Tense	Active Voice	Passive Voice

Present	1. portāns, portantis
	  carrying
	2. movēns, moventis
	  moving
	3. mittēns, mittentis
	  sending
	  iaciēns, iacientis
	  throwing
	4. audiēns, audientis
	  hearing	

Perfect		1. portātus, -a, -um
		  (having been) carried
		2. mōtus, -a, -um
		  (having been) moved
		3. missus, -a, -um
		  (having been) sent
		  iactus, -a, -um
		  (having been) thrown
		4. audītus, -a, -um
		  (having been) heard

Future	1. portātūrus, -a, -um
	  about to carry
	2. mōtūrus, -a, -um
	  about to move
	3. missūrus, -a, -um
	  about to send
	  iactūrus, -a, -um
	  about to throw
	4. audītūrus, -a, -um
	  about to hear	

NOTES

1. The present and future participles are active in form and meaning.
2. The perfect participle is passive in form and meaning.
3. The present participle of **īre** (*to go*) is **iēns, euntis**. The participles of the other irregular verbs are formed regularly, e.g., **volēns, volentis**. There is no present participle of **esse** (*to be*).
4. The future participle of **īre** is **itūrus, -a, -um**.
5. The future participle of **esse** is **futūrus, -a, -um**.
6. Other possible translations of the future participle include: *going to, likely to, intending to, determined to, on the point of…-ing.*

7. Although the participles of
   deponent verbs have the
   same endings as those of
   non-deponent verbs, all the
   meanings are active:

Present Participle	1. cōnāns, cōnantis, *trying* 2. verēns, verentis, *fearing* 3. loquēns, loquentis, *speaking* ēgrediēns, ēgredientis, *going out* 4. experiēns, experientis, *testing*
Perfect Participle	1. cōnātus, -a, -um, *having tried* 2. veritus, -a, -um, *having feared* 3. locūtus, -a, -um, *having spoken* ēgressus, -a, -um, *having gone out* 4. expertus, -a, -um, *having tested*
Future Participle	1. cōnātūrus, -a, -um, *about to try* 2. veritūrus, -a, -um, *about to fear* 3. locūtūrus, -a, -um, *about to speak* ēgressūrus, -a, -um, *about to go out* 4. expertūrus, -a, -um, *about to test*

Exercise 45b

Give the present, perfect, and future participles of the following verbs in the
nominative feminine singular. Translate each form you give:

1. amō
2. moneō
3. aspergō
4. cōnspiciō
5. sentiō

6. rixor
7. polliceor
8. sequor
9. prōgredior
10. experior

polliceor, pollicērī, pollicitus sum, *to promise*

Exercise 45c

Read aloud and translate. Then identify each participle, give its tense,
gender, case, and number, say whether it is active or passive in meaning, and
tell what it modifies:

1. Multīs hominibus subsequentibus, fūr effugere nōn potuit.
2. Sextus fūrem effugere cōnantem subsequēbātur.
3. Puerī calōrem breve modo tempus passī ē caldāriō exiērunt.
4. Sextus domum profectūrus ab omnibus laudātus est.
5. Thisbē moritūra ad terram cecidit.
6. Fūr vestīmenta surreptūrus in thermās ingressus est.
7. Pȳramus ad illam arborem prōgrediēns vēstīgia leōnis vīdit.
8. Vēlāmine relictō, Thisbē in spēluncam cōnfūgit.
9. Ad rīmam inter sē sēcrētō colloquentēs amōrem exprimēbant.
10. Pȳramus Thisbēn secūtūrus ex urbe profectus est.
11. Sōle oriente, mercātōrēs profectī sunt ad Āfricam nāvigātūrī.
12. Multa virginī pollicitus, Pȳramus eī valedīxit.

orior, orīrī, ortus sum, *to rise*

OVID'S METAMORPHOSES

The title of Ovid's great poem, the *Metamorphoses*, is Greek for *changes of form*. In this highly original poem in fifteen books, Ovid describes or alludes to a change in form of a god or a human being in every story from the creation of the universe to the deification of Julius Caesar in 42 B.C. It has been one of the most important sources of mythology for all writers since Ovid's time. These stories have delighted readers for over 2,000 years. Here are four of these stories told briefly in English.

BAUCIS AND PHILEMON

Baucis and Philemon, an aged couple who did not have much in the way of worldly goods, welcomed Jupiter and Mercury, who were traveling on earth disguised as mortals. One thousand homes had turned the gods away and would not grant them hospitality, but this pious couple prepared a meal for their guests with the very best that they had and shared everything with these strangers—the epitome of hospitality. In return Jupiter granted their wish to die at the same moment, when their time had come, by turning them into two trees growing from one trunk.

ACTAEON

Actaeon and his friends had been hunting one morning with great success. At noon, since it was very hot, Actaeon urged his friends to go home with their spoils and return the next morning.

In a secret glade through which ran a sparkling stream, the goddess Diana used to bathe when she was tired of hunting. On this day she had given her bow and arrows, her

Ovid among the Scythians, by Delacroix
Oil on canvas, National Gallery, London, England

robe, and her sandals to her attendant nymphs, let down her hair, and stepped into the pool. Actaeon, wandering through the unfamiliar woods, came upon the goddess as she was bathing. As he gazed awestruck at her, she splashed water into his face and said, "Now you are free to tell anyone that you have seen me undressed—if you can." As she spoke, Actaeon was changed into a spotted stag with fear in his heart. He fled but his own hounds caught his scent and gave chase. He tried to cry out, "I am your master, Actaeon," but he no longer had a human voice. He was finally caught, and his pack of hounds killed him. The goddess Diana had no pity for him until the hounds had torn his life out.

NIOBE

Niobe, the daughter of Tantalus, refused to honor Latona, mother of Apollo and Diana, and insulted her by ridiculing the fact that Latona only had two children while she herself had fourteen—seven boys and seven girls. Latona was angry and asked her children, Apollo and Diana, to make Niobe pay for insulting her divinity. Immediately Apollo and Diana went to Thebes and with bow and arrow killed the seven sons of Niobe. Niobe's grief-stricken husband, Amphion, killed himself with a dagger. In spite of all this, Niobe still insisted that she had triumphed over Latona as she still had more children than the goddess. At once as the daughters stood grieving for their brothers, they were killed one by one by the arrows of Apollo and Diana. Finally realizing the enormity of her crime, Niobe sat among the bodies of her children and slowly changed into stone. She was taken by a whirlwind to Maeonia, her native land, where she became part of the rocky mountains from which a trickling stream of tears flows eternally.

CALLISTO

Callisto was a beautiful nymph of Arcadia and a follower of the goddess Diana. When Jupiter caught sight of her wandering in the woods, he desired her very much. He assumed the dress and form of the goddess Diana and so was able to overcome her fear of men and then force her to his will. Her shame and fear of her secret becoming known by Diana and the other nymphs made her flee away from them deeper into the woods. When her son Arcas was born, Juno was no longer able to contain her jealousy and took revenge by taking away Callisto's human form and changing her into a huge black bear. Because she still had human feelings, Callisto fled both the hunters and the other bears and wandered lonely through the woods. Out hunting one day, Arcas, now fifteen years old, happened upon his mother in the forest. As he was about to kill her with his spear, Jupiter stopped him, snatched them both up, and placed them in the sky as Ursa Major and Ursa Minor. Juno was even more angry at seeing Callisto and Arcas so honored and went straight to Tethys and Oceanus, gods of the sea, and asked them to bar these two from ever coming into the stream of Ocean. The gods assented, and Ursa Major and Ursa Minor move constantly around the pole but are never allowed to go below the horizon into the stream of Ocean.

LOVERS' GRAFFITI

I

Rōmula hīc cum Staphylō morātur.
Romula hangs around here with Staphylus.

II

Restitūtus multās saepe dēcēpit puellās.
Restitutus has often deceived many girls.

III

Vibius Restitūtus hīc sōlus dormīvit et Urbānam suam dēsīderābat.
Vibius Restitutus slept here—alone—and longed for his Urbana.

IV

Successus textor amat caupōniae ancillam, nōmine Hīredem, quae quidem illum nōn cūrat. Sed ille rogat illa commiserētur. Scrībit rīvālis. Valē.
Successus the weaver is in love with the hostess's maid, Iris by name, who of course doesn't care about him. But he asks that she take pity (on him). His rival is writing (this). Farewell.

V

Quisquis amat, valeat; pereat quī nescit amāre!
  Bis tantō pereat, quisquis amāre vetat!
Whoever's in love, may he succeed; whoever's not, may he perish!
  Twice may he perish, whoever forbids me to love!

A FAMOUS POEM OF CATULLUS

Odī et amō. Quare id faciam, fortasse requīris.
  Nesciō, sed fierī sentiō et excrucior.

                    —LXXXV

I love and I hate. Perhaps you ask why I do this.
  I do not know, but I feel it happening and I am tormented.

WORD STUDY XI

Diminutive Suffixes

When added to the base (occasionally the nominative singular) of a Latin noun or adjective, the suffixes *-ulus* (*-olus* after a vowel), *-(i)culus*, and *-ellus* (sometimes *-illus*) alter the meaning of the word by diminishing its size or importance:

Noun or Adjective	Base (or Nom. Sing.)	Suffix		Diminutive
puer, -ī, m., *boy*	**puer-** +	*-ulus*	=	**puerulus, -ī**, m., *little boy, young slave boy*
parvus, -a, -um, *small*	**parv-** +	*-ulus*	=	**parvulus, -a, -um**, *little, tiny*

Diminutives were sometimes used affectionately:

fīlia, -ae, f., *daughter*	**fīli-** +	*-ola*	=	**fīliola, -ae**, f., *little daughter, darling daughter*

but they could also be disparaging:

mulier, mulieris, f., *woman*	**mulier-** +	*-cula*	=	**muliercula, -ae**, f., *a little, weak, foolish woman*

Some diminutives had special meanings:

ōs, ōris, n., *mouth*	**ōs-** +	*-culum*	=	**ōsculum, -ī**, n., *a kiss*

Adjectives formed with diminutive suffixes have endings of the 1st and 2nd declensions; diminutive nouns are in either the 1st or 2nd declension, and the gender is usually the same as that of the original noun:

novus, -a, -um, *new*	**nov-** +	*-ellus*	=	**novellus, -a, -um**, *young, tender*
pars, partis, f., *part*	**part-** +	*-icula*	=	**particula, -ae**, f., *a little part*

English words derived from these Latin diminutives usually end in *-le, -ule, -ole, -cle, -cule, -el,* or *-il*, e.g., *particle, novel.*

Exercise 1

Give the meaning of the following Latin diminutives. Consult a Latin dictionary to determine what (if any) special meanings these diminutives may have had for the Romans:

1. **servulus, -ī**, m.
2. **oppidulum, -ī**, n.
3. **amīcula, -ae**, f.
4. **lectulus, -ī**, m.
5. **capitulum, -ī**, n.
6. **cistella, -ae**, f.
7. **ancillula, -ae**, f.
8. **libellus, -ī**, m.
9. **lapillus, -ī**, m.
10. **puellula, -ae**, f.

Exercise 2
Give the English word derived from each of the following Latin diminutives:

1. **mūsculus, -ī,** m., *little mouse*
2. **circulus, -ī,** m., *a round figure*
3. **corpusculum, -ī,** n., *a little body*
4. **rīvulus, -ī,** m., *a little stream*
5. **minusculus, -a, -um,** *somewhat small*
6. **tabernāculum, -ī,** n., *tent*

Exercise 3
Look up the Roman emperor Caligula in an encyclopedia and find out why he was known by this diminutive nickname.

Frequentative Verbs

Frequentative verbs are formed from other Latin verbs and denote repeated or intensified action. (They are also called intensive verbs.) They are usually in the first conjugation, e.g., **dictō, -āre,** *to say often, repeat* (from **dīcō, -ere,** *to say*). Often the special frequentative meaning has been lost and the frequentative verb has nearly the same meaning as the original verb, e.g., **cantō, -āre,** *to sing* (from **canō, -ere,** *to sing*). Frequentative verbs are formed from other verbs in one of two ways:

1. by adding *-ō* to the stem of the fourth principal part, e.g., **acceptō, -āre,** *to receive* (from **acceptus,** perfect passive participle of **accipiō**)
2. by adding *-itō* to the base of the present infinitive (occasionally to the stem of the fourth principal part), e.g., **rogitō, -āre,** *to ask frequently or earnestly* (from **rogāre**), and **ēmptitō, -āre,** *to buy up* (from **ēmptus,** perfect passive participle of **emō**)

Exercise 4
Give the original Latin verb to which each of the following frequentative verbs is related:

1. iactō, -āre	5. haesitō, -āre	9. exercitō, -āre	13. tractō, -āre
2. cessō, -āre	6. cursō, -āre	10. dormitō, -āre	14. agitō, -āre
3. habitō, -āre	7. vīsitō, -āre	11. clāmitō, -āre	
4. ventitō, -āre	8. scrīptitō, -āre	12. ductō, -āre	

Exercise 5
Look up each of the frequentative verbs in Exercise 4 in a Latin dictionary. Identify each frequentative verb whose meaning differs significantly from the meaning of the original verb.

Exercise 6
Form a frequentative verb from each of the following Latin verbs by adding *-ō* to the stem of the fourth principal part. Look up the frequentative verb in a Latin dictionary and compare its meaning with that of the original verb:

1. excipiō	3. olfaciō	5. adiuvō	7. gerō
2. reprehendō	4. expellō	6. terreō	8. capiō

REVIEW X: CHAPTERS 43–45

Exercise Xa: Imperfect and Pluperfect Subjunctives

Give the imperfect and pluperfect subjunctives of the following verbs in the third person singular (give both active and passive forms for numbers 1–5):

1. amō
2. moneō
3. dūcō
4. capiō
5. inveniō

6. moror
7. vereor
8. sequor
9. ingredior
10. experior

Exercise Xb: Participles

Give the present, perfect, and future participles of the verbs in Exercise Xa in the nominative and accusative singular feminine.

Exercise Xc: Translation

Read aloud and translate:

CAESAR VISITS BRITAIN

Gaius Iūlius Caesar, dux praeclārus Rōmānōrum, in Galliā pugnāns multa dē Britanniā cognōvit. Mercātōrēs enim ē Britanniā ad Galliam trānsgressī multa emēbant ac vēndēbant; et Britannī auxilium Gallīs Caesarī resistentibus semper mittēbant. Caesar igitur, Gallīs victīs et nāvibus parātīs, in Britanniam trānsgredī cōnstituit. Profectūrī tamen mīlitēs, magnā tempestāte coortā, nāvēs   5
cōnscendere vix poterant. Complūribus post diēbus, cum tempestāte nāvēs paene dēlētae essent, Rōmānī Britanniae appropinquantēs incolās in omnibus collibus īnstructōs cōnspexērunt. Ēgredientēs Rōmānōs Britannī, pīlīs coniectīs, dēpellere cōnātī sunt; sed, quamquam multōs Rōmānōrum vulnerāvērunt, tandem superātī sunt.   10

1 **dux, ducis,** m., *general*
pugnō, -āre, -āvī, -ātūrus, *to fight*

8 **īnstructus, -a, -um,** *drawn up, deployed*
pīlum, -ī, n., *javelin*

6 **cōnscendō, cōnscendere, cōnscendī, cōnscēnsus,** *to board (ship)*
9 **dēpellō, dēpellere, dēpulī, dēpulsus,** *to drive away*

Exercise Xd: Identification

In the story in Exercise Xc, identify the following in sequence:

1. a present active participle
2. a perfect participle of a deponent verb
3. a present active participle
4. an ablative absolute
5. a future active participle
6. an ablative absolute
7. a **cum** circumstantial clause
8. a present active participle
9. a perfect passive participle
10. a present participle of a deponent verb
11. an ablative absolute

Exercise Xe: Substitution

Choose the phrase or clause that could be substituted for the words quoted from the story in exercise Xc and that would keep the same sense. Then translate the sentence, substituting the new phrase or clause for the original words:

1. **in Galliā pugnāns**
   a. in Galliā pugnātūrus
   b. quī in Galliā pugnābat
   c. in Galliā pugnant
2. **ē Britanniā ad Galliam trānsgressī**
   a. quī ē Britanniā ad Galliam trānsgredientur
   b. ē Britanniā ad Galliam trānsgressūrī
   c. quī ē Britanniā ad Galliam trānsgressī erant
3. **Gallīs victīs et nāvibus parātīs**
   a. cum Gallī victī essent et nāvēs essent parātae
   b. Gallōs victūrus et nāvēs parātūrus
   c. Gallōs vincēns et nāvēs parāns
4. **profectūrī tamen mīlitēs**
   a. profectīs tamen mīlitibus
   b. mīlitēs tamen quī proficīscī in animō habēbant
   c. mīlitēs tamen quī profectī essent
5. **cum tempestāte nāvēs paene dēlētae essent**
   a. tempestāte nāvēs paene dēlente
   b. quod tempestāte nāvēs paene dēlētae sunt
   c. nāvibus tempestāte paene dēlētīs
6. **quamquam multōs Rōmānōrum vulnerāvērunt**
   a. multīs Rōmānīs vulnerātīs
   b. multōs Rōmānōrum vulnerātūrī
   c. multī Rōmānōrum vulnerātī

Exercise Xf: Reading Comprehension

Read the following story from Ovid and answer the questions with full sentences in English:

ARACHNĒ ET MINERVA

Lȳdia Arachnē, perītissima omnium puellārum quae tēlās texēbant, per urbēs Lȳdiās arte suā erat praeclārissima. Iter ex urbibus vīcīnīs faciēbant multī, quī cūriōsī Arachnēn tēlās texentem spectāre volēbant. Etiam nymphae, silvīs et montibus et undīs relictīs, ad casam Arachnēs veniēbant. Omnēs mīrābantur nōn modo tēlās textās sed etiam artem quā texēbat. Minerva ipsa Arachnēn docuisse dīcēbātur, sed 5 puella hoc vehementer negāvit. "Nūlla dea," inquit, "mihi magistra fuit! Sī dea ipsa advēnerit, certāmen nōn vītābō!"

Quō audītō, Minerva Arachnēn vīsitātūra anum simulāvit et baculō innixa ad puellam superbam vēnit. In casam ingressa sīc locūta est: "Audī mē monentem! Fāmam pete inter mortālēs sed cēde deae veniamque tuīs dictīs, temerāria, rogā! 10 Veniam dabit dea rogantī."

"Abī, anus!" clāmāvit Arachnē. "Nōlī mē monēre!" Mīrāta tamen est cūr dea ipsa nōn vēnisset, cūr certāmen vītāret. Tum dea, "Vēnī!" inquit et fōrmam simulātam dēposuit. Quamquam dea sē ostenderat, puella tamen nōn timuit, immō certāmen prōposuit. 15

Tum ambae, cum ad tēlās cōnsēdissent, pictūrās pulcherrimās texere coepērunt. Operibus cōnfectīs, tēla Minervae nūllō modō melior erat tēlā Arachnēs. Minerva autem rēs ā dīs bene gestās texuerat, Arachnē rēs male gestās. Quō vīsō, īrātissima facta est dea. Arachnē, ferōciter ā deā castīgāta, sē laqueō suspendit.

Puellae pendentis miserita est Minerva, quae sīc locūta est: "Vīve, superba! Sed 20 vīve, fōrmā arāneae sūmptā!"

Arachnē, capite statim dēminūtō, ipsa tōtō corpore parva facta est. Adhūc tamen fīlum dēdūcēns arānea tēlam texit.

1 **Lȳdius, -a, -um,** *from Lydia (a country in Asia Minor), Lydian*	**innixus, -a, -um** +abl., *leaning on*
perītus, -a, -um, *skilled*	9 **superbus, -a, -um,** *proud, arrogant*
tēla, -ae, f., *web, fabric, loom*	10 **venia, -ae,** f., *pardon, forgiveness*
2 **cūriōsus, -a, -um,** *curious*	**dicta, -ōrum,** n. pl., *words*
3 **nympha, -ae,** f., *nymph, nature spirit*	16 **ambō, ambae, ambō,** *both*
4 **mīror, -ārī, -ātus sum,** *to admire, wonder at, wonder*	17 **opus, operis,** n., *work, product*
6 **negō, -āre, -āvī, -ātus,** *to deny*	19 **laqueus, -ī,** m., *noose*
7 **certāmen, certāminis,** n., *contest*	20 **misereor, -ērī, -itus sum** + gen., *to pity*
8 **anus, -ūs,** f., *old woman*	21 **arānea, -ae,** f., *spider*
simulō, -āre, -āvī, -ātus, *to pretend, take the form of*	23 **fīlum, -ī,** n., *thread*
	dēdūcēns, *drawing out, spinning*

10 **cēdō, cēdere, cessī, cessūrus** + dat., *to yield to, give in to*
14 **ostendō, ostendere, ostendī, ostentus,** *to show*
18 **gerō, gerere, gessī, gestus,** *to wear; to carry on, perform, do*
19 **suspendō, suspendere, suspendī, suspēnsus,** *to suspend, hang*
20 **pendeō, pendēre, pependī,** *to be suspended, hang*
22 **dēminuō, dēminuere, dēminuī, dēminūtus,** *to reduce in size*

1. For what was Arachne most famous?
2. What did curious people do?
3. What did the nymphs do?
4. What did they admire?
5. Who was said to have taught Arachne?
6. What challenge to the goddess did Arachne make?
7. What form did the goddess assume?
8. What advice did she give?
9. What did Arachne say in reply?
10. Who proposed the contest?
11. Whose woven fabric was better?
12. What had Minerva and Arachne woven?
13. Why did Arachne hang herself?
14. How did Minerva react?
15. What does Arachne continue to do in her transformed state?

Minerva

chariots—followed possibly by a swim across the Tiber.

A RAINY DAY

Many of the games that children play today were also played by Roman children. They built toy houses and rode on long sticks; they had spinning tops, hoops that they bowled along with a stick, and dolls (**pūpae**); they tossed coins, calling out "heads or ships" (**capita aut nāvia**); and they played at being soldiers or judges or consuls. They also harnessed mice to toy carts.

Several children's games used nuts. In one a nut was balanced on three others, and children competed at knocking them down with a fruit pit. The winner got all the nuts. They also competed at tossing nuts into a narrow-necked vase placed some distance away. A very popular game was to ask your partner to guess whether the number of nuts (or pebbles or other similar objects) hidden in your hand was odd or even (**pār impār**). In another popular game two players each showed (or "flashed") a number of fingers on their right hands (**digitīs micāre**) and simultaneously called out how many fingers altogether they believed had been shown. The round was won by the player who first guessed correctly five times. This game is still played in Italy under the name of *morra*.

Both adults and children played a game that resembled checkers or chess (**lūdus latrunculōrum,** *game of bandits*), in which they moved two sets of pieces on a checkered board. They also played a game of chance with knucklebones (**tālī**). Older children and young men took exercise on the Campus Martius—wrestling, riding, and driving chariots—followed possibly by a swim across the Tiber.

As we rejoin our story, Marcus, Cornelia, and Sextus are spending a rainy day at home.

Roman children at play

"Ēheu!" mussāvit Marcus. "Cūr 'ēheu'?" rogāvit Sextus.

"Semper pluit!" respondit Marcus. "Ego in animō habēbam ad Campum Mārtium hodiē dēscendere et ad palaestram īre, sed pater nōs domī manēre iussit. Putō patrem esse crūdēlem."

Eō ipsō tempore Eucleidēs ingressus puerōs rogāvit cūr tam trīstēs essent. "In 5
palaestram īre cupiēbāmus," inquit Marcus, "sed pater hoc vetuit."

Cui Eucleidēs, "Bonō animō este!" inquit. "Ego vōs docēbō latrunculīs lūdere. Putō hunc lūdum esse optimum."

Duās ferē hōrās ita lūdēbant. Postrēmō Sextus exclāmāvit, "Hic lūdus mē nōn iam dēlectat. Ego putō hunc lūdum esse pessimum. Age, Marce! Nōnne vīs pār impār lūdere 10
vel digitīs micāre?"

Statim clāmāre coepērunt ambō. Simul Marcus, "Quīnque!" simul Sextus, "Novem!" Deinde Marcus, "Octō!" Sextus, "Sex!"

"Tacēte, puerī!" interpellāvit Eucleidēs. "Nōlīte clāmōribus vestrīs vexāre mātrem et Cornēliam! Putō vōs esse molestissimōs hodiē." At puerī eī nōn pārēbant. Itaque 15
Cornēlia, clāmōribus audītīs, in ātrium ingressa rogāvit quid facerent.

"Nōlī nōs vexāre!" inquit Sextus. "Abī! Sed cūr pūpam in manibus habēs? Num pūpā lūdis?"

(continued)

3 **putō, -āre, -āvī, -ātus,** *to think,*
   consider
8 **lūdus, -ī,** m., *school, game*
9 **ferē,** adv., *almost, approximately*
   postrēmō, adv., *finally*

12 **ambō, ambae, ambō,** *both*
17 **pūpa, -ae,** f., *doll*
   Num...? *Surely...not...?* (introduces
   a question that expects the
   answer "no")

Exercise 46a
Respondē Latīnē:

1. Cūr erat Marcus trīstis?
2. Cūr Marcus patrem crūdēlem esse putat?
3. Quid Eucleidēs puerōs docuit?
4. Quid Sextus post duās hōrās facere voluit?
5. Quōs Marcus et Sextus clāmōribus vexābant?
6. Quis in ātrium ingressa est?
7. Quid in manibus habuit?

"Stultus es, Sexte! Pūpa nōn est mea. Num crēdis mē pūpā lūdere? Hanc pūpam, quam ego ipsa fēcī, filiae Dāvī dōnō dabō. Hodiē est diēs nātālis eius." 20

Subitō Sextus, pūpā abreptā, in peristȳlium aufūgit. Quō vīsō, Eucleidēs Sextō clāmāvit, "Nōlī pūpam laedere! Statim eam refer!"

Eō ipsō tempore ingressus est Cornēlius. Cum audīvisset quid Sextus fēcisset, "Sexte!" clāmāvit. "Venī hūc!" Puer, iam timidus, in ātrium regressus pūpam Cornēliae reddidit. Tum Cornēlius Sextum sēcum ex ātriō ēdūxit. 25

Quō factō, Marcus rogāvit, "Quid pater faciet? Quid Sextō fiet?"

Cui Cornēlia, "Putō," inquit, "patrem in animō habēre Sextum verberāre."

20 **dōnum, -ī,** n., *gift*
  dōnō (dat.) **dare,** *to give as a gift*
  diēs nātālis, diēī nātālis, m., *birthday*

21 **peristȳlium, -ī,** n., *peristyle, (courtyard surrounded with a colonnade)*

26 **Quid Sextō fiet?** *What will happen to Sextus?*

21 **abripiō, abripere, abripuī, abreptus,** *to snatch away*
22 **laedō, laedere, laesī, laesus,** *to harm*

Respondē Latīnē:

1. Lūdēbatne pūpā Cornēlia?
2. Cuius erat diēs nātālis?
3. Quid Sextus, pūpā vīsā, fēcit?
4. Cui Sextus pūpam reddidit?
5. Quid Cornēlius factūrus erat?

BUILDING THE MEANING
Accusative and Infinitive (Indirect Statement) I

The following sentences occurred in the story:

Putō **hunc lūdum esse** optimum. (46:7–8)
*I think **that this game is** very good.*

Putō **vōs esse** molestissimōs. (46:15)
*I think **that you are** very annoying.*

Num crēdis **mē pūpā lūdere?** (46:19)
*Surely you do not believe **that I am playing** with a doll?*

In such sentences, you are being given two pieces of information:

(1) I think
  Putō

(2) what I think
  hunc lūdum esse optimum.
  (that) this game is very good.

You will see that, in the second part, the Latin subject is expressed in the *accusative* case and the verb is in the *infinitive*, where English says *that this game* and *is*. Similarly:

Sciō		**vōs esse** molestissimōs.
I know	*that*	*you are* very troublesome.
Vidēmus		**Dāvum** in agrīs **labōrāre.**
We see	*that*	*Davus is working* in the fields.
Audiō		**eum** domī **morārī.**
I hear	*that*	*he is staying* at home.

Other verbs that may be followed by the *accusative and infinitive* construction include **dīcō** (*I say*), **spērō** (*I hope*), and **sentiō** (*I feel*).

Sextus sentit <u>**sē** aegrum **esse.**</u>
*Sextus feels **<u>that he is ill</u>**.*

In translating this Latin construction, the next English word after verbs such as *I think, I know, I see, I hear,* and *I feel* will most often be *that*.

This accusative and infinitive construction in which something is being reported indirectly is known as *indirect statement*.

Exercise 46b
Read aloud and translate:

1. Eucleidēs dīcit lūdum latrunculōrum esse optimum.
2. Sciō Cornēlium esse senātōrem Rōmānum.
3. Nōs omnēs scīmus Cornēliam esse puellam Rōmānam.
4. Putō Sextum puerum temerārium esse.
5. Audiō Cornēlium ad Cūriam festīnāre.
6. Scit ancillās cēnam parāre.
7. Videō haud longam esse viam.
8. Audiō caupōnem esse amīcum Eucleidis.
9. Putāmus in agrīs labōrāre servōs.
10. Crēdō Aurēliam in urbem dēscendere.
11. Dīcunt Marcum dormīre.
12. Scīmus semper ēsurīre puerōs.
13. Audiō Titum mappam nōn habēre.
14. Cornēlia putat pūpam esse pulcherrimam.

Exercise 46c

Select, read aloud, and translate:

1. Aliī putant (Sextus/Sextum) esse bonum, aliī putant eum (est/erat/esse) molestum.
2. Dāvus quidem scit omnēs (puerōs/puerum/puerī) saepe esse (molestum/molestī/molestōs).
3. At Aurēlia putat Marcum et Sextum semper bonōs (sunt/esse/erant).
4. Sextus Marcō dīcit Dāvum (esse/est/sum) īrācundum.
5. Respondet Marcus (Dāvī/Dāvō/Dāvum) nōn semper (esse/est) īrācundum.
6. Dīcit Dāvum in agrīs strēnuē (labōrāre/labōrāvit/labōrat).
7. Sextus respondet Dāvum sub arbore cotīdiē post merīdiem (dormīs/dormiēbat/dormīre).
8. Cornēlia putat (puerī/puerīs/puerōs) haud strēnuē (labōrāvērunt/labōrant/labōrāre).
9. Dīcit Cornēlia Marcum et (Sextī/Sextum/Sextus) saepe in lectīs diū (iacēre/iacent/iacēmus).
10. Flāvia, amīca Cornēliae, putat (Cornēlia/Cornēliam/Cornēliae) puellam pulcherrimam (esse/sunt/est).

Exercise 46d

Using story 46 and the information on indirect statement as guides, give the Latin for:

1. Marcus says that his father is cruel.
2. Eucleides says that the game of bandits is the best, but Sextus thinks it is the worst.
3. Eucleides says that the children are very annoying today.
4. Sextus believes that Cornelia is playing with the doll.
5. Eucleides thinks that Sextus is harming the doll.

GAMES PLAYED BY CHILDREN AND ADULTS

Descriptions of games played by Roman children are preserved in the writings of ancient authors. They are often difficult for us to interpret, although they were probably perfectly clear to ancient readers who would have been familiar with the games and their rules. In the following passage the poet Ovid describes games boys played with nuts (**nucēs**). See if you can figure out how many games Ovid describes and how they were played. We give both the Latin and an English translation of each couplet. You may want to look up some of the Latin words in a dictionary:

Hās puer aut certō rēctās dīlāminat ictū
  aut prōnās digitō bisve semelve petit.
These (nuts), as they stand upright, a boy splits with certain aim,
  or, as they lie on their side, strikes with his finger once or twice.

Quattuor in nucibus, nōn amplius, ālea tōta est,
  cum sibi suppositīs additur ūna tribus.
In four nuts, and no more, is all his hazard,
  when one is added to the three beneath it.

Per tabulae clīvum lābī iubet alter et optat
  tangat ut ē multīs quaelibet ūna suam.
Another has them roll down a sloping board, and prays
  that one out of many, whichever it may be, may touch his own.

Est etiam, pār sit numerus quī dīcat an impār,
  ut dīvīnātās auferat augur opēs.
Then there is (a boy) who guesses whether the number be odd or even,
  that the augur may bear away the wealth he has divined.

Fit quoque dē crētā, quālem caeleste figūram
  sīdus et in Graecīs littera quarta gerit.
Then too there is drawn in chalk a shape, such as a heavenly
  constellation or the fourth Greek letter bears.

Haec ubi distīncta est gradibus, quae cōnstitit intus
  quot tetigit virgās, tot capit ipsa nucēs.
When this has been marked with stages, the nut that stops within it
  gains itself as many nuts as it has touched lines.

Vās quoque saepe cavum spatiō distante locātur,
  in quod missa levī nux cadat ūna manū.
Often too a hollow vessel is placed at a distance,
  into which a nut flung by a skillful hand may fall.

—Ovid, *Nux* 73–86

The next two passages refer to playing **pār impār** by flashing the fingers (**micāre**):

When they praise a man's honesty, they say, "He is a man with whom you can safely play at odd and even in the dark."

—Cicero, *De officiis* III. 77

"Suppose there were two men to be saved from a sinking ship—both of them wise men—and only one small plank. Should both seize it to save themselves? Or should one give way to the other?"

"Why, of course one should give way to the other, but that other must be the one whose life is more valuable, either for his own sake or for that of his country."

"But what if these considerations are of equal weight in both?"

"Then there will be no contest, but one will give place to the other, as if the point were decided by lot or at a game of odd and even."

—Cicero, *De officiis* III. 90

GAMBLING WITH KNUCKLEBONES

From a personal letter of the Emperor Augustus:

I dined, dear Tiberius, with the same company; we had besides as guests Vinicius and the elder Silius. We gambled like old men during the meal both yesterday and today. When the knucklebones were thrown, whoever turned up the "dog" or the six put a denarius in the pool for each one of the knucklebones and the whole was taken by anyone who threw the "Venus."

From a personal letter of the Emperor Augustus to his daughter:

I send you two hundred and fifty denarii, the sum that I gave each of my guests, in case they wished to play at knucklebones or at odd and even during the dinner.

—Suetonius, *Augustus* LXXI.2, 4

Girls playing knucklebones

THE LAST MOVE IN A GAME OF CHESS

Julius Canus, after a long dispute with the Emperor Caligula, was ordered by the capricious emperor to be executed. Seneca the moralist praises the bravery of Canus under sentence of death:

> Will you believe that Canus spent the ten intervening days before his execution in no anxiety of any sort? What the man said, what he did, how tranquil he was, passes all credence. He was playing chess when the centurion who was dragging off a whole company of victims to death ordered that he also be summoned. Having been called, he counted the pawns and said to his partner: "See that after my death you do not claim falsely that you won." Then nodding to the centurion, he said, "You will bear witness that I am one pawn ahead."
>
> —Seneca, *De tranquillitate* XIV 6–7

Quid est tam incertum quam tālōrum iactus? *What is so uncertain as a cast of dice?*
(Cicero, *De divinatione* II.121)
nucēs relinquere *to leave childhood behind* (Persius, *Satires* I.10)

FORMS
The Irregular Verb *fīō, fierī, factus sum*

This irregular verb, meaning *to become, be made,* or *happen,* serves as the passive of **faciō**. Note that the verb has only three principal parts: **fīō,** *I become;* **fierī,** *to become,* and **factus sum,** *I became.* Some of its forms were introduced in Exercise 34h. You saw an example in the story at the beginning of this chapter:

"Quid pater faciet? Quid Sextō **fiet**?" (46:26)
*"What will father do? What **will happen** to Sextus?"*

Its forms in the present, imperfect, and future tenses are as follows:

		Present	Imperfect	Future
	1	fīō	fiē*bam*	fī*am*
S	2	fīs	fiē*bās*	fī*ēs*
	3	fit	fiē*bat*	fī*et*
	1	fī*mus*	fiē*bāmus*	fī*ēmus*
P	2	fī*tis*	fiē*bātis*	fī*ētis*
	3	fīu*nt*	fiē*bant*	fī*ent*

Learn the above forms thoroughly.

Exercise 46e
Read aloud and translate:

1. Titus vīnum bibit et paulātim ēbrius fit.
2. Sī Titus plūs vīnī bibet, magis ēbrius fiet.
3. Aurēlia Titum in diēs molestiōrem fierī putat.
4. Quid Titō fiet sī etiam plūs vīnī nunc bibet?
5. Aliquid malī certē eī fiet.

THE EARLY EMPIRE

Augustus died at the age of seventy-six in A.D. 14, in the month named for him in 27 B.C. At the time of his death, the mood in Rome was one of contentment. The frontiers of the empire were secure, the state bureaucracy was operating well, the **equitēs** were satisfied with the expansion of trade and the new careers that were open to them in political and military service, and the urban population was happy to have enough food and entertainment. Augustus had also left behind a strong national consciousness of the strength and glorious achievements of the Roman Empire, a perception that the *Aeneid* and other works of literature had helped to create.

Growth of the Roman Empire, 44 B.C.–A.D. 180

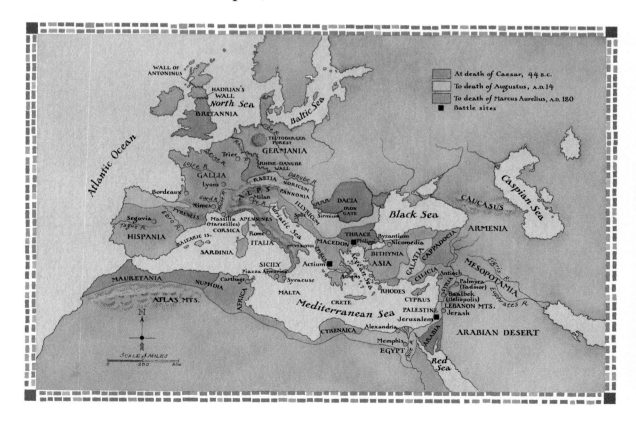

For almost half a century, the Roman world had been ruled by a single master who held all real authority in his own hands, despite the trappings of republican government. Only an extraordinary individual could maintain that kind of control. Inevitably, upon his death, trouble was bound to come. What made matters even worse was that Augustus intended the office of emperor to be hereditary, but in order to maintain the illusion of republicanism it could not officially be made hereditary. Unfortunately, he had failed to produce a son of his own, whom he could have maneuvered into a position to be accepted as emperor after his death. Therefore, Augustus had to use the children and grandchildren of his sister, Octavia; his daughter, Julia; and his wife's first husband, T. Claudius Nero, as substitutes. That is why the dynasty of emperors who ruled the first century of the Roman Empire is called the Julio-Claudian dynasty. Because of Augustus' maneuverings to procure an heir from his own family, many different people could claim a right to succeed to Augustus' principate. Therefore, family intrigue and murder were prominent in the history of this dynasty.

THE JULIO-CLAUDIAN DYNASTY

The personal lives of the Julio-Claudian dynasty inspired much scandal and malicious rumor that were gleefully reported by ancient writers such as the biographer Suetonius. Much of it has been dramatized in modern novels and films such as Robert Graves' *I Claudius* and *Claudius the God*. Even after the falsehoods have been eliminated, the truth still sometimes sounds like a soap opera.

The man who ultimately succeeded Augustus was his stepson Tiberius, who had been a loyal and effective subordinate in military and political affairs. Unfortunately, he had never been Augustus' first choice as a successor, and he was old and disillusioned by the time Augustus had no one else old enough left to succeed him. Tiberius' biggest problems were that he instinctively disdained many of the old families in the Senate and let himself be too influenced by Sejanus, corrupt head of the Praetorian Guard. Sejanus had tried to eliminate other members of the Julio-Claudian family and take control through marrying Tiberius' niece. By the time Tiberius found out about Sejanus' plottings and had him executed, only his nephew Caligula was in a position to succeed.

Caligula had suffered a very abnormal childhood. At first he was spoiled by his father, Germanicus, who had been in line to succeed Tiberius. When Gaius was a small boy, his father's soldiers had made him their mascot dressed in a soldier suit and had named him Caligula, "Little Boot," after the tiny army boots (**caligae**) he wore. When he arrived in Rome to head the state, his personality and generosity made a good first impression: He gave the praetorians a large cash bonus, provided the people with grand spectacles, and even displayed interest in the government. He had no real training for the job, however, and before long began to show bad temper, arrogance, and irrational fear of plots against him. As emperor he lived in terror of losing his life in palace intrigue, and he finally ended up in Tiberius' eccentric refuge on the Isle of Capri. Despite a promising start, he quickly proved unfit to rule and was assassinated in A.D. 41.

The Praetorian Guard proclaimed Caligula's uncle Claudius as the new emperor. Born prematurely with mental and physical infirmities, Claudius had not previously been seen as suited to rule. He was more able than many had realized, however. Unfortunately, lack of affection as a child made him easily susceptible to scheming wives who tried to use him to promote their family interests. His fourth wife, Agrippina the Younger, probably killed him with poisoned mushrooms in order to obtain the throne for her son, Nero, after she had brought about the murder of Claudius' own son, Britannicus.

Nero Claudius Caesar was sixteen years old when he became emperor. Agrippina encouraged him to devote himself to music, drama, and chariot races so that she could be the power behind the throne. Eventually, he tired of her dominance and had her murdered. He spent more and more time and money on the circus, theater, and musical contests while he neglected the finances and the provincial armies. After a great fire destroyed much of Rome in A.D. 64, he rebuilt the city and erected a new palace called the **Domus Aurea** *(Golden House)*, on such a lavish scale that he was accused of starting the fire to have the chance of showing off. He

Claudius
Marble head, Louvre, Paris, France

deflected attention to the Christians in Rome by accusing them and condemning many to horrible deaths. His cowardice and brutality alienated many Romans, but the final straw was a costly tour of Greece, where he competed as a performing artist in public competitions in A.D. 67 and 68. When Nero returned to Rome, he faced a thoroughly hostile Senate and armies who were rebelling because they had not been paid. Under the threat of troops coming to carry out the Senate's decree of execution, Nero took his own life.

Despite their personal deficiencies and their inability to get along with the Senate, which resented the increasingly centralized power of the emperor, the Julio-Claudians had provided the Roman Empire with two generations of peace and prosperity. Tiberius promoted public careers for the **equitēs** and consolidated the military gains of Augustus, while Claudius added the province of Britain through conquest in 43. Claudius further professionalized the imperial bureaucracy by using loyal freedmen and promoted economic growth by building roads, bridges, and harbors. During most of Nero's reign, capable advisors such as the philosopher Seneca kept things outside of Rome on an even keel.

THE FLAVIAN DYNASTY

Powerful generals from the provinces had already begun to maneuver against Nero before his death. The years A.D. 68 and 69 saw the rapid succession of four emperors in a series of assassinations and civil wars: Galba, Otho, Vitellius, and Vespasian. Fortunately for Rome and the empire, Vespasian was able to stop the slide into chaos and establish his own Flavian dynasty firmly in power. Vespasian was an **eques** of Sabine origin who had become a successful general in the conquest of Britain and in subduing a major insurrection by the Jews of Judaea. He quickly restored the principate on the model of Augustus. To show the new direction of his reign, he tore down Nero's **Domus Aurea** and began construction of the Flavian Amphitheater (the Colosseum) on part of the site for the benefit of the public.

Vespasian's elder son, Titus, who had captured Jerusalem in A.D. 70, had served as his father's loyal Praetorian prefect until Vespasian died in A.D. 79. Titus' popularity grew during his brief reign when he promptly provided relief to the victims of Mt. Vesuvius' eruption in A.D. 79 and of a plague and great fire at Rome in A.D. 80. He completed the Flavian Amphitheater and dedicated it with magnificent games. His death from a fever caused great mourning. He was honored by the Arch of Titus in the Forum, which depicts his triumph over Judaea.

Titus' younger brother, Domitian, had always resented his more popular brother and used his own power as emperor to settle the score for real or imagined hurts earlier in life. His autocratic behavior and paranoid treatment of "enemies" unleashed a cycle of assassination plots and oppression among the senatorial class that finally resulted in his murder in A.D. 96. Despite his bad points, however, Domitian had followed many of the successful policies of his father and brother. Like them, he had kept the support of the lower classes through generous treatment, preserved peace on the frontier, and kept a good surplus in the treasury.

THE FIVE GOOD EMPERORS

The senators who had plotted against Domitian had tried to break the pattern of dynastic succession established by Augustus and Vespasian. They elected as emperor a childless and elderly senator named Nerva. To protect himself against being overthrown by the Praetorian Guard and provincial armies, however, Nerva had to create a dynastic heir by adopting Trajan, the powerful general of Lower Germany. Before Trajan could even get to Rome to greet his new father, Nerva died.

Trajan
Marble bust, Ephesus Museum, Turkey

Trajan showed great respect for the Senate, and grateful senators gave him the title **Optimus Prīnceps**. He revived the expansionism of the old republic by conquering Dacia, Armenia, Mesopotamia, and Assyria. Dacia was rich in gold, but Trajan's rapid expansion dangerously overextended the empire's borders and exhausted him. Just before his heart failed in 177, he adopted his son-in-law Hadrian as his heir.

Hadrian upset many senators when he concluded that it was necessary to abandon most of Trajan's conquests except Dacia. He concentrated his efforts on building strong, fixed defensive boundaries such as his famous wall in Britain. His one major war was fought in Judaea against a new rebellion. After his victory, he founded a Roman colony on the site of Jerusalem and further scattered the Jewish people from their ancient home. Hadrian had taken more power away from the Senate, and when he suppressed a senatorial plot near the end of his life, he alienated the Senate even more. When he died, the senators tried to withhold the honor of deification.

Since Hadrian had no children, he had adopted Titus Aurelius Antoninus as his heir. Antoninus earned the **cognōmen** Pius by persuading hostile senators to deify Hadrian in return for concessions that would restore some of the Senate's lost prestige. Antoninus ruled benignly and lived a simple life of Roman modesty. The momentum that had been built up by Trajan and Hadrian carried the empire safely through his long and peaceful reign, and he left the biggest surplus that the treasury had ever seen. Unfortunately, while he was content to stay in Italy and tend his country estate, hostile forces were massing just beyond the imperial frontiers. His son-in-law and adopted son Marcus Aurelius had to deal with the first in a series of unprecedented military crises that almost led to the empire's destruction during the third century A.D.

During the reign of the Five Good Emperors, the Roman Empire reached the height of its peace and prosperity under rulers who promoted the public welfare and patronized literature and the arts: Nerva and Trajan established the **alimenta,** a welfare program for orphans that also provided investment for agricultural development. Trajan and Hadrian founded and beautified cities all over the empire. Many monuments such as Trajan's Column, which depicts the Dacian War, Trajan's Market, Hadrian's villa at Tivoli, his domed Pantheon, his temple to Venus and Rome, and his tomb, the Castel Sant' Angelo, still stand. The emperors' concerns for good government are revealed in the letters of Pliny the Younger, who was favored by Trajan. Marcus Aurelius was devoted to Stoic philosophy, and in his *Meditations* he left behind a much-admired testament to his fortitude and commitment to a moral life in the face of continuous warfare against barbarian enemies, a disastrous plague, court intrigue, and treachery.

Marcus Aurelius
Gold aureus, private collection

LOOKING FORWARD TO THE GAMES

Postrīdiē, dum Gaius Cornēlius in tablīnō scrībit, subitō intrāvit Titus, frāter eius. "Salvē, Gaī!" clāmāvit Titus. "Quid agis?"

"Bene!" respondit Cornēlius. "Sed semper sum, ut vidēs, negōtiōsus."

Cui Titus, "Prō certō habeō tē crās nōn labōrātūrum esse. Omnēs enim cīvēs Rōmānī ad mūnera itūrī sunt. Spērō tē quoque ad mūnera itūrum esse." 5

At Cornēlius, "Mūnera?" inquit. "Quid dīcis, mī Tite?"

"Prō dī immortālēs!" exclāmāvit Titus. "Crās Caesar amphitheātrum aperiet novum. Tū tamen rogās quid dīcam?"

Cornēlius autem cum rīsū, "Nōnne sentīs mē per iocum hoc dīxisse? Certē hic diēs maximē omnium memorābilis erit. Cōnstat servōs strēnuē labōrāvisse et amphitheātrum 10 summā celeritāte cōnfēcisse. Mārtiālis epigrammata dē spectāculīs iam scrībit. Plūrimī gladiātōrēs mox clāmābunt, 'Avē, imperātor, moritūrī tē salūtant!' "

Cui Titus, "Mehercule! Tōtum populum continēbit hoc amphitheātrum. Crās māne viae erunt plēnae hominum quī ab omnibus partibus ad spectāculum congredientur."

"Ita!" inquit Cornēlius. "Putō tamen Aurēliam eō nōn itūram esse. Scīs enim 15 Aurēliam neque mūnera neque sanguinem amāre. Aurēlia domī manēre māvult. Marcum tamen mēcum sum ductūrus. Iam adulēscēns est et mox togam virīlem sūmet. Sextus autem, quod adhūc puer est, domī manēbit; nam, ut docet Seneca, 'Quō maior populus, eō plūs perīculī.' Quotā hōrā tū ad amphitheātrum crās māne es itūrus?"

(continued)

3	**negōtiōsus, -a, -um,** *busy*	12	**imperātor, imperātōris,** m.,
4	**prō certō habēre,** *to be sure*		*commander, emperor*
5	**mūnera, mūnerum,** n. pl., *games*	16	**māvult,** *(she) prefers*
	spērō, -āre, -āvī, -ātus, *to hope*	18	**quō maior…, eō plūs…,** *the*
10	**cōnstat,** *it is agreed*		*greater…, the more…*
11	**epigramma, epigrammatis,** n., *epigram*		

13 **contineō, continēre, continuī, contentus,** *to confine, hold*
16 **mālō, mālle, māluī,** irreg., *to prefer*

Exercise 47a
Respondē Latīnē:

1. Quandō intrāvit Titus tablīnum Gaiī?
2. Quālis vir est Cornēlius?
3. Quō cīvēs Rōmānī crās ībunt?
4. Quid Caesar crās faciet?
5. Quālis diēs erit crās?
6. Quid servī aedificāvērunt?
7. Unde hominēs ad spectāculum congredientur?
8. Cūr Aurēlia domī manēre māvult?
9. Quis cum Cornēliō ad mūnera ībit?
10. Cūr Sextus domī manēbit?

"Prīmā lūce," respondit Titus, "nam mātūrē advenīre in animō habeō. Quandō tū et 20
Marcus eō perveniētis?"

"Haud mātūrē," inquit Cornēlius, "sed prō certō habeō nōs tē in amphitheātrō
vīsūrōs esse. Nunc haec epistula est cōnficienda. Valē!"

"Valē!" inquit Titus. "Nōs abitūrī tē salūtāmus!"

20 **mātūrē**, adv., *early*   23 **epistula est cōnficienda,** *the letter*
must be finished

Respondē Latīnē:

1. Quotā hōrā Titus ad amphitheātrum crās ībit?
2. Quem putat Cornēlius sē in amphitheātrō crās vīsūrum esse?
3. Quid Cornēlius nunc cōnficere vult?

BUILDING THE MEANING
Accusative and Infinitive (Indirect Statement) II

The future infinitive and the perfect infinitive are also used in indirect statements.
Look at the following examples:

>Putō Aurēliam eō nōn **itūram esse**. (47:15)
>*I think that Aurelia **will** not **go** there.*

>Prō certō habeō nōs tē **vīsūrōs esse**. (47:22–23)
>*I am sure that we **will see** you.*

The phrases **itūram esse** and **vīsūrōs esse** are *future active infinitives*. You will recognize this form as **esse** with the future participle, which appears in the accusative case
agreeing with the subject of the infinitive clause in gender, case, and number. (For the future participle, see Chapter 45.)

>Cōnstat servōs strēnuē **labōrāvisse** et amphitheātrum summā celeritāte
>**cōnfēcisse**. (47:10–11)
>*It is agreed that slaves **worked** hard and **finished** the amphitheater very quickly.*

The *perfect active infinitive* of non-deponent verbs (e.g., **labōrāvisse** and **cōnfēcisse**
above) can be recognized by the ending **-isse**, which is added to the perfect stem. (See
Chapter 41.)

The *perfect infinitive* of deponent verbs consists of the perfect participle plus the infinitive of the verb *to be*, **esse**. The perfect infinitive of deponent verbs is active in meaning:

> locūtus esse, *to have spoken*
> secūtus esse, *to have followed*

Thus:

> Titus dīcit hominēs ab omnibus partibus Rōmam **congressōs esse.**
> *Titus says that men from all regions **have come together** to Rome.*

Note that the participle **congressōs** agrees with the subject of the indirect statement, **hominēs**.

When **sē** is used in the accusative and infinitive construction in indirect statements, it is translated *he, she,* or *they* and refers to the subject of the verb of *saying, thinking,* or *hearing*:

> Titus dīxit **sē** ad amphitheātrum itūrum esse.
> *Titus said that **he** would go to the amphitheater.*

The use of **sē** in this sentence shows that *he* refers to Titus. If the *he* had referred to someone else, **eum** would have been used instead of **sē**.

Adulēscēns spērat sē diū vīctūrum esse; senex potest dīcere sē diū vīxisse. *A young man hopes that he will live a long time; an old man is able to say that he has lived a long time.* (adapted from Cicero, *On Old Age* XIX.68)

Exercise 47b
Read aloud and translate:

1. Putāmus servōs strēnuē labōrātūrōs esse.
2. Putāsne patruum tuum ad amphitheātrum pervēnisse?
3. Cōnstat illum diem memorābilem fuisse.
4. Scīs Cornēliam domī mānsūram esse.
5. Cornēlius audit Titum domum nōn vēnisse.
6. Cornēlius putat Aurēliam in peristȳlium ingressam esse.
7. Scīmus Sextum ad patrem suum epistulam mīsisse.
8. Audīmus Caesarem amphitheātrum novum aperuisse.
9. Scīmus omnēs cīvēs Rōmānōs ad mūnera itūrōs esse.
10. Spērat Aurēlia Cornēlium domum festīnātūrum esse.

Exercise 47c

Select, read aloud, and translate:

1. Prō certō habeō puerum (locūtus esse/locūtum esse/locūtūrōs esse).
2. Putāmus mīlitēs tribus diēbus (adventūrōs/adventūrās/adventūram) esse.
3. Spērō tē, Cornēlia, mox (reditūrus/reditūram/reditūrum) esse.
4. Scīmus (eam/eōs/eum) mox ingressūram esse.
5. Putat (omnēs/nēminem/paucōs) discessūrum esse.
6. Sciō (eōs/eum/eam) nōs secūtōs esse.
7. Putō puellās heri (ēgredī/ēgressās esse/ēgressūrās esse).
8. Audīvī servōs paucīs diēbus amphitheātrum (cōnficere/cōnfectūrum esse/cōnfectūrōs esse).
9. Respondent servī sē heri quam celerrimē (currere/cucurrisse/cursūrōs esse).
10. Eucleidēs dīcit sē epistulam crās (cōnficere/cōnfēcisse/cōnfectūrum esse).

Exercise 47d

Using story 47 and the information on indirect statement as guides, give the Latin for:

1. I know that all the Roman citizens will go to the games tomorrow.
2. Titus says that Caesar will open the new amphitheater tomorrow.
3. Cornelius says that slaves worked hard and finished the amphitheater very quickly.
4. Titus says that the amphitheater will hold the whole population (people).
5. Cornelius says that he has not yet finished his letter.

CIRCUS AND ARENA

The Romans did not have regular sporting events as we have on weekends or organized entertainment available every day as we have in the theater or movies. Instead, to celebrate religious festivals, commemorate great national victories, or honor the emperor, there were public holidays. These lasted a varying number of days, during which entertainments were presented in the circus and the arena. The number of these festivals increased as time went on until, by the reign of Claudius, 159 days of the year were holidays.

Admission to the shows was free, and all the emperors made sure there was plenty of entertainment. According to Fronto:

> Trajan sensibly always paid attention to the idols of the theater, the circus, or the arena because he knew that the entertainment of the people was very important to the government; doling out corn or money might keep individuals quiet, but shows were necessary to keep the mob happy.

> —Fronto, *Preamble to History* 17

The Colosseum as it looks today

Juvenal, too, refers to the demand of the Roman mob for **pānem et circēnsēs**—the bread-dole and games in the circus.

The cost of the public games was met by the state. Often, magistrates added to the grant from their own pockets in order to increase their popularity and the chance of success in their careers. To do this they even ran into debt:

> Julius Caesar spent money so recklessly that many thought he was paying a high price to create a short-lived sensation, but really he was buying very cheaply the most powerful position in the world. Before entering politics he was thirteen hundred talents in debt. As aedile he staged games with 320 pairs of gladiators fighting in single combat. In this and his other extravagance in presenting theatrical performances, processions, and public banquets, he completely outdid all previous efforts to obtain publicity in this way.
>
> —Plutarch, *Caesar* 5

THE COLOSSEUM

When the family of Cornelius returned to Rome, the great building of the Colosseum was nearing completion. Until this time, Rome's amphitheaters had usually been temporary wooden structures, and these caused some frightful disasters, as at Fidenae near Rome in A.D. 27, when a wooden amphitheater collapsed, killing or maiming 50,000 people. Wooden structures continued to be built even after the completion of the magnificent architectural monument known to its contemporaries as the **Amphitheātrum Flāvium** but familiar to us as the Colosseum, so named from the nearby colossal statue of Nero, converted by Vespasian into a statue of the sun-god.

Begun by Vespasian, the Colosseum was dedicated in A.D. 80 by his son Titus, who, to speed up its construction, had used Jewish prisoners taken in the capture of Jerusalem ten years before. The massive elliptical building rose in four tiers and measured overall 620 x 512 feet or 189 x 156 meters. With seating space estimated at 45,000, it could be covered over by a massive awning in excessive heat or rain—though Gaius Caligula is said to have taken delight in opening such awnings of earlier wooden amphitheaters in times of extreme heat and forbidding anyone to leave! It took 1,000 sailors of the imperial fleet to raise the awning over the Colosseum.

Admission was free and open to men, women, and children, slave or free, so long as places were available. Women were confined to the topmost area, and their view must certainly have been restricted.

The floor of the Colosseum was of timber, strewn with sand, and had numerous trapdoors. Under the arena, and extending beyond it, was a vast complex of subterranean cells and passages, which now lie open and exposed to view. Remains can be seen of lifts and machinery (worked by counterweights) used to raise, at various points in the arena, caged animals, scenery, and other apparatus needed for wild beast hunts.

On the occasion of the dedication of the Colosseum, Titus held a festival for 100 days and during the celebrations staged a very lavish gladiatorial show.

For more than 1900 years, the Colosseum has stood as the most imposing monument in the city of Rome and has been almost synonymous with the city itself. A medieval writer, the Venerable Bede (c. A.D. 673–735), quoted the following pilgrims' proverb or prophecy linking the fate of the Colosseum with that of Rome and of the world:

> Quam diū stat Colyssaeus, stābit et Rōma.
> Quandō cadet Colyssaeus, cadet et Rōma.
> Quandō cadet Rōma, cadet et mundus.
>
> *While stands the Coliseum, Rome shall stand;*
> *When falls the Coliseum, Rome shall fall;*
> *And when Rome falls—the World.*

—translated by Lord Byron

MARTIAL'S EPIGRAMS

Born in Bilbilis, Spain, about A.D. 40, Martial went to Rome in A.D. 64, the year of the Great Fire, when Nero was emperor. His fame as a keen observer of life in the city and as a composer of biting, satirical epigrams **(epigrammata)** rests on poems he published in great numbers between A.D. 86 and 98. In A.D. 80, the year in which the Flavian Amphitheater was dedicated, Martial wrote a group of epigrams that he published under the title *De spectaculis*, in which he describes many of the memorable combats that took place in the arena that year. Translations of the first three poems in the collection are given below. In the first, Martial tries to assess the importance of the Amphitheater as an architectural monument. In the second he describes the joy of the Roman people in the building program of Vespasian and Titus that replaced the hated **Domus Aurea** of Nero with structures of more use to the people. In the third he pictures the influx of people from all over the Roman world who came to the dedication ceremonies.

(I)

Do not let barbarian Memphis tell of the wonder of her Pyramids, nor Assyrian toil vaunt its Babylon; let not the soft Ionians be praised for Trivia's temple; let the altar built of many horns keep its Delos hidden; let not Carians exalt to the skies with excessive praise the Mausoleum poised on empty air. The results of all these labors of man yield to Caesar's Amphitheater. One work in place of all shall Fame rehearse.

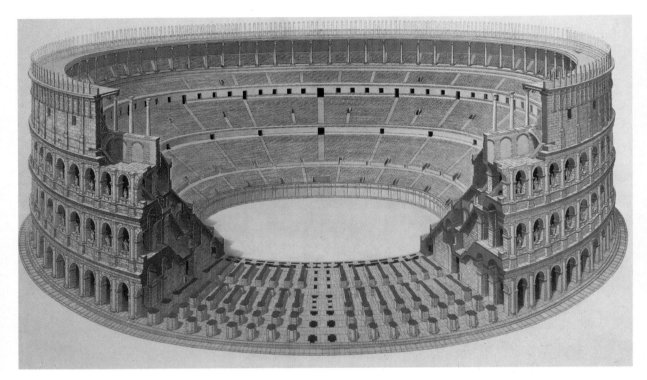

Reconstruction of the Colosseum

(II)

Here where, rayed with stars, the Colossus has a close view of heaven, and in the middle of the way tall scaffolds rise, hatefully gleamed the palace of a savage king, and only a single House then stood in all the City. Here, where the far-seen Amphitheater lifts its mass august, was Nero's lake. Here where we admire the warm baths, a gift swiftly built, a proud domain had robbed the poor of their dwellings. Where the Claudian Colonnade extends its outspread shade, the Palace ended in its farthest part. Now Rome is restored to itself, and under your rule, Caesar, what had been the delight of a tyrant is now the delight of the people.

(III)

What nation is so far distant, what people so barbarous, Caesar, that a spectator has not come from one of them to your city? A farmer of Rhodope has come from Orphic Haemus; a Sarmatian fed on draughts of horses' blood has come; and he who drinks at its source the stream of first-found Nile, and he whose shore the wave of farthest Tethys beats; the Arab has hurried here, Sabaeans have hurried, and Cilicians have here been drenched in their own saffron dew. With hair twined in a knot Sygambrians have come, and Aethiopians with their locks twined in other ways. The languages of the peoples are varied, yet they are one when you are acclaimed your country's true father.

FORMS
The Irregular Verb *mālō, mālle, māluī*

The verb **malō** is a compound of the adverb **magis** and the irregular verb **volō**, and it means *to wish more, wish rather,* or *prefer*. It has no imperative. In the story at the beginning of this chapter, you saw:

> Aurēlia domī manēre **māvult.** (47:16)
> *Aurelia **prefers** to stay at home.*

The forms of this verb in the present, imperfect, and future tenses are as follows:

		Present	Imperfect	Future
	1	mál**ō**	mālé**bam**	mál**am**
S	2	máv**ī**s	mālé**bās**	mál**ēs**
	3	máv**ul**t	mālé**bat**	mál**et**
	1	málu**mus**	mālēbá**mus**	mālé**mus**
P	2	māvúl**tis**	mālēbá**tis**	mālé**tis**
	3	málu**nt**	mālé**bant**	mál**ent**

Learn the above forms thoroughly.

Note carefully when the third letter is *l* and when it is *v* in the present tense. The imperfect, future, and the tenses formed from the perfect stem are regular.

Review the forms of **volō** and **nōlō** in the Forms section at the end of this book before doing the following exercise.

Exercise 47e

Read aloud and translate. Then for each form of the verb **volō**, substitute the corresponding form of the verb **nōlō**, read aloud, and translate. Then substitute the corresponding forms of **mālō**, read aloud, and translate:

1. Titus trigōne lūdere volēbat.
2. Puerī ad thermās īre volunt.
3. "In silvam convenīre volumus," inquiunt Pȳramus et Thisbē.
4. "Ad amphitheātrum crās īre volam," inquit Marcus.
5. Titus prīmā lūce ad amphitheātrum īre vult.
6. Sciō puerōs prīmā lūce surgere velle.
7. Cūr pār impār lūdere vīs, Marce?
8. "Vultisne latrunculīs lūdere, puerī?" inquit Eucleidēs.
9. "Dormīre volō," inquit Sextus.
10. Cornēliī ad vīllam rūsticam mox redīre volent.
11. Sciō Aurēliam herī domī manēre voluisse.

▬ ▬ ▬ ▬

**Dīmidium dōnāre Linō quam crēdere tōtum
quī māvult, māvult perdere dīmidium.**
*Whoever prefers to give Linus half rather than trust him
with the whole, prefers to lose the half.* (Martial, *Epigrams* I.75)

▬ ▬ ▬ ▬

A DAY AT THE COLOSSEUM

A day at the Colosseum was a great occasion. Tickets (**tesserae**), shown to the gate-keepers (**appāritōrēs**), were numbered according to the seating areas in the amphitheater. Seventy-six main entrances and numerous marble plaques illustrating the seating areas enabled the spectators to move swiftly and efficiently through a network of passages, stairs, and ramps to their correct place. The officiating magistrate, usually the emperor in Rome, would go to the imperial seat of honor (**pulvīnar**), and then the show could begin. The gladiators would parade and stop before the **pulvīnar**; they would greet the emperor with the words: "Hail, emperor, those about to die salute you!" (**Avē, imperātor, moritūrī tē salūtant.**) Next the trumpet-players and horn-players (**tubicinēs** and **cornicinēs**) would strike up. Then came the games. Pairs (**paria**) of gladiators would fight, urged on by the trainers (**lanistae**). The people joined in with roars of "Thrash him!" (**Verberā!**), "Murder him!" (**Iugulā!**), "He's hit!" (**Hoc habet!**), "Let him go!" (**Mitte!**). The savagery reached a peak with the midday fighters (**merīdiānī**), usually condemned criminals.

Avē, imperātor, moritūrī tē salūtant, depicted by Jean Leon Gerome
Yale University Art Gallery, New Haven, Connecticut, Gift of C. Ruxton Love, Jr.

Marcus and his father go to the amphitheater early in the morning as planned:

Prope amphitheātrum omnēs viae erant plēnae hominum quī ad spectāculum veniēbant. Undique clāmor ac strepitus; undique cīvēs, fēminae, servī. Multī tōtam noctem extrā amphitheātrī portās morātī erant. Nunc adfuit hōra spectāculī.

Cornēlius, cum tesserās appāritōribus ostendisset, ad locum senātōribus reservātum cum Marcō ā servō ductus est. Marcus tot et tam variōs hominēs numquam vīderat. Dum 5 attonitus circumspicit, subitō vīdit Titum iam cōnsēdisse. Patruum rogāre cupiēbat quandō pervēnisset, nam sciēbat Titum sērō ē lectō surgere solēre. Sed, quod pater aderat, Marcus nihil dīxit. Quam ingēns erat amphitheātrum! Quanta erat spectātōrum turba! Marcus coniciēbat quot spectātōrēs amphitheātrō continērī possent cum subitō fuit silentium. Omnēs ad pulvīnar oculōs convertērunt. 10

"Ecce!" clāmāvit Titus. "Iam intrat Caesar, amor ac dēliciae generis hūmānī!"

Tum, clāmōre sublātō, spectātōrēs prīncipem ūnā vōce salūtāvērunt. Stupuit Marcus, admīrātiōne captus. Iam gladiātōrēs cūnctī contrā pulvīnar cōnstiterant. "Avē, imperātor!" clāmāvērunt. "Moritūrī tē salūtant." Exiērunt gladiātōrēs. Mox tubicinēs et cornicinēs. Postrēmō gladiātōrum paria in arēnam intrāvērunt. 15

(continued)

5 **tot**, indecl. adj., *so many*	**contrā**, prep. + acc., *against, opposite,*
11 **dēliciae, -ārum**, f. pl., *delight*	*in front of, facing*
13 **admīrātiō, admīrātiōnis**, f.,	
amazement	

4 **ostendō, ostendere, ostendī, ostentus**, *to show, point out*
9 **coniciō, conicere, coniēcī, coniectus**, *to throw, throw together; to figure out, guess*
10 **convertō, convertere, convertī, conversus**, *to turn (around)*
12 **tollō, tollere, sustulī, sublātus**, irreg., *to lift, raise*
13 **cōnsistō, cōnsistere, cōnstitī**, *to halt, stop, stand*

Exercise 48a
Respondē Latīnē:

1. Quō hominēs veniēbant?
2. Quid Cornēlius appāritōribus ostendit?
3. Quō Cornēlius ductus est?
4. Quid Marcus coniciēbat?
5. Quid spectātōrēs fēcērunt postquam Caesar intrāvit?
6. Quid gladiātōrēs clāmāvērunt?

Nunc undique erat clāmor, tumultus, furor. Lanistae hūc illūc concursantēs, "Verberā!" "Iugulā!" clāmābant; turba, "Hoc habet!" aut, "Mitte!" aut, "Iugulā!" Marcus nihil tāle prius vīderat. Complūrēs hōrās ācriter pugnābātur; haud minus ferōciter ā spectātōribus clāmābātur.

Subitō Cornēlius, "Nunc," inquit, "domum nōbīs redeundum est. Mox enim   20
pugnābunt merīdiānī, quōs aliās tū, Marce, vidēbis."

"Nōnne tū quoque discēdere vīs, patrue?" clāmāvit Marcus.

Cui respondit Titus sē discēdere nōlle; sē nōndum satis vīdisse; merīdiānōs mox in arēnam ventūrōs esse. Brevī tempore Marcus cum Cornēliō in lectīcā per urbem portābā-tur et sēcum cōgitābat, "Quid ego prīmum Sextō nārrābō?"   25

16	**furor, furōris,** m., *frenzy*	20	**nōbīs redeundum est,** *we must return*
18	**ācriter,** adv., *fiercely*	21	**aliās,** adv., *at another time*
	pugnābātur, *the fighting went on*	24	**arēna, -ae,** f., *sand, arena*

Respondē Latīnē:

1. Quid clāmābant lanistae?
2. Quōmodo pugnābātur?
3. Quōmodo ā spectātōribus clāmābātur?
4. Quōs gladiātōrēs Marcus aliās vidēbit?
5. Quid Marcus in lectīcā cōgitābat?

▬ ▬ ▬ ▬

Quot hominēs, tot sententiae. *Everyone has his own opinion.* (Terence, *Phormio* 454)

▬ ▬ ▬ ▬

Exercise 48b
Read aloud and translate:

1. Titus respondet sē domum redīre nōlle.
2. Nōs omnēs scīmus Marcum ad amphitheātrum īsse.
3. Prō certō habēmus Titum sērō perventūrum esse.

BUILDING THE MEANING
Accusative and Infinitive (Indirect Statement) III

So far, the verbs of *thinking, knowing, saying,* and *seeing* introducing indirect state-ments have usually been in the present tense. Now look carefully at these sentences and compare them with the three sentences in Exercise 48b:

> Titus respondit sē domum redīre **nōlle.**
> *Titus replied that he **was unwilling** to return home.*

Nōs omnēs sciēbāmus Marcum ad amphitheātrum **īsse.**
*We all knew that Marcus **had gone** to the amphitheater.*

Prō certō habēbāmus Titum sērō **perventūrum esse.**
*We were sure that Titus **would arrive** late.*

After the past tenses **respondit, sciēbāmus,** and **habēbāmus,** although the accusative and infinitive clauses are exactly the same in Latin as they were in Exercise 48b, in English

> the present infinitive is translated by *was unwilling,*
> the perfect infinitive is translated by *had gone,* and
> the future infinitive is translated by *would arrive.*

In all indirect statements, whether introduced by verbs in the present or a past tense,

> the present infinitive = action going on at the *same time* as the action
> of the main verb;
> the perfect infinitive = action that was completed *before* the action
> of the main verb;
> the future infinitive = action that will take place *after* the action of
> the main verb.

Exercise 48c

Read aloud and translate each sentence, with the main verb first in the present tense and then in the past tense:

1. Titus spērat (spērāvit) puerōs ad mūnera itūrōs esse.
2. Marcus dīcit (dīxit) patrem epistulam cōnfēcisse.
3. Audiō (audīvī) Cornēlium ad Cūriam festīnāre.
4. Cornēlius dīcit (dīxit) sē Marcum sēcum ductūrum esse.
5. Num crēdis (crēdidistī) Cornēliam pūpā lūdere?
6. Prō certō habeō (habēbam) Aurēliam nōbīscum nōn itūram esse.
7. Aurēlia scit (sciēbat) Cornēliam pūpam fīliae Dāvī dedisse.
8. Patruus meus respondet (respondit) sē manēre mālle.
9. Sextus dīcit (dīxit) Marcum domum mātūrē reditūrum esse.
10. Marcus putat (putāvit) sē numquam tot et tam variōs hominēs vīdisse.

━━ ━━ ━━ ━━

Sōcratēs tōtīus mundī sē incolam et cīvem arbitrābātur. *Socrates thought himself an inhabitant and a citizen of the whole world.* (Cicero, *Tusculan Disputations* 5.108)

━━ ━━ ━━ ━━

Exercise 48d

MARCUS REPORTS BACK

Read the following passage aloud and answer the questions that follow with
full sentences in Latin:

Marcus iam domum regressus omnia quae vīderat Sextō nārrābat:
"Cum amphitheātrō appropinquārēmus, vīdimus magnam hominum
multitūdinem per portās intrāre. Nōs ipsī ingressī vīdimus multa mīlia cīvium
iam cōnsēdisse. Ego nōn crēdidissem tot hominēs amphitheātrō continērī posse.
Patruum exspectāre voluī, sed pater mihi dīxit Titum sine dubiō iam adesse. Et   5
rēctē dīxit; nam cum ad locum senātōribus reservātum vēnissēmus, vīdimus
Titum eō iam ductum esse.
    Subitō undique clāmātum est. Deinde vīdī imperātōrem ā gladiātōribus
salūtārī. Quam fortiter incēdēbant hī gladiātōrēs! Multī tamen eōrum moritūrī
erant. Ubi pugnam commīsērunt, spectābam obstupefactus. Nihil tāle prius   10
vīderam. Vīdī multōs vulnerārī atque complūrēs quidem occīdī. Quam fortēs
erant gladiātōrēs!
    Maximē dolēbam quod ante merīdiem domum nōbīs redeundum erat. Titus
dīxit sē mālle manēre, cum cuperet merīdiānōs vidēre. Spērō patrem mē ad
amphitheātrum iterum ductūrum esse. Fortasse tē quoque dūcet."   15

3 **mīlia, mīlium,** n. pl., *thousands*	10 **pugna, -ae,** f., *fight, battle*
4 **crēdidissem,** *I would have believed*	**pugnam committere,** *to join battle*
8 **clāmātum est,** *there was shouting*	**obstupefactus, -a, -um,** *astounded*

9 **incēdō, incēdere, incessī,** *to go in, march in*

Exercise 48e
Respondē Latīnē:

1. Quandō Marcus hominum multitūdinem vīdit?
2. Quid Marcus vīdit postquam amphitheātrum intrāvit?
3. Quid Marcus nōn crēdidisset?
4. Quid Cornēlius Marcō dīxit?
5. Quem ad locum Marcus vīdit Titum ductum esse?
6. Quōmodo Marcus pugnam spectābat?
7. Quid Marcus in gladiātōrum pugnā fierī vīdit?
8. Cūr Marcus dolēbat?
9. Quid Titus dīxit?
10. Quid Marcus spērat?

Accusative and Infinitive (Indirect Statement) IV

Passive infinitives and infinitives of deponent verbs are also used in this construction:

> Vīdī multōs **vulnerārī** atque complūrēs quidem **occīdī.** (48d:11)
> *I saw that many **were being wounded** and several actually **were being killed.***

> Titus dīxit omnēs Rōmānōs dē amphitheātrō **loquī.**
> *Titus said that all the Romans **were talking** about the amphitheater.*

The present passive infinitive is already familiar from Chapter 31. It can be recognized by the ending *-rī* in the 1st, 2nd, and 4th conjugations and the ending *-ī* in the 3rd conjugation.

For the perfect tense, the passive infinitive consists of the perfect participle and **esse:**

> Vīdimus Titum eō iam **ductum esse.** (48d:6–7)
> *We saw that Titus **had** already **been taken** there.*

> Audīvimus omnēs Rōmānōs dē amphitheātrō **locūtōs esse.**
> *We heard that all the Romans **had been talking** about the amphitheater.*

Note that the perfect participle agrees in gender, case, and number with the subject of the infinitive.

Exercise 48f

Form the present passive and the perfect passive infinitives of the following verbs. For the perfect passive infinitives, make the participles feminine accusative singular:

1. salūtō, -āre, -āvī, -ātus
2. videō, vidēre, vīdī, vīsus
3. ostendō, ostendere, ostendī, ostentus
4. coniciō, conicere, coniēcī, coniectus
5. sepeliō, sepelīre, sepelīvī, sepultus

Exercise 48g

Form the perfect infinitives of these deponent verbs. Make the participles masculine accusative singular:

1. moror, -ārī, -ātus sum
2. vereor, -ērī, -itus sum
3. loquor, loquī, locūtus sum
4. ingredior, ingredī, ingressus sum
5. experior, experīrī, expertus sum

Exercise 48h

Read aloud and translate:

1. Eucleidēs vīdit Cornēliam ā puerīs vexārī.
2. Sextus nescit vōcem suam audītam esse.
3. Vīdimus complūrēs nāvēs nōs sequī.
4. Putātis vestīmenta ā servō custōdīrī.
5. Scīvī mīlitēs in Britanniam profectōs esse.
6. Scīvī fūrēs in apodytērium ingressōs esse.
7. Cornēlius vīdit pūpam ā Sextō abreptam esse.
8. Cornēlius scīvit fīliam ā Sextō saepe vexārī.
9. Cōnstat amphitheātrum celeriter ā servīs cōnfectum esse.
10. Marcus Sextō dīcit sē ā patre ad amphitheātrum ductum esse.

One type of gladiator was the *net man*, who fought using only a net and trident.

FORMS
Verbs: Infinitives (Consolidation)

You have now met the following forms of the infinitive:

		Present		Perfect		Future
		Active	Passive	Active	Passive	Active
1		portáre	portári	portāvísse	portátus, -a, -um ésse	portātúrus, -a, -um ésse
2		movére	movéri	mōvísse	mótus, -a, -um ésse	mōtúrus, -a, -um ésse
3		míttere	mítti	mīsísse	míssus, -a, -um ésse	missúrus, -a, -um ésse
-iō		iácere	iáci	iēcísse	iáctus, -a, -um ésse	iactúrus, -a, -um ésse
4		audíre	audíri	audīvísse	audítus, -a, -um ésse	audītúrus, -a, -um ésse

Deponent Verbs

The present and perfect infinitives of deponent verbs are passive in form; the future infinitive is active in form:

Present	Perfect	Future
cōnári	cōnátus, -a, -um ésse	cōnātúrus, -a, -um ésse
séqui	secútus, -a, -um ésse	secūtúrus, -a, -um ésse

NOTES
1. The future passive infinitive rarely appears in Latin and will not be taught in this book.
2. Translations of the various forms of the infinitive are not given in the charts above because they will vary according to the use of the infinitive in the sentence. The infinitives of deponent verbs in all three tenses are active in meaning.

Exercise 48i
Using the story in Exercise 48d and the information in this chapter on indirect statement as guides, give the Latin for:

1. Marcus said that a great multitude of men had entered through the gates. (Use **ingredior**.)
2. Marcus said that he had seen nothing of this sort before.
3. Marcus said that many gladiators had been wounded.
4. Marcus said that Titus stayed and saw the midday fighters.
5. Marcus hopes that his father will take him to the amphitheater again.

GLADIATORS

Criminals sentenced to death could be purchased cheaply and thrown to the beasts or made to fight to the death, unarmed, in the arena. But those convicted of lesser crimes, for which the mines or deportation was the penalty, might instead go to a gladiatorial school. Slaves acquired through war or piracy were another source of recruitment, and occasionally volunteers, including Roman citizens, actually took up the gladiatorial trade. All gladiators bound themselves to their trade by an oath that laid down the severest penalties for backsliders or runaways: "to be burnt with fire, shackled with chains, beaten with rods, and killed with steel" (**ūrī, vincīrī, verberārī, ferrōque necārī**).

After thorough training in the barracks, the gladiator was ready for the arena. Successful gladiators, like chariot drivers, were popular heroes. This is an inscription from Pompeii:

> The girls' heart-throb, the Thracian Celadus, (property) of Octavius, three wins out of three.

Victorious gladiators were richly rewarded and, after a period of service, might win the wooden sword of freedom, even if slaves. Veteran gladiators could also be employed as overseers in the gladiatorial schools.

The fate of a defeated gladiator rested with the spectators. If he had won favor, the spectators might wave their handkerchiefs, and the emperor or presiding magistrate might then signal for his release. Otherwise, a turn of the thumb indicated that the fallen gladiator should speedily be killed.

**Gilded glass fragment
showing a gladiator**
British Museum, London, England

There were various classes of gladiators—these included the heavily armed Samnite with oblong shield, visored helmet, and short sword; the Thracian carrying a small round shield and curved scimitar; the **murmillō**, or *fish man*, who wore a helmet with a fish emblem on it and was armed with a sword and large shield; and the **rētiārius,** or *net man*, who was unarmed but for a great net and sharp trident. Each had his own supporters: the Emperor Titus, for example, supported the Thracians, as did Caligula. Local rivalry, too, was common, as is borne out by this inscription from Pompeii:

> Luck to the people of Puteoli and all those from Nuceria; down with the Pompeians.

Such rivalry could lead to trouble, as this incident in the reign of Nero illustrates:

> About this time there was a serious riot involving the people of Pompeii and Nuceria. It started with a small incident at a gladiatorial show. Insults were being exchanged, as often happens in these disorderly country towns. Abuse changed to stone-throwing, and then swords were drawn. The games were held in Pompeii and the locals came off best. Many badly wounded Nucerians were taken to their city. Many parents and children were bereaved. The Emperor ordered the Senate to inquire into the matter, and the Senate passed it on to the consuls. As a result of their report, the Senate banned Pompeii from holding any similar event for ten years.

> —Tacitus, *Annals* XIV.17

Gladiators were not used to fight animals (**bēstiae**) in the wild-beast hunts. For this, special fighters, **bēstiāriī**, were employed. In these shows, such animals as lions, tigers, bears, bulls, hippopotami, elephants, crocodiles, deer, pigs, and even ostriches were made to fight each other or the **bēstiāriī** or else driven to attack condemned criminals, who were sometimes chained or nailed to stakes. When Trajan held four months of festivities to celebrate his Dacian wars, some 10,000 gladiators and over 11,000 animals appeared in the arena over this period.

Even before the time of the emperors we read of the provinces being scoured for animals for these shows. Caelius, in a letter to his friend Cicero, wrote:

> Curio is very generous to me and has put me under an obligation; for if he had not given me the animals which had been shipped from Africa for his own games, I would not have been able to continue with mine. But, as I must go on, I should be glad if you would do your best to let me have some animals from your province—I am continually making this request.

> —Cicero, *Letters to his Friends* VIII.8

OTHER SHOWS IN THE ARENA

While dedicating the Amphitheater, the Emperor Titus also held a sea fight (**naumachia**) on the old artificial lake of Augustus and afterwards used the empty basin of the lake for still more gladiatorial bouts and a wild-beast hunt (**vēnātiō**) in which over 5,000 animals of different kinds died in a single day. His brother and imperial successor, Domitian, was not to be outdone; he even used the Amphitheater itself as a lake! Suetonius, in his life of Domitian, writes:

> Domitian constantly gave lavish entertainments both in the Amphitheater and in the Circus. As well as the usual races with two-horse and four-horse chariots, he put on two battles, one with infantry and one with cavalry; he also exhibited a naval battle in his amphitheater. He gave hunts of wild beasts and gladiatorial fights at night by torchlight, and even fights between women.

> He staged sea battles with almost full-sized fleets. For these he had a pool dug near the Tiber and seats built around it. He even went on watching these events in torrential rain.

—Suetonius, *Domitian* 4

A drawing of a sea fight staged in an arena. Notice the rams on the front of the boats.

GRAFFITI AND INSCRIPTIONS

Written at night on the facade of a private house in Pompeii:

D. Lucrētī Satrī Valentis flāminis Nerōnis Caesaris Aug. fīlī perpetuī gladiātōrum paria XX et D. Lucrētī Valentis fīlī glad. paria X, pug. Pompēīs VI V IV III pr. Īdūs Apr. Vēnātiō legitima et vēla erunt.

Twenty pairs of gladiators provided by Decimus Lucretius Satrius Valens priest for life of Nero, son of Caesar Augustus, and ten pairs of gladiators provided by the son of Decimus Lucretius Valens, will fight at Pompeii on April 8, 9, 10, 11, and 12. There will be a regular hunt and awnings.

Scratched on the columns in the peristyle of a private house in Pompeii:

Suspīrium puellārum Tr. Celadus Oct. III III.

The girls' heart-throb, the Thracian Celadus, (property) of Octavius, three wins out of three.

A curse against a **bēstiārius**:

Occīdite extermināte vulnerāte Gallicum, quem peperit Prīma, in istā hōrā in amphiteātrī corōnā. Oblīgā illī pedēs membra sēnsūs medullam; oblīgā Gallicum, quem peperit Prīma, ut neque ursum neque taurum singulīs plāgīs occīdat neque bīnīs plāgīs occīdat neque ternīs plāgīs occīdat taurum ursum; per nōmen deī vīvī omnipotentis ut perficiātis; iam iam citō citō allīdat illum ursus et vulneret illum.

Kill, destroy, wound Gallicus whom Prima bore, in this hour, in the ring of the amphitheater. Bind his feet, his limbs, his senses, his marrow; bind Gallicus whom Prima bore, so that he may slay neither bear nor bull with single blows, nor slay (them) with double blows, nor slay with triple blows bear (or) bull; in the name of the living omnipotent god may you accomplish (this); now, now, quickly, quickly let the bear smash him and wound him.

Sepulchral inscription of a **rētiārius**:

D. M. Vītālis invictī rētiārī, nātiōne Bataus, hīc suā virtūte pariter cum adversāriō dēcidit, alacer fu. pugnīs III. Convīctor eius fēcit.

To the deified spirits of Vitalis, a net-fighter who was never beaten; a Batavian by birth, he fell together with his opponent as a result of his own valor; he was a keen competitor in his three fights. His messmate erected (this monument).

Exercise 48j

The poet Martial, whose epigrams you have already met, found much to write about in the contests taking place in the Amphitheater. In the following poem he praises the gladiator Hermes, who excelled in no fewer than three fighting roles: as a **vēles** lightly armed with a spear, as a **rētiārius** with net and trident, and as a **Samnīs** heavily armed with visored helmet. This explains why he is called **ter ūnus** in the last line. The meter is hendecasyllabic.

Read aloud and translate:

> Hermēs Mārtia saeculī voluptās,
> Hermēs omnibus ērudītus armīs,
> Hermēs et gladiātor et magister,
> Hermēs turba suī tremorque lūdī,
> Hermēs quem timet Hēlius, sed ūnum,　　5
> Hermēs cui cadit Advolāns, sed ūnī,
> Hermēs vincere nec ferīre doctus,
> Hermēs suppositīcius sibi ipse,
> Hermēs dīvitiae locāriōrum,
> Hermēs cūra laborque lūdiārum,　　10
> Hermēs belligerā superbus hastā,
> Hermēs aequoreō mināx tridente,
> Hermēs casside languidā timendus,
> Hermēs glōria Mārtis ūniversī,
> Hermēs omnia sōlus, et ter ūnus.　　15

—Martial, *Epigrams* V.24

1　**Hermēs:** the gladiator has adopted the name of the Greek god Hermes (= Mercury, the messenger god who conducts souls of the dead to the underworld)
　Mārtius, -a, -um, *connected with Mars (the god of war and combat)*
　saeculum, -ī, n., *age, era*
　voluptās, voluptātis, f., *pleasure, delight*
4　**turba, -ae,** f., *crowd; cause of confusion/turmoil*
　suī...lūdī, *of his school (of gladiators)*
　tremor, tremōris, m., *cause of fright, terror*
5　**Hēlius,** Greek word for *Sun,* and **Advolāns,** literally, *Flying to (the Attack)*—two distinguished gladiators
　sed ūnum, *but the only one*

7 **feriō, -īre, -īvī, -ītus,** *to strike, kill*

8 **suppositīcius sibi ipse,** *himself his only substitute*

9 **dīvitiae, -ārum,** f. pl., *wealth, riches*
locārius, -ī, m., *scalper (a person who buys up seats,* **loca,** *in the amphitheater and then sells them for as high a price as he can get)*

10 **cūra, -ae,** f., *care;* here, *the favorite*
labor, labōris, m., *work, toil;* here, *a cause of suffering/distress, "heart-throb"*
lūdia, -ae, f., *female slave attached to a gladiatorial school*

11 **belliger, belligera, belligerum** (cf. the phrase **bellum gerere,** *to wage war*), *warlike*
superbus, -a, -um, *proud, arrogant*
hasta, -ae, f., *spear*

12 **aequoreō...tridente** (cf. **aequor, aequoris,** n., *the sea*), *with his sea trident*
mināx, minācis, *menacing*

13 **cassis, cassidis,** f., *plumed metal helmet*
languidus, -a, -um, *drooping (describing the crest of the helmet drooping down over the eyes)*
timendus, -a, -um, *to be feared*

14 **Mārtis ūniversī,** *of every kind of combat*

15 **ter,** adv., *three times*

▬▬▬▬▬

Gladiātor in arēnā cōnsilium capit. *The gladiator adopts a plan in the arena.* (Seneca, *Epistulae Morales* XXII)
Nōn tē petō, piscem petō. Quid mē fugis, Galle? *It is not you I am aiming at, but the fish. Why do you flee from me, Gallus?* (spoken by the adversary of a murmillō; quoted by Festus, 285M, 358L)

▬▬ ▬▬ ▬▬▬

CHAPTER 49

ANDROCLES AND THE LION

Ōlim in Circō Maximō lūdus bēstiārius populō dabātur. Omnēs spectātōribus admīrātiōnī fuērunt leōnēs, sed ūnus ex eīs vidēbātur saevissimus. Ad pugnam bēstiāriam intrōductus erat inter complūrēs servus quīdam cui Androclēs nōmen fuit. Quem cum ille leō procul vīdisset, subitō quasi admīrāns stetit ac deinde lentē et placidē hominī appropinquābat. Tum caudam clēmenter et blandē movēns, manūs hominis, prope iam   5
metū exanimātī, linguā lambit. Androclēs, animō iam recuperātō, leōnem attentius spectāvit. Tum, quasi mūtuā recognitiōne factā, laetī ibi stābant et homō et leō.

Ea rēs tam mīrābilis turbam maximē excitāvit. Androclem ad pulvīnar arcessītum rogāvit Caesar cūr ille saevissimus leō eī sōlī pepercisset. Tum Androclēs rem mīrābilem nārrāvit: 10

"Dum ego in Āfricā cum dominō meō habitō," inquit, "propter eius crūdēlitātem fugere coāctus in spēluncam cōnfūgī. Haud multō post ad eandem spēluncam vēnit hic

(continued)

---

2 **admīrātiōnī esse,** *to be a source of amazement (to)*
3 **Androclēs, Androclis,** m., *Androcles*
4 **quasi,** adv., *as if*
   admīror, -ārī, -ātus sum, *to wonder (at)*
   placidē, adv., *gently, peacefully, quietly, tamely*

5 **clēmenter,** adv., *in a kindly manner*
   blandē, adv., *in a coaxing/winning manner*
6 **exanimātus, -a, -um,** *paralyzed*
7 **mūtuus, -a, -um,** *mutual*
11 **crūdēlitās, crūdēlitātis,** f., *cruelty*

6 **lambō, lambere, lambī,** *to lick*
9 **parcō, parcere, pepercī** + dat., *to spare*
12 **cōgō, cōgere, coēgī, coāctus,** *to compel, force*

Exercise 49a
Respondē Latīnē:

1. Quālis vidēbātur ūnus ē leōnibus?
2. Quis ad pugnam intrōductus erat?
3. Quid fēcit leō cum hominem vīdisset?
4. Quid leō linguā lambit?
5. Quōmodo Androclēs leōnem spectāvit?
6. Quid Caesar fēcit?
7. Ubi Androclēs habitābat?
8. Quālem dominum habēbat?
9. Quō cōnfūgit?

leō gemēns et dolēns, ūnō pede claudus. Atque prīmō quidem terrōris plēnus latēbam. Sed leō, cum mē cōnspexisset, mītis et mānsuētus appropinquāvit atque pedem mihi ostendit, quasi auxilium petēns. Stirpem ingentem, quae in eius pede haerēbat, ego 15 extrāxī ac iam sine magnō timōre vulnus lāvī. Tum ille, pede in manibus meīs positō, recubuit et dormīvit.

"Trēs annōs ego et leō in eādem spēluncā habitābāmus, eōdem cibō vēscentēs. Posteā captus ā mīlitibus, reductus sum ad dominum quī mē statim ad bēstiās condemnāvit."

Prīnceps, fābulā servī audītā, maximē admīrābātur. Androclēs omnium cōnsēnsū 20 līberātus est, datusque eī leō.

13 **doleō, -ēre, -uī, -itūrus,** *to be sorry,*
    be sad, be in pain
    claudus, -a, -um, *lame*
    lateō, -ēre, -uī, *to lie in hiding*
14 **mītis, -is, -e,** *gentle*

    mānsuētus, -a, -um, *tame*
15 **stirps, stirpis,** gen. pl., **stirpium,** f.,
    thorn
20 **cōnsēnsus, -ūs,** m., *agreement*

18 **vēscor, vēscī** + abl., *to feed (on)*

Respondē Latīnē:

1. Quālis erat leō?
2. Quid leō hominī ostendit?
3. Quid in pede leōnis haerēbat?
4. Quam diū Androclēs et leō in eādem spēluncā habitābant?
5. Quis Androclem ad bēstiās condemnāvit?
6. Quid Androclēs omnium cōnsēnsū accēpit?

BUILDING THE MEANING
What to Expect with the Verb *audiō*

Look at the following sentences:

Audīvit cūr pater advēnisset.
He heard why his father had arrived.

Clāmōrēs servōrum audīvit.
He heard the shouts of the slaves.

Audīvit patrem ad urbem advēnisse.
He heard that his father had reached the city.

You will see that the sense after *heard* can develop in three different ways:

He heard why, who, what, how....   *indirect question* (with verb in the subjunctive)

He heard something/someone.   *direct object* (accusative case)

He heard that....   *indirect statement* (with accusative and infinitive)

When you meet **audiō**, you must expect one of these three possibilities:

1. **Audiō cūr, quis, quid, quōmodo...:** translate straight on:

   Audīvī quid dīcerēs.
   I heard what you were saying.

2. **Audiō** *accusative*...: wait to see if there is also an *infinitive*. If there is no infinitive, the accusative is the direct object of **audiō**:

   Audiō servōs.
   I hear the slaves.

   Audiō servōs in viīs clāmantēs.
   I hear the slaves shouting in the streets.

3. If there is an infinitive, insert *that* and continue with the translation of the accusative:

   Audiō servōs cēnam parāvisse.
   I hear (that) the slaves have prepared dinner.

The following verbs have to be treated in the same way:

sciō, *I know*   **videō**, *I see*
intellegō, *I understand, realize*   **sentiō**, *I feel, notice, realize*

Exercise 49b

Read aloud and translate:

1. Puerī audīvērunt gladiātōrēs prīncipem salūtantēs.
2. Eucleidēs nōn sēnsit ubi essent puerī.
3. Marcus vīdit gladiātōrēs iam in arēnam intrāvisse.
4. Spectātōrēs nōn intellēxērunt cūr leō manūs servī lamberet.
5. Cornēlius sciēbat locum senātōribus reservātum esse.
6. Androclēs dīxit sē stirpem ē pede leōnis extrāxisse.
7. Pȳramus crēdēbat Thisbēn ā leōne occīsam esse.
8. Nōnne audīs illōs leōnēs strepitum maximum facientēs?
9. Ita vērō! Leōnēs audiō; sed cīvēs maiōrem strepitum facere videntur.
10. Cīvēs intellegēbant servōs saepe fugere cōgī.

Exercise 49c

Read aloud and translate:

1. Puer nesciēbat quot gladiātōrēs vulnerātī essent.
2. Androclēs dīxit leōnem ūnō pede claudum ad spēluncam vēnisse.
3. Scīvistīne bēstiās sub arēnā continērī? Ipse eās audīvī.
4. Cīvēs prō certō habēbant nūllōs gladiātōrēs effugere cōnātūrōs esse.
5. Spectātōrēs vīdērunt leōnem caudam clēmenter moventem.

Exercise 49d

Using story 49 and the information on **audiō** and other verbs as guides, give the Latin for:

1. We have never heard that a lion had spared a man.
2. No one understood why the lion was licking the man's hand.
3. Androcles suddenly realized that he had lived with this lion in Africa.
4. He saw that a huge thorn was sticking in its foot.
5. Everyone knew why the lion had been given to him.

**The legend of overpowering a lion was an important one throughout antiquity.
Pictured: the nymph Cyrene taming a lion and being crowned by Libya**
British Museum, London, England

quid pro quo literally, *"something for something," one thing in exchange for another.*
Manus manum lavat. *One hand washes the other* or *One good turn deserves another.*
Ab aliō expectēs alterī quod fēceris. *Expect (the same treatment from another) that you give to your neighbor.* (Publilius Syrus 2)

How do these sayings fit the moral of the story of Androcles and the lion?

Exercise 49e Take parts, read aloud, and translate:
Scene I: In the Amphitheater

(Licinius Caeliusque, duo spectātōrēs in amphitheātrō sedentēs, inter sē loquuntur.)
LICINIUS: Ecce! In arēnam veniunt bēstiāriī! Scīsne quot sint?
CAELIUS: Minimē vērō! Scīsne tū quot leōnēs, quot tigrēs adsint? Ego audīvī multōs
leōnēs ingentēs ab Āfricā allātōs esse et sub arēnā in caveīs tenērī.

(Intrat Postumius quī sērō venīre solet.)   5
POSTUMIUS: Videō prīncipem iam advēnisse et ā cīvibus salūtārī.
CAELIUS: Ecce! Iam bēstiāriī eum salūtant! Ēheu! Sciunt sē moritūrōs esse.
POSTUMIUS: Tacēte! Audiō bēstiās! Vidētisne leōnēs in arēnam immittī?
LICINIUS: Ecce bēstia immānis! Servō illī parvō numquam parcet! Iam pugnāre
incipiunt. Euge!   10
POSTUMIUS: Euge! At cōnstitit leō! Mīror cūr leō cōnstiterit!
CAELIUS: Num crēdis eum rē vērā cōnstitisse? Prō certō habeō eum mox impetum
ferōciter factūrum esse.
LICINIUS: At videō leōnem lentē et placidē hominī appropinquantem. Mehercule!
Vidēsne eum manūs hominis linguā lambentem? Sciō leōnem esse saevis-   15
simum. Nesciō cūr hominem nōn occīdat.
CAELIUS: Vidēsne servum leōnem spectantem? Timēre nōn vidētur.
POSTUMIUS: Videō servum ā prīncipe arcessītum esse. Mīror quid dīcat.

Scene II: Leaving the Amphitheater

LICINIUS: Nōn poteram intellegere cūr leō impetum nōn faceret. Mīrum quidem
erat spectāculum.   20
CAELIUS: Audīvī leōnem ā prīncipe hominī darī.
POSTUMIUS: Ita vērō! Sed ecce! Paetus venit. Salvē, Paete!
PAETUS: Cūr hunc tantum clāmōrem facitis?
CAELIUS: Hoc vix crēdēs! Vīdimus leōnem, bēstiam saevissimam, servī manūs lam-
bentem! Nescīmus cūr manūs nōn dēvorāverit.   25
PAETUS: Quid? Nōnne audīvistis causam? Leō ille sēnsit sē hominem anteā vīdisse.
Homō prīncipī nārrāvit quōmodo stirpem ōlim ē pede leōnis extrāxisset.
Nārrāvit sē et leōnem in Āfricā in eādem spēluncā trēs annōs habitāvisse.
Ubi captus est, putāvit sē numquam iterum leōnem vīsūrum esse. Nesciē-
bat quō leō īsset.   30
POSTUMIUS: Agite! Sērō est. Ēsuriō! Domum redeāmus. Fortasse vidēbimus servum
leōnem per viās dūcentem.

4 **cavea, -ae,** f., *cage*   12 **rē vērā,** *really, actually*
9 **immānis, -is, -e,** *huge*   **impetus, -ūs,** m., *attack*
11 **mīror, -ārī, -ātus sum,** *to wonder*   31 **redeāmus,** *let us return*

8 **immittō, immittere, immīsī, immissus,** *to send in, release*
10 **incipiō, incipere, incēpī, inceptus,** *to begin*
19 **intellegō, intellegere, intellēxī, intellēctus,** *to understand, realize*

OPPOSITION TO THE GAMES

Sometimes high-born Romans were so enthusiastic about the combats in the arena that they took part themselves as gladiators. The Roman poet Juvenal, and Romans generally, strongly disapproved:

> There in the arena you have a disgrace to the city: Gracchus fighting not in the arms of a **murmillō** with shield and saber, for he scorns and rejects such equipment; nor does he hide his face with a visor. Look! It's a trident he sports; he shakes his trailing net in his right hand, casts, and misses. Then he holds up his naked face for all to see and runs frantically around the whole arena, easily recognizable!
>
> —Juvenal, *Satires* VIII.199–206

Some Romans protested the brutality of gladiatorial shows. Seneca writes about the midday "interval" between the morning and afternoon sessions. In this interval criminals were forced to fight in the arena until everyone was dead:

> By chance I attended a midday exhibition, expecting some fun, wit, and relaxation—an exhibition at which men's eyes have respite from the slaughter of their fellow-men. But it was quite the reverse. The previous combats were the essence of compassion; but now all the trifling is put aside and it is pure murder. The men have no defensive armor. They are exposed to blows at all points, and no one ever strikes in vain. Many persons prefer this program to the usual pairs and to the bouts "by request." Of course they do; there is no helmet or shield to deflect the weapon. What is the need of defensive armor, or of skill? All these mean delaying death. In the morning they throw men to the lions and the bears; at noon, they throw them to the spectators. The spectators demand that the slayer shall face the man who is to slay him in his turn; and they always reserve the latest conqueror for another butchering. The outcome of every fight is death, and the means are fire and sword.
>
> —Seneca, *Epistulae morales* VII

After Seneca, others came out against the institution of the games. Among those were Christian writers such as Tertullian and Augustine. The Emperor Constantine made a decree of abolition, but this seems not to have been enforced. Gladiatorial shows were finally suppressed by Honorius (Emperor of the West, A.D. 395–423), though other blood-sports in the arena continued for several centuries after this.

TRIER

The story of Lucius and Helge is a fictional account of the very real and significant historic process of Romanization in northern Europe. The history of the city of Trier, situated in what is now Rheinland-Pfalz, Germany, testifies eloquently to the factual record of that process.

Situated on a broad expanse of lush meadow in the Moselle valley, the city had its origins as the tribal capital of the Treveri, a Celtic clan. The Roman beginnings date from the time of Julius Caesar, to whom the Treveri supplied cavalry troops. A civilian settlement grew up around the small Roman fort. The actual Roman city dates from the reign of Augustus, who founded Augusta Treverorum to establish a supply base for the armies on the Rhine, and to spread urban civilization to the frontier of northern Europe by establishing a model city there.

Trier

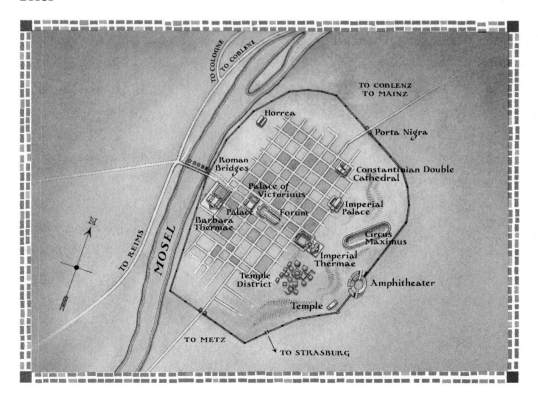

Located at a crossroads, the city became a commercial center for trade in food, wine, textiles, leather goods, pottery, and building materials. In time, it began to possess all the characteristics of a Roman city. The grid of cross-streets intersecting at a forum was probably laid out during the reign of Claudius (A.D. 41–54). There were baths, a residence for the Roman procurator, and an amphitheater, built around A.D. 100, with a seating capacity of about 20,000. That amphitheater, a smaller version of the Flavian Amphitheater in Rome, was a hallmark of Trier's Romanization. At the same time, a bathing complex was constructed, and temples were built, not only to gods the Romans brought with them, such as Mithras, the Indo-Iranian god so popular with Roman soldiers, but also to Lenus Mars, a local deity who combined a Celtic god with the Roman Mars.

The peaceful development of the city was interrupted a number of times in its Roman history, but it always recovered. Tragedy struck when the Alemanni crossed the Rhine and sacked the city and other centers of urban civilization about 275. However, Probus (reigned 276–282) drove the barbarians back over the Rhine and restored order.

In A.D. 293 the Emperor Diocletian made sweeping changes in the administrative structure of the Roman empire. There were to be two emperors, **Augustī:** Maximian in the West and Diocletian himself in the East. Each **Augustus** was to have a co-regent, a **Caesar,** thus forming a tetrarchy or rule of four princes. Constantius Chlorus, father of Constantine the Great, was named by Diocletian to be **Caesar** of the West and took up residence at Augusta Treverorum, now called Treveri. Recovering from the destruction eighteen years earlier, it became a capital city again. Twelve years later Constantius became the **Augustus** of the West.

As befits a capital city, unprecedented building took place. The magnificent Imperial Baths, equalled only by the baths of Caracalla and Diocletian at Rome, and a circus for chariot races were built, and the amphitheater was repaired and enlarged. Constantine, who succeeded his father as Caesar of the West and who resided from time to time at Treveri, built a monumental gateway and completed one of the most impressive building complexes, the Aula Palatina, a law-court (**basilica**). Later when Constantine became sole Augustus, he founded Constantinople in the East as the new capital of the Empire.

Constantine the Great died in 337. Valentinian (reigned 364–375) left his brother to rule in Constantinople and took up his own residence at Treveri. His son, Gratian (reigned 367–383), also resided there. He renovated the baths; a new sewage system was built, the streets were repaved and lined with porticos, and the double church that forms the ancient nucleus of the present-day cathedral was constructed.

Treveri was also a center of learning. In 365 Valentinian engaged Decimus Magnus Ausonius, a professor of rhetoric at the University of Burdigala (Bordeaux), to serve as tutor to his son, Gratian. Gratian maintained a lifelong friendship with Ausonius, elevating him to a consulship. Ausonius is the author of a poem extolling the beauty of the Moselle and another in which he acknowledges Treveri as a city that "feeds, clothes, and arms the empire's troops."

In 383 Gratian was slain by a usurper to the throne, and his brother, Valentinian II, was the last ruler to reside at Treveri. Roman troops were withdrawn from the Rhine, and Treveri went into a state of decline, finally being overrun by Franks.

What is especially noteworthy about the many years of prestige and prosperity that Trier enjoyed (as Augusta Treverorum and as Treveri), is that most of its inhabitants were not Italians or Romans but Celts, a proud people native to that area of northern Europe. The Celts, who had their own traditions, engaged at times in rebellion against Roman rule. However, once they accepted the benefits of Roman urban civilization, the people of Treveri thrived in the prosperity of the Pax Romana for over four hundred years.

ADDITIONAL READING:
The Romans Speak for Themselves: Book II: "Alypius Catches Gladiator Fever," pages 63–71.

WORD STUDY XII

Suffixes *-ārium* and *-ōrium*

The addition of the suffix **-ārium** (neuter form of the adjectival suffix **-ārius**; see Word Study V) to the base of a Latin noun or adjective creates a 2nd declension neuter noun meaning *a place for...*, e.g., **libr-** (base of **liber**, *book*) + **-ārium** = **librārium, -ī,** n., *a place for books* or *a bookcase*. English sometimes uses this Latin suffix to create new words, such as *aquarium* (literally, "a place for water," from Latin **aqua**), but most English words derived from Latin words with the suffix **-ārium** end in *-ary*, e.g., *library*.

Similarly, the suffix **-ōrium** (neuter form of **-ōrius**, an adjectival suffix similar to **-ārius**), when added to the stem of the fourth principal part of a Latin verb, forms a 2nd declension neuter noun that denotes a place where the action of the verb takes place, e.g., **audīt-** (perfect passive participial stem of **audīre**, *to hear*) + **-ōrium** = **auditōrium, -ī,** n., *a place for listening, lecture-room*.

Exercise 1

Give the meaning of each of the following Latin nouns, using the words in parentheses as guides. Confirm the meanings in a Latin dictionary:

1. caldārium (**calidus**)
2. repositōrium (**repōnere**)
3. armārium (**arma**)
4. aviārium (**avis,** *bird*)
5. sōlārium (**sōl,** *sun*)
6. Tabulārium (**tabula,** *tablet, record*)

Exercise 2

Give the meaning of each of the following English nouns, and give the Latin root word from which each is derived:

1. dormitory
2. infirmary
3. lavatory
4. terrarium
5. laboratory
6. diary

Suffix *-ūra*

The suffix **-ūra** may be added to the stem of the fourth principal part of a Latin verb to form a 1st declension noun that means the *act of* or *result of...*, e.g., **scrīpt-** (perfect passive participial stem of **scrībere,** *to write*) + **-ūra** = **scrīptūra, -ae,** f., *a writing.* English words derived from these nouns generally end in *-ure,* e.g., *scripture.*

Exercise 3

Give the Latin noun ending in **-ūra** that is formed from the stem of the fourth principal part of each of the following verbs. Give the English derivative of each noun formed. Consult an English dictionary as needed:

1. colō
2. coniciō
3. adveniō
4. stō
5. pōno
6. capiō
7. misceō
8. nāscor

Exercise 4

Give the meaning of each of the following English nouns and give the Latin verb from which each is derived. Consult an English dictionary as needed:

1. lecture
2. creature
3. pasture
4. aperture
5. rupture
6. stricture

Suffix *-mentum*

When the suffix **-mentum** is added to the present stem of a Latin verb, a 2nd declension neuter noun is formed that means the *result of* or *means of* the action of the verb, e.g., **impedī-** (pres. stem of **impedīre,** *to hinder*) + **-mentum** = **impedīmentum, -ī,** n., *a hindrance;* pl., *baggage.* English derivatives of these nouns end in *-ment,* e.g., *impediment.* Latin nouns ending in **-mentum** frequently alter the spelling of the present stem of the root verb, e.g., **documentum,** from **docēre.**

Exercise 5

Give the Latin noun ending in *-mentum* formed from the present stem of each of the following verbs. Give the meaning of the noun and of its English derivative:

1. compleō
2. ligō
3. paviō, -īre, *to pound, tamp down*

Exercise 6

Give the meaning of each of the following English words and give the Latin root verb from which each is derived. Consult an English dictionary as needed:

1. sediment
2. monument
3. sentiment
4. regiment
5. momentum
6. augment

Inceptive Verbs

Latin verbs that end in *-scō* are called *inceptive* (from **incipiō**, *to begin*) since they denote an action in its beginning stages, e.g., **conticēscō**, *to become silent*. Compare the simple verb, **taceō**, *to be silent*. Inceptive verbs belong to the 3rd conjugation. Often the inceptive is related to a noun or adjective rather than to another verb, e.g., **advesperāscit**, *it grows dark*, from **vesper**, *evening*.

Exercise 7

Using the words in parentheses as guides, give the meaning of each of the following inceptive verbs:

1. quiēscō (**quiēs, quiētis**, f., *rest, quiet*)
2. convalēscō (**valeō**, *to be strong*)
3. senēscō (**senex**, *old*)
4. ingravēscō (**ingravō**, *to burden;* cf. **gravis**, *heavy*)
5. aegrēscō (**aeger**, *sick*)
6. stupēscō (**stupeō**, *to be amazed*)
7. proficīscor (**faciō**, *to make, do*)
8. adolēscō (**adulēscēns**, *a young man*)

Exercise 8

The present participial stem of an inceptive verb often becomes an English word. Give the meaning of the following English words, derived from inceptive verbs in Exercise 7. Consult an English dictionary as needed:

1. convalescent
2. quiescent
3. adolescent
4. senescent

REVIEW XI: CHAPTERS 46-49

Exercise XIa: The Irregular Verb *fīō, fierī, factus sum*

Give the forms of this verb in the second person singular in each of the following tenses. Translate each form you give:

1. Present
2. Imperfect
3. Future
4. Perfect
5. Pluperfect
6. Future Perfect

Exercise XIb: The Irregular Verb *mālō, mālle, māluī*

Give the forms of this verb in the third person singular in the tenses listed above. Translate each form you give.

Exercise XIc: Infinitives

Give the present active and passive, the perfect active and passive, and the future active infinitives of the following verbs. Translate each form you give:

1. amō
2. moneō
3. dūcō
4. iaciō
5. inveniō

Exercise XId: Infinitives

Give the present, perfect, and future infinitives of the following deponent verbs. Translate each form you give:

1. moror
2. vereor
3. loquor
4. ingredior
5. experior

Exercise XIe: Translation and Identification

Read aloud and translate. Identify each indirect statement, indirect question, ablative absolute, and **cum** circumstantial clause:

1. Aurēlia servōs in culīnā loquentēs audīvit.
2. Cornēlia Valerium ad Italiam regressum esse nōn audīverat.

3. Spectātōrēs nōn audīverant cūr servus līberātus esset.
4. Stirpe ē pede extractā, leō recubuit et dormīvit.
5. Prīnceps, fābulā audītā, cōnstituit servō parcere. Negāvit enim sē umquam prius tālem fābulam audīvisse.
6. Audīvimus spectātōrēs, cum leōnem hominis manūs lambentem vidērent, attonitōs esse.
7. Cornēlius putāvit Titum domum sē secūtum esse; sed mox intellēxit eum in amphitheātrō morātum esse.
8. Sextō vīsō, fūr effugere cōnāns in pavīmentō lāpsus est.
9. "Ēheu!" inquit Thisbē. "Putō meum vēlāmen tē perdidisse." Quibus verbīs dictīs, sē occīdere cōnāta est.
10. Dīcitur duōs amantēs in eōdem sepulcrō sepultōs esse.

negō, -āre, -āvī, -ātus, *to say that...not*

Exercise XIf: Translation and Identification

Read aloud and translate. Identify the tense and voice of each participle and of each infinitive:

1. Sciēbāmus multōs fūrēs vestīmenta ē balneīs surrepta in urbe vēndere.
2. Pȳramus, vēstīgiīs leōnis vīsīs, putāvit puellam necātam esse.
3. Thisbē, corpore Pȳramī vīsō, dīcit ipsam sē occīsūram esse.
4. Ex urbe profectūrī audīvimus viam Appiam clausam esse. Nesciēbāmus quandō Baiās perventūrī essēmus.
5. Puerī ex ātriō ēgredientēs, vōce Eucleidis audītā, sē in cubiculum cōnfugitūrōs esse mussāvērunt.
6. Sextus ē lūdō domum missus sciēbat Cornēlium sē pūnītūrum esse.
7. Titō rogantī Cornēlius respondit Aurēliam ad amphitheātrum nōn itūram esse; eam domī manēre mālle.
8. Marcus Titum cōnspectum rogāvit quot spectātōrēs amphitheātrō continērī possent.
9. Gladiātōrēs pugnātūrī Caesarem salūtāre solent. Sciunt multōs moritūrōs esse.
10. Post pugnās in amphitheātrō factās spectātōrēs multōs gladiātōrēs occīsōs esse vīdērunt.

THE SIEGE OF JERUSALEM

In A.D. 69, Vespasian was forced to withdraw from suppressing a growing rebellion in Judea to return to Rome and assert his claims to the imperial throne. The next year, however, he sent his son Titus back to Judea to end the revolt by whatever means necessary. Titus besieged the city of Jerusalem for four months before it was finally captured and destroyed. Many Jews were taken prisoner and sent back to Rome in slavery. Now, forty years after the destruction of the city, a young Jewish boy from the city of Caesarea has written a letter to his grandfather, who was captured during the siege and taken to Rome as a slave. The grandfather, now a **lībertus**, writes a letter back with his memories of the siege of Jerusalem.

Read the following letter and answer the questions in English:

Appius Iūlius Giora nepōtī suō S. P. D.:

Salvē, Simōn! Quam laetus epistulam tuam accēpī. Gaudeō quod valēs. Spērō etiam valēre et patrem tuum et mātrem et sorōrēs et omnēs quī tēcum Caesarēae habitent. In epistulā tuā multa dē Hierosolymīs ā Titō imperātōre obsessīs rogābās. Difficile est mihi hās trīstissimās rēs referre sed, cum omnia cognōscere velīs, ut poēta ille dīxit, 5 "Quamquam animus meminisse horret lūctūque refūgit, incipiam."

Quōmodo nōs Iūdaeī abhinc quadrāgintā annōs, rebelliōne contrā Rōmānōs factā, Gessium Flōrium, prōcūrātōrem illum Iūdaeae pessimum, ex urbe Hierosolymīs expulerimus, iam bene scīs. Ego ipse forte Hierosolyma paulō ante advēneram, nam diēbus fēstīs sānctissimīsque rem dīvīnam facere volēbam. Cum scīrēmus, Gessiō expulsō, 10 Rōmānōs regressūrōs esse, urbem dēfendere parābāmus.

Urbs autem Hierosolyma nātūrā arteque mūnītissima erat: moenia enim ab Hērōde aedificāta erant, templum ā Solomōne rēge, arx ā Rōmānīs ipsīs. Sed ēheu! Eō tempore Iūdaeī sibi paene exitiō erant. Mīlitēs enim nostrī in trēs dīversās factiōnēs dīvidēbantur, quārum ducēs inter sē cotīdiē rixābantur, nam aliī alia cōnsilia capere volēbant. Itaque, 15 antequam Rōmānī regressī sunt, multī Iūdaeī iam necātī erant, multum cibī dēlētum erat.

T. Flāvius Vespāsiānus, prīnceps Rōmānōrum, quod urbem recipere cōnstituerat, Titum fīlium cum quattuor legiōnibus mīsit. Castrīs extrā Hierosolyma positīs, Rōmānī quattuor mēnsēs urbem mūrō circumdatam obsidēbant. Tandem, multīs proeliīs factīs multīsque utrimque necātīs, Iūdaeī cibō carēbant. Multīs famē pereuntibus, Iūdaeī tamen 20 sē nōn trādidērunt. Titus igitur urbem summīs vīribus adortus est: arce dēlētā, templō incēnsō, omnēs cīvēs aut captī aut necātī sunt.

Ego ipse, prīmō mēnse ā Rōmānīs proeliō captus, nōn necātus sum. In servitūtem tamen abstractus sum, neque fīnem obsidiōnis ipse vīdī. Dīcitur Titus urbī populōque Iūdaeō parcere voluisse. Ferunt quoque templum Titō invītō dēlētum esse. Id tamen vix 25 crēdere possum. Rōmānī enim nec mōrēs nostrōs nec sacra ūllō modō intellēxērunt, immō semper reprehendērunt. Sēnsit tamen Titus templum esse sēdem sēditiōnis atque prō certō habēbat, templō dēlētō, Iūdaeōs mox arma trāditūrōs esse.

Aliter autem rem nārrant sapientēs nostrī, apud quōs legimus Deum, īrātum quod Iūdaeī nōn iam piī essent, eōs pūnīre cōnstituisse. Itaque et urbem et templum dēlēre Rōmānōs sīvit, immō adiūvit! Sīc pūnīvit Deus populum suum. Valē! 30

1 **nepōs, nepōtis,** m., *grandson*
3 **Caesarēa, -ae,** f., *Caesarea (a town in Palestine, on the Mediterranean Sea)*
4 **Hierosolyma, -ōrum,** n. pl., *Jerusalem*
6 **meminisse,** *to remember*
   horreō, -ēre, -uī, *to shudder, be unwilling*
   lūctus, -ūs, m., *grief, mourning*
7 **Iūdaeī, Iūdaeōrum,** m. pl., *the Jews*
   quadrāgintā, *forty*
8 **prōcūrātor, prōcūrātōris,** m., *procurator, governor*
   Iūdaea, -ae, f., *Judaea*
9 **paulō,** adv., *a little*
10 **fēstus, -a, -um,** *festival/feast (day)*
   sānctus, -a, -um, *holy, sacred*
   rēs dīvīna, reī dīvīnae, f., *religious rite*
12 **mūnītus, -a, -um,** *fortified*
   Hērōdēs, Hērōdis, m., *Herod (the Great, king of Judaea, 40–4 B.C.)*
13 **Solomōn, Solomōnis,** m., *Solomon (son of David and third king of Israel)*
   arx, arcis, f., *citadel, fortress*
14 **exitiō esse,** *to be a source of destruction*

   dīversus, -a, -um, *different, opposed*
15 **dux, ducis,** m., *leader*
18 **legiō, legiōnis,** f., *legion (a division of the Roman army)*
   castra pōnere, *to pitch camp*
19 **proelium, -ī,** n., *battle*
20 **utrimque,** adv., *on both sides*
   famēs, famis, abl., **famē,** f., *hunger, starvation*
21 **vīrēs, vīrium** (pl. of **vīs**), f. pl., *military forces*
24 **obsidiō, obsidiōnis,** f., *siege*
25 **ferunt,** *they say*
26 **mōs, mōris,** m., *custom;* pl., *character*
   sacra, -ōrum, n. pl., *religious rites*
   ūllus, -a, -um, *any*
27 **sēdēs, sēdis,** gen. pl., **sēdium,** f., *seat, center (of some activity)*
   sēditiō, sēditiōnis, f., *political strife, rebellion*
29 **aliter,** adv., *differently*
   sapiēns, sapientis, m., *wise man*
30 **pius, -a, -um,** *dutiful, worshipful*

5 **referō, referre, rettulī, relātus,** *to bring back, report, write down*
6 **refugiō, refugere, refūgī,** *to shrink back, recoil*
17 **recipiō, recipere, recēpī, receptus,** *to receive, recapture*
19 **circumdō, circumdare, circumdedī, circumdatus,** *to surround*
20 **pereō, perīre, periī, peritūrus,** *to perish, die*
24 **abstrahō, abstrahere, abstrāxī, abstractus,** *to drag away, carry off*

1. Who is writing to whom?
2. What had Simon asked about?
3. When had the Jews revolted?
4. Who was expelled from Jerusalem?
5. Why was the author in Jerusalem?
6. How well was Jerusalem fortified?
7. How were the Jews almost destroyed?
8. What did the Jewish factions do?
9. Who was sent against the city?
10. How long was the city besieged?
11. Did the Jews surrender?
12. Why was the author not killed?
13. What is said about Titus?
14. Why did Titus destroy the Temple?

NOTHING EVER HAPPENS

Sōl caelō serēnō lūcēbat. Cantābant avēs. Nātūra ipsa gaudēre vidēbātur. Trīstī vultū tamen sedēbat Cornēlia sōla in peristȳliō. Sēcum cōgitābat: "Mē taedet sōlitūdinis. Cūr nēmō mē observat? Cūr mēcum nēmō loquitur? Pater tantum temporis in tablīnō agit ut eum numquam videam. Māter tam occupāta est ut mēcum numquam loquātur. Marcus et Sextus suīs lūdīs adeō dēditī sunt ut nihil aliud faciant. Nōn intellegō cūr nūper etiam 5 servae mē neglēxerint, cūr Eucleidēs ille verbōsus verbum nūllum mihi dīxerit. Ō mē miseram!"

Cornēliae haec cōgitantī, "Heus tū, Cornēlia!" clāmāvit Marcus quī tum intrāvit in peristȳlium. "Pater iubet tē in tablīnō statim adesse. Festīnāre tē oportet."

Cornēlia, cum in tablīnum intrāvisset, vīdit adesse et patrem et mātrem, id quod erat 10 eī admīrātiōnī et cūrae.

(continued)

1 **sōl, sōlis,** m., *sun*
  serēnus, -a, -um, *clear; bright*
  avis, avis, gen. pl., **avium,** m./f., *bird*
3 **observō, -āre, -āvī, -ātus,** *to watch, pay attention to*
5 **adeō,** adv., *so much, to such an extent*
  dēditus, -a, -um, *devoted, dedicated*

  nūper, adv., *recently*
8 **Heus!** *Hey there!*
10 **id quod,** *that/a thing which*
11 **cūrae esse,** *to be a cause of anxiety (to)*

1 **lūcet, lūcēre, lūxit,** *it is light, it is day; (it) shines*
2 **taedet, taedēre, taesum est,** *it bores, makes one* (acc.) *tired of something* (gen.)
  Mē taedet sōlitūdinis, *It tires me of…, I am tired of/bored with…*
6 **neglegō, neglegere, neglēxī, neglēctus,** *to neglect, ignore*
9 **oportet, oportēre, oportuit,** *it is fitting; ought*
  Festīnāre tē oportet, *That you hurry is fitting, You ought to hurry.*

Exercise 50a
Respondē Latīnē:

1. Cūr Cornēlia trīstis est?
2. Ubi pater multum temporis agit?
3. Quam occupāta est Aurēlia?
4. Quibus rēbus sunt Marcus et Sextus dēditī?
5. Loquunturne aut servae aut Eucleidēs cum Cornēliā?
6. Quis Cornēliae clāmāvit?
7. Quō Cornēliam īre oportet?

Tum pater gravī vultū, "Ōlim, Cornēlia," inquit, "Pūblius Cornēlius Scīpiō Āfricānus, vir praeclārissimus gentis nostrae, dīcitur inter epulās senātōrum fīliam suam Tiberiō Gracchō dēspondisse. Post epulās, cum Scīpiō domum regressus uxōrī dīxisset sē fīliam dēspondisse, illa maximā īrā erat commōta. 'Nōn decet patrem,' inquit, 15 'dēspondēre fīliam, īnsciā mātre.' At pater tuus nōn est Pūbliō Cornēliō similis, nam ūnā cōnstituimus et ego et māter tua iuvenī cuidam nōbilī tē dēspondēre. Quīntus Valerius, adulēscēns ille optimus, vult tē in mātrimōnium dūcere, id quod nōbīs placet. Placetne tibi, Cornēlia?"

Cornēlia adeō perturbāta erat ut vix loquī posset, sed tandem submissā vōce, "Mihi 20 quoque placet," respondit.

Cui Cornēlius, "Estō! Crās aderit Valerius ipse."

13 **gēns, gentis,** gen. pl., **gentium,** f., *family, clan*
    epulae, -ārum, f. pl., *banquet, feast*
16 **similis, -is, -e** + dat., *similar (to), like*

17 **iuvenis, iuvenis,** m., *young man*
20 **submissus, -a, -um,** *quiet, subdued, soft*

14 **dēspondeō, dēspondēre, dēspondī, dēspōnsus,** *to betroth, promise in marriage*
15 **decet, decēre, decuit,** *it is becoming, fitting; should*
    Nōn decet patrem dēspondēre fīliam, *That a father should betroth his daughter is not fitting, A father should not betroth his daughter.*

Respondē Latīnē:

1. Quō in locō Pūblius Cornēlius Scīpiō fīliam suam dēspondisse dīcitur?
2. Quōmodo uxor eius commōta erat?
3. Cūr commōta erat?
4. Quid Cornēlius et Aurēlia facere cōnstituerant?
5. Quis Cornēliam in mātrimōnium dūcere vult?
6. Placetne ille Cornēliō et Aurēliae?
7. Placetne ille Cornēliae?

BUILDING THE MEANING
Result Clauses

When you meet these words—

adeō, adv., *so much, to such an extent*
ita, adv., *thus, in such a way*
sīc, adv., *thus, in this way*
tālis, -is, -e, *such*

tam, adv., *so*
tantus, -a, -um, *so great*
tantum, adv., *so much*
tot, indecl. adj., *so many*

—you will often find the word **ut** later in the sentence meaning *that*, followed by a clause indicating *result*:

> **Adeō** perturbāta erat **ut** vix loquī posset. (50:20)
> *She was **so** confused **that** she could hardly speak.*

> **Tam** occupāta est **ut** mēcum numquam loquātur. (50:4)
> *She is **so** busy **that** she never speaks to me.*

If the result clause is negative, **ut** is followed by **nōn:**

> **Adeō** perturbāta est **ut** loquī **nōn** possit.
> *She is **so** confused **that** she can**not** speak.*

The verb in the result clause is in the subjunctive and is translated into the equivalent tense of the English indicative. The verbs **loquātur** and **possit** in the examples above are *present subjunctives*.

FORMS
Verbs: Present and Perfect Subjunctive

The imperfect and pluperfect subjunctives were tabulated in the Forms section of Chapter 43. The following is the tabulation of the other two tenses of the subjunctive, the present and perfect:

Present Subjunctive
Active Voice

		1st Conjugation	2nd Conjugation	3rd Conjugation		4th Conjugation
S	1	pórt*em*	móve*am*	mítt*am*	iáci*am*	aúdi*am*
	2	pórt*ēs*	móve*ās*	mítt*ās*	iáci*ās*	aúdi*ās*
	3	pórt*et*	móve*at*	mítt*at*	iáci*at*	aúdi*at*
P	1	portḗ*mus*	moveā*mus*	mittā*mus*	iaciā*mus*	audiā*mus*
	2	portḗ*tis*	moveā*tis*	mittā*tis*	iaciā*tis*	audiā*tis*
	3	pórt*ent*	móve*ant*	mítt*ant*	iáci*ant*	aúdi*ant*

Passive Voice

		1st Conjugation	2nd Conjugation	3rd Conjugation		4th Conjugation
S	1	pórt*er*	móve*ar*	mítt*ar*	iáci*ar*	aúdi*ar*
	2	portḗ*ris*	moveā*ris*	mittā*ris*	iaciā*ris*	audiā*ris*
	3	portḗ*tur*	moveā*tur*	mittā*tur*	iaciā*tur*	audiā*tur*
P	1	portḗ*mur*	moveā*mur*	mittā*mur*	iaciā*mur*	audiā*mur*
	2	portḗ*minī*	moveā*minī*	mittā*minī*	iaciā*minī*	audiā*minī*
	3	portḗ*ntur*	moveā*ntur*	mittá*ntur*	iaciá*ntur*	audiá*ntur*

Deponent Verbs

S	1	cóner etc.	vérear etc.	lóquar etc.	regrédiar etc.	expériar etc.

Irregular Verbs

		ésse
S	1	sim
	2	sīs
	3	sit
P	1	símus
	2	sítis
	3	sint

So also **póssim, vélim, nólim, málim**

		íre
S	1	éam
	2	éās
	3	éat
P	1	eámus
	2	eátis
	3	éant

So also **féram, fíam**

Perfect Subjunctive
Active Voice

S	1	portáverim	móverim	míserim	iécerim	audíverim
	2	portáveris	móveris	míseris	iéceris	audíveris
	3	portáverit	móverit	míserit	iécerit	audíverit
P	1	portāvérimus	mōvérimus	mīsérimus	iēcérimus	audīvérimus
	2	portāvéritis	mōvéritis	mīséritis	iēcéritis	audīvéritis
	3	portáverint	móverint	míserint	iécerint	audíverint

Passive Voice

S	1	portátus sim etc.	mótus sim etc.	míssus sim etc.	iáctus sim etc.	audítus sim etc.

Deponent Verbs

S	1	cōnátus sim etc.	véritus sim etc.	locútus sim etc.	regréssus sim etc.	expértus sim etc.

Irregular Verbs

		ésse
S	1	fúerim etc.

So also **potúerim, volúerim, nōlúerim, mālúerim, íerim,** and **túlerim.** The perfect subjunctive of **fíō** is **fáctus sim**.

Be sure to learn the above forms thoroughly.

Exercise 50b

Here are sample forms of all the tenses of the subjunctive, active and passive, of a regular verb and sample forms of the subjunctives of a deponent verb:

Regular Verb:

Present Active
parem

Present Passive
parer

Perfect Active
parāverim

Perfect Passive
parātus sim

Imperfect Active
parārem

Imperfect Passive
parārer

Pluperfect Active
parāvissem

Pluperfect Passive
parātus essem

Deponent Verb:

Present
cōner

Perfect
cōnātus sim

Imperfect
cōnārer

Pluperfect
cōnātus essem

Give subjunctive forms of the following verbs in the designated person and number, following the pattern above. For deponent verbs give only passive forms:

1. observō, -āre, -āvī, -ātus: 3rd pl.
2. dēspondeō, dēspondēre, dēspondī, dēspōnsus: 1st sing.
3. neglegō, neglegere, neglēxī, neglēctus: 1st pl.
4. proficīscor, proficīscī, profectus sum: 3rd sing.
5. ēgredior, ēgredī, ēgressus sum: 2nd pl.

A betrothal ring

BUILDING THE MEANING
Sequence of Tenses

Compare the following pairs of sentences containing indirect questions:

1. a. Nōn intellegō cūr servae mē **neglegant**.
   *I do not understand why the slave-girls **neglect** me.*

   b. Nōn intellegō cūr servae mē **neglēxerint**.
   *I do not understand why the slave-girls **neglected** me.*

2. a. Nōn intellēxī cūr servae mē **neglegerent**.
   *I did not understand why the slave-girls **were neglecting** me.*

   b. Nōn intellēxī cūr servae mē **neglēxissent**.
   *I did not understand why the slave-girls **had neglected** me.*

When the verb in the main clause is in the *present tense* (as in 1a and 1b above), a *present subjunctive* in the indirect question (as in 1a above) indicates an action going on at the same time as (or after) that of the main verb, and a *perfect subjunctive* in the indirect question (as in 1b above) indicates an action that took place before that of the main verb.

When the verb in the main clause is in a *past tense* (as in 2a and 2b above), an *imperfect subjunctive* in the indirect question (as in 2a above) indicates an action going on at the same time as (or after) that of the main verb, and a *pluperfect subjunctive* in the indirect question (as in 2b above) indicates an action that took place before that of the main verb.

This relationship between the tense of the verb in the main clause and the tense of the subjunctive in the subordinate clause is called *sequence of tenses*. The sequence is said to be *primary* when the verb in the main clause is in a primary tense, i.e., *present* or *future* or *future perfect*, as in 1a and 1b above. The sequence is said to be *secondary* when the verb in the main clause is in a secondary tense, i.e., *imperfect* or *perfect* or *pluperfect*, as in 2a and 2b above.

SEQUENCE OF TENSES		
	Main Clause Indicative	**Subordinate Clause** Tense of Subjunctive *Time of Action Relative to Main Clause*
Primary Sequence	Present Future Future Perfect	Present = *Same time or after* Perfect = *Time before*
Secondary Sequence	Imperfect Perfect Pluperfect	Imperfect = *Same time or after* Pluperfect = *Time before*

Exercise 50c

Read aloud and translate each sentence, and then explain the sequence of tenses between the main and the subordinate clauses:

1. Tam laetae cantant avēs ut nātūra ipsa gaudēre videātur.
2. Tam laetae cantābant avēs ut nātūra ipsa gaudēre vidērētur.
3. Tot spectātōrēs ad lūdōs conveniunt ut Circus vix omnēs contineat.
4. Tot spectātōrēs ad lūdōs convēnerant ut Circus vix omnēs continēret.
5. Cornēlia nōn rogat cūr pater sē Valeriō dēsponderit.
6. Cornēlia nōn rogāvit cūr pater sē Valeriō dēspondisset.

Sequence of Tenses in Result Clauses

In result clauses a present subjunctive will usually be used in primary sequence and an imperfect or perfect subjunctive in secondary sequence. The imperfect subjunctive in result clauses is used to emphasize the natural or logical connection between the main clause and the result:

> Leō tantus et tam ferōx erat <u>ut servus metū exanimātus **caderet**.</u>
> *The lion was so large and so fierce <u>that the slave (as could be expected) **fell down** paralyzed with fear</u>.*

The perfect subjunctive would emphasize the fact that the result actually did take place:

> Leō tantus et tam ferōx erat <u>ut servus metū exanimātus **ceciderit**.</u>
> *The lion was so large and so fierce <u>that the slave (actually) **fell down** paralyzed with fear</u>.*

Exercise 50d

Read aloud and translate each sentence, and make your translations show the difference in meaning between the use of the imperfect and the perfect subjunctives:

1. Tanta tempestās coorta erat ut sērō Brundisium advenīrēmus.
2. Tanta tempestās coorta erat ut sērō Brundisium advēnerimus.
3. Pater tam gravī vultū locūtus est ut Cornēlia mīrārētur quid accidisset.
4. Pater tam gravī vultū locūtus est ut Cornēlia mīrāta sit quid accidisset.
5. Cornēlia Flāviae scrīpsit: "Tam laeta eram ut vix loquī possem."
6. Cornēlia Flāviae scrīpsit: "Tam laeta eram ut vix loquī potuerim."

ROMAN WEDDINGS

When a Roman girl reached marriageable age—somewhere between twelve and fourteen—her father set about finding her a husband.

When a friend asked the writer Pliny to help him find a suitable match for his niece, Pliny wrote back to say that a certain Acilianus would be just the man. After speaking highly of Acilianus' father, his grandmother on his mother's side, and his uncle, he describes the prospective bridegroom as follows:

> Acilianus himself is a person of very great energy and application, but at the same time exceedingly modest. He has held the offices of quaestor, tribune, and praetor with very great distinction, and this relieves you of the need to canvass

A girl of marriageable age in a courtyard in Pompeii
Oil on canvas "In a Courtyard in Pompeii" by Luigi Bazzani, Waterhouse and Dodd, London, England

on his behalf. His expression is frank and open; his complexion is fresh and he has a healthy color; his whole bearing is noble and handsome, with the dignity of a senator. I don't know whether I should add that his father has ample means; for, when I picture you and your brother for whom we are seeking a son-in-law, I think there is no need for me to say more on that subject; and yet, when I consider the attitudes of people nowadays and even the laws of the country, which judge a man's income as of primary importance, I'm probably right in thinking that even a reference to his father's means should not be omitted. Certainly, if one thinks of the children of the marriage and their children, one must take the question of money into account when making a choice.

—Pliny, *Letters* I.14

When we remember that a Roman would be nearly forty before he attained the praetorship, Pliny's candidate (if we read between the lines) was probably red-faced, stout, and middle-aged, but Pliny seems to consider these points less important than having good family connections and plenty of money.

So our thirteen-year-old Cornelia might find herself engaged to a mere boy (minimum age fourteen) or to someone three times her age, but she was not expected to raise any objections to what was simply a legal contract between families.

Before the actual wedding, a betrothal ceremony (**spōnsālia**) often took place, witnessed by relatives and friends. The father of the girl was asked formally if he "promised" his daughter and replied that he did. (Question: **Spondēsne?** Answer: **Spondeō.**) Gifts were then given to the bride-to-be, including a ring (**ānulus**) either of gold or of iron set in gold. This was worn on the third finger of the left hand, from which it was believed a nerve ran straight to the heart. Aulus Gellius, a Roman scholar and writer of the second half of the second century A.D., explains:

I have heard that the ancient Greeks wore a ring on the finger of the left hand which is next to the little finger. They say, too, that the Roman men commonly wore their rings in that way. Apion in his *Egyptian History* says that the reason for this practice is that, upon cutting into and opening human bodies, it was found that a very fine nerve proceeded from that finger alone of which we have spoken, and made its way to the human heart; that it therefore seemed quite reasonable that this finger in particular should be honored with such an ornament, since it seems to be joined, and as it were united, with that supreme organ, the heart.

—Aulus Gellius, *Attic Nights* X.10

Before the betrothal ceremony, the two families had usually already discussed the terms of the dowry (**dōs**), a sum of money or property given by the bride's father along with his daughter. The dowry was returnable in the event of a divorce.

Exercise 50e

Read aloud and translate:

Omnia iam diū ad spōnsālia parāta erant, īnsciā Cornēliā. Valerius enim, cum prīmum Brundisiī ē nāve ēgressus est, ad Cornēlium scrīpserat sē velle Cornēliam in mātrimōnium dūcere; deinde Cornēlius rescrīpserat sē libenter fīliam Valeriō dēspōnsūrum esse; tum Aurēlia Vīniam, mātrem Flāviae, invītāverat ut prōnuba esset. Ad spōnsālia igitur Valerius et Vīnia et Flāvia Rōmam iam advēnerant.   5

Aderat diēs spōnsālium. Quīntā hōrā omnēs Cornēliī atque propinquī amīcīque in ātrium convēnērunt. Deinde, silentiō factō, Cornēlia vultū dēmissō ingressa in ātrium dēducta est. Tum Valerius, quī contrā Cornēlium in mediō ātriō stābat, eī, "Spondēsne," ait, "tē fīliam tuam mihi uxōrem datūrum esse?"   10

Cui Cornēlius, "Spondeō."

Quō dictō, Valerius ad Cornēliam conversus ānulum aureum tertiō digitō sinistrae manūs eius aptāvit. Tum ōsculum eī dedit. Omnēs spōnsō et spōnsae grātulātī sunt.

1	**spōnsālia, spōnsālium,** n. pl., *betrothal ceremony*	12	**conversus, -a, -um,** *having turned, turning*
	ad spōnsālia, *for the betrothal*		**ānulus, -ī,** m., *ring*
5	**prōnuba, -ae,** f., *bride's attendant*	13	**sinister, sinistra, sinistrum,** *left*
7	**propinquus, -ī,** m., *relative*		**aptō, -āre, -āvī, -ātus,** *to place, fit*
10	**ait,** *(he/she) says, said*	14	**grātulor, -ārī, -ātus sum** + dat., *to congratulate*

8 **dēmittō, dēmittere, dēmīsī, dēmissus,** *to let down, lower*
10 **spondeō, spondēre, spopondī, spōnsus,** *to promise solemnly, pledge*

––––

Sīqua volēs aptē nūbere, nūbe parī. *If you wish a suitable marriage, marry an equal.* (Ovid, *Heroides* IX.32)

––––

MARCUS COMES OF AGE

Coming of age was an important occasion for a Roman boy, and it was marked both by an official ceremony (**officium togae virīlis**) and by family celebrations. The ceremony usually took place when the boy had reached the age of sixteen but not on his birthday. It was common for it to be celebrated at the **Līberālia** (the festival of Liber or Bacchus, the god of wine) on March 17. It began with the boy dedicating (**cōnsecrāre**) the luck-charm (**bulla**) which he had worn since he was a baby and the toga with the purple edge (**toga praetexta**). These he placed before the shrine of the household gods (**larārium**), which was usually in the **ātrium** of the house. From this time on he wore the plain white toga (**toga virīlis** or **toga pūra**) indicating that he was no longer a boy but a man. After the ceremony members of his family and friends escorted him to the Forum (**in Forum dēdūcere**). There, in the building where the public records were housed (**Tabulārium**), his name was entered in the records (**tabulae,** literally, *tablets*). The official ceremony was now completed, and the family entertained their friends at a private celebration.

The time has now come for Marcus to assume the **toga virīlis.**

Gold bulla
Museo e Gallerie Nazionali
di Capodimonte, Naples, Italy

Iam aderat mēnsis Mārtius. Erat diēs Līberālium quō diē adulēscentēs Rōmānī togam pūram sūmere solēbant. Abhinc complūrēs mēnsēs Marcus sēdecim annōs complēverat; nunc togam virīlem sumptūrus erat. Itaque Cornēlius amīcōs clientēsque omnēs invītāverat ut eō diē apud sē convenīrent. Omnēs sciēbant patrem Marcī dīvitissimum esse; omnēs prō certō habēbant eum optimam cēnam amīcīs datūrum esse. 5

Domus Gaiī Cornēliī plēna erat tumultūs, strepitūs, clāmōris. Tot et tam variī hominēs eō conveniēbant ut iānitor, ab iānuā prōgressus, in ipsō līmine sollicitus stāret. Sī quis appropinquābat, eum magnā vōce rogābat quis esset et quid vellet. Aliōs rogābat ut in domum prōcēderent, aliīs praecipiēbat ut in viā manērent. Nōnnūllī autem, quī neque amīcī Cornēliī erant neque clientēs, domuī appropinquāvērunt, quod spērābant 10 Cornēlium sē ad cēnam invītātūrum esse. Hī iānitōrem ōrābant nē sē dīmitteret; ille autem eīs imperābat ut statim discēderent.

Tandem, omnibus rēbus parātīs, Cornēlius tōtam familiam rogāvit ut in ātrium convenīrent. Aderant propinquī; aderant multī amīcī; aderant plūrimī clientium; aderant omnēs servī lībertīque Cornēliōrum. Cūnctī inter sē colloquēbantur, cūnctī gaudēbant 15 quod ad hoc officium togae virīlis invītātī erant.

In ātriō ante larārium stābat Marcus togam praetextam bullamque auream in manibus tenēns. Sēnsit oculōs omnium in sē conversōs esse. Conticuērunt omnēs. Marcus prīmum togam praetextam atque bullam ante larārium dēpositās Laribus familiāribus cōnsecrāvit. "Nunc," inquit, "hās rēs puerīlēs hīc dēpōnō. Nunc vōbīs, ō 20 Larēs familiārēs, haec libenter cōnsecrō."

(continued)

2	**pūrus, -a, -um,** *spotless, clean, plain white*	11	**ōrō, -āre, -āvī, -ātus,** *to beg*
	sūmere, *to assume (i.e., put on for the first time)*		**nē sē dīmitteret,** *not to send them away*
4	**invītāverat ut,** *he had invited (them) to*	12	**imperō, -āre, -āvī, -ātus** + dat., *to order*
7	**līmen, līminis,** n., *threshold, doorway*	19	**Larēs, Larum,** m. pl., *household gods*
8	**sī quis,** *if anyone*	20	**familiāris, -is, -e,** *belonging to the family/household*
9	**nōnnūllī, -ae, -a,** *some*		

9   **praecipiō, praecipere, praecēpī, praeceptus** + dat., *to instruct, order*
11   **dīmittō, dīmittere, dīmīsī, dīmissus,** *to send away*

Exercise 51a Respondē Latīnē:

1. Quī mēnsis erat?
2. Quot annōs complēverat Marcus?
3. Quid hodiē factūrus erat?
4. Quid omnēs amīcī clientēsque Cornēliī prō certō habēbant?
5. Cūr iānitor sollicitus erat?
6. Quid iānitor rogābat appropinquantēs?
7. Quid iānitor rogābat ut quīdam ex appropinquantibus facerent?
8. Quid aliīs praecipiēbat?
9. Quid iānitor iubēbat eōs facere quī neque amīcī Cornēliī neque clientēs erant?
10. Quō tōta familia convēnit?
11. Cūr cūnctī gaudēbant?
12. Quid Marcus Laribus familiāribus cōnsecrāvit?

Quō factō, pater servō cuidam imperāvit ut togam virīlem Marcō indueret. Deinde parentēs eum amplexī sunt et cēterī eī grātulātī sunt. Nunc Marcus, multīs comitantibus, in Forum ā patre est dēductus.

Quō cum pervēnissent, Marcō ad Tabulārium ductō, pater eōs quī comitābantur 25
rogāvit ut extrā Tabulārium manērent. Ipse ūnā cum fīliō et paucīs propinquīs in Tabulārium ingressus est, nam ibi nōmen Marcī in tabulīs pūblicīs erat īnscrībendum.

Quibus rēbus cōnfectīs, omnēs adstantēs Marcum iam ēgressum magnō clāmōre salūtāvērunt. Deinde cum Marcus omnibus grātiās ēgisset propter tantam ergā sē bene-
volentiam, omnēs domum Cornēliōrum rediērunt, nam Cornēlius multōs invītāverat ut 30
apud sē eō diē cēnārent.

23 **comitor, -ārī, -ātus sum,**
   to accompany
27 **erat īnscrībendum,** *had to*
   be registered

29 **grātiās agere** + dat., *to thank*
   ergā, prep. + acc., *toward*
   benevolentia, -ae, f., *kindness*

23 **amplector, amplectī, amplexus sum,** *to embrace*

Respondē Latīnē:

1. Quid Cornēlius servō cuidam imperāvit ut faceret?
2. Quō est Marcus dēductus?
3. Quī in Tabulārium ingressī sunt?
4. Quid in Tabulāriō factum est?
5. Quid ut facerent Cornēlius multōs invītāverat?

BUILDING THE MEANING
Telling to, Asking to: Indirect Commands

Compare the following pairs of sentences:

1. a. Aliōs rogat **ut** in domum **prōcēdant**. (cf. 51:8–9)
      *He asks some **to go forward** into the house.*

   b. Aliōs rogāvit **ut** in domum **prōcēderent**. (cf. 51:8–9)
      *He asked some **to go forward** into the house.*

2. a. Hī iānitōrem ōrant **nē** sē **dīmittat**. (cf. 51:11)
      *They keep begging the doorkeeper **not to send them away**.*

   b. Hī iānitōrem ōrābant **nē** sē **dīmitteret**. (51:11)
      *They kept begging the doorkeeper **not to send them away**.*

In these sentences **ut** is translated by *to*; **nē** is translated by *not to*. The subordinate clauses in the sentences above, introduced by **ut** or **nē** and with their verbs in the subjunctive, are called *indirect commands*.

A *present subjunctive* will be found in primary sequence (examples 1a and 2a above), and an *imperfect subjunctive* will be found in secondary sequence (examples 1b and 2b above).

Verbs such as the following may introduce indirect commands:

hortor, *to encourage, urge*   **moneō,** *to advise, warn*   **praecipiō,** *to instruct, order*
imperō, *to order*   **persuādeō,** *to persuade*
invītō, *to invite*
obsecrō, *to beseech, beg*
ōrō, *to beg*
rogō, *to ask*

Note that most of the verbs that introduce indirect commands take a direct object in the accusative case:

Aliōs rogābat <u>ut in domum prōcēderent</u>. (51:8–9)
*He was asking **some** <u>to go forward into the house</u>.*

The verbs **imperō, praecipiō,** and **persuādeō,** however, take the dative case:

Coquō imperāvit (praecēpit/persuāsit) <u>ut in ātrium venīret</u>.
*He ordered (instructed/persuaded) **the cook** <u>to come into the atrium</u>.*

Another arrangement is also possible:

Imperāvit ut coquus in ātrium venīret.
He ordered that the cook come into the atrium.

Here the order was issued not to the cook but to someone else (not specified).

Exercise 51b

In story 51, locate nine subordinate clauses that express indirect commands.

1. Translate the sentences in which these indirect commands occur.
2. Tell in English what the direct command (or request) was or would have been that is being reported indirectly in each case.
3. Locate one example of a subordinate clause with *indirect questions* (rather than indirect commands or requests) in story 51, and tell in English what the direct questions were that are here being reported indirectly.

Ego vōs hortor ut amīcitiam omnibus rēbus hūmānīs antepōnātis.
I urge you to set friendship before all other human affairs. (Cicero, *On Friendship* V.17)

Exercise 51c

Read aloud and translate each sentence, identify the type of each subordinate clause, and then identify the tense of each verb in the subjunctive:

1. Cornēlius convīvās omnēs invītat ut in ātrium prōcēdant.
2. Tum Cornēlius Marcō imperāvit ut rēs puerīlēs Laribus cōnsecrāret.
3. Cornēlius Marcum togā pūrā indūtum rogāvit ut ad Forum sēcum proficīscerētur.
4. In Tabulāriō pater rogat ut nōmen Marcī in tabulīs pūblicīs īnscrībātur.
5. Cornēlius omnēs convīvās invītāvit ut apud sē cēnārent.
6. Tē ōrō atque obsecrō ut domum veniās.
7. Iānitor iam iānuam claudēbat: tam dēfessus erat ut dormīre cuperet.
8. Asellus iānitōrem vīsum rogāvit quid eō diē fēcisset.
9. "Tibi dīcō," inquit iānitor, "plūrimōs hominēs ā mē aut ad iānuam acceptōs esse aut dīmissōs."
10. "Nōlī ibi morārī," inquam, "nam dominus imperāvit ut iānua claudātur."

Note that in sentence 10 present time is clearly in the speaker's mind when using the verb **imperāvit,** *has ordered.* When the perfect tense is used in this way, the sequence is primary, and therefore a present subjunctive is used in the indirect command.

Exercise 51d

Select, read aloud, and translate:

1. Nōlī mē hortārī ut ad illam urbem (īrem/eam).
2. Tē semper moneō nē in mediā viā (ambulēs/ambulārēs).
3. Abhinc multōs mēnsēs Valerius Cornēliō persuāsit ut Cornēliam sibi (spondēret/spondeat).
4. Plūrimī hominēs cum ad domum Cornēliī pervēnissent rogābant ut intrāre (liceat/licēret).
5. Prīmō omnēs hominēs hortor ut in viā (maneant/manērent).
6. Deinde amīcōs propinquōsque Cornēliī rogāvī ut (intrārent/intrent).
7. Clientibus praecēpī nē statim in domum (prōcēderent/prōcēdant).
8. Nōnnūllī, quōs nōn prius vīdī, mē ōrant nē sē (dīmitterem/dīmittam).
9. Eōs monuī nē ad iānuam (morārentur/morentur).
10. Tandem coāctus sum servōs rogāre ut eōs baculīs (repellant/repellerent).

Exercise 51e

Using story 51 and the information on indirect commands as guides, give the Latin for the following. Use present subjunctives in all of the indirect commands:

1. Cornelius is inviting all his friends and clients to come together at his house.
2. The doorkeeper asks some people to go forward into the house.
3. Others he orders to stay in the street.
4. Others he orders to depart immediately.
5. Cornelius orders a certain slave to put a toga of manhood on Marcus.

COMING-OF-AGE CEREMONIES

When Cicero, the great statesman and orator (106–43 B.C.), was governor of Cilicia, an area of southern Asia Minor, he wrote the following in a letter to his friend Atticus (50 B.C.) about his nephew Quintus and his son Marcus:

> Cicerōnēs puerī amant inter sē, discunt, exercentur, sed alter
> frēnīs eget, alter calcāribus. Quīntō togam pūram Līberālibus
> cōgitābam dare; mandāvit enim pater.

> My son and nephew are fond of one another, learn their lessons,
> and take their exercise together; but the one needs the rein and
> the other the spur. I intend to celebrate Quintus' coming of age
> on the feast of Bacchus. His father asked me to do this.

> —Cicero, *Letters to Atticus* VI.1

The following year Cicero planned to give the **toga pūra** to his own son, Marcus, in his hometown of Arpinum to the southeast of Rome:

> Volō Cicerōnī meō togam pūram dare, Arpīnī putō.

> I wish to celebrate my son's coming of age. Arpinum, I think, will
> be the place.

> —Cicero, *Letters to Atticus* IX.17

On 31 March, 49 B.C., Cicero, barred from Rome for political reasons, wrote with pride from Arpinum:

> Ego meō Cicerōnī, quoniam Rōmā carēmus, Arpīnī potissimum
> togam pūram dedī, idque mūnicipibus nostrīs fuit grātum.

> Since Rome was out of bounds, I celebrated my son's coming of
> age at Arpinum in preference to any other place, and so doing
> delighted my fellow townsmen.

> —Cicero, *Letters to Atticus* IX.19

THE LATE EMPIRE

The Late Empire was beset with enormous problems that were political, administrative, economic, financial, and military all at once. Throughout this period the matter of succession between one emperor and the next was a bloody one. The frontiers of the empire were under attack everywhere by encroaching barbarian tribes. The Roman economy was in decline, overburdened by the enormous combined costs of maintaining continuous wars of defense along all the frontiers and dealing with uprisings in many provinces, supporting an enormous slave population, and paying the salaries and expenses of a huge administrative bureaucracy that had spread to every corner of the empire. In addition, former provinces and allies were developing into economic centers that competed with rather than supported Rome.

Below are brief descriptions of some of the emperors who tried to rule the empire and hold it together.

CARACALLA, A.D. 211–217

Caracalla enacted a measure that granted full Roman citizenship to all freeborn people throughout the empire. His motive was a practical one: Since all citizens were subject to inheritance taxes, increasing their numbers increased the revenues of the state. Caracalla was such a ruthless tyrant, however, that his Praetorian prefect had him put to the sword.

DIOCLETIAN, A.D. 284–305

Diocletian, who claimed Jupiter as his protector, formed a tetrarchy, a government ruled by four leaders. He assumed the title **Augustus** for himself and took charge of the eastern provinces. He named Maximian the **Augustus** in command of Italy and Africa. The two **Augustī,** in turn, appointed two **Caesarēs** as their junior partners: Galerius looked after the Danube provinces and Constantius the western districts. This restructuring was an effort to deal with the fact that the empire had become too large for a single

Caracalla—Roman marble bust

Marble cuirassed bust, Louvre, Paris, France

Amethyst cameo of Constantine II

Carved amethyst cameo, British Museum, London, England

ruler to control. Each member of the tetrarchy achieved military success in his own realm, while Diocletian took the lead in creating new laws that made the state more important than the individual citizen. The emperor was no longer a **prīnceps** working along with others, but a **dominus** surrounded by a royal court, who dictated his orders to a bureaucracy reorganized into four prefectures, twelve dioceses, and about 100 provinces. In addition, there was a gradual move to tie people by heredity to specific trades and tracts of land, as well as an unsuccessful attempt at price-fixing, a measure by which Diocletian hoped to improve the poor economic conditions in the empire.

CONSTANTINE, A.D. 324–337

In A.D. 305, Diocletian and Maximian, the two **Augustī,** abdicated, and the rival **Caesarēs**, Galerius and Constantius Chlorus, became the two new **Augustī.** Constantine, the son of Constantius, was then a hostage in Galerius' court. Constantine escaped, however, and went to Eboracum (York) in England and joined his father shortly before Constantius died. After the troops in England proclaimed Constantine their new leader, Galerius allowed him to remain in power as **Caesar** of Britain and Gaul. Driven by an ambition to acquire even greater power, Constantine waited for the right moment and then invaded Italy. On his way to Rome in A.D. 312, as the Christian historian Eusebius tells the story, Constantine saw the symbol of the cross in the sky together with the words, **In hōc signō vincēs** (*Under this sign you will win*). This apparition inspired him to order his soldiers to mark this Christian emblem on their shields. Shortly thereafter Constantine defeated Maxentius, the self-proclaimed **Augustus** of the West, in a pitched battle at the Mulvian Bridge outside Rome and became lord of the western half of the empire. Convinced that the Christian God had granted him his victory, Constantine persuaded the Augustus of the East, Licinius, to join him in issuing the Edict of Milan, which gave Christians the right to worship as they chose and thus ended their years of persecution.

After sharing the rule of the empire for a time, however, the two **Augustī,** Constantine and Licinius, went to war against each other. In A.D. 324, Constantine defeated Licinius and became the one and only leader of the reunified Roman Empire. For the rest of his reign, Constantine worked to further the reforms of Diocletian, displaying even more fully his talents as general, administrator, and legislator. Because of the accomplishments of these two emperors, the Roman Empire would continue to exist for more than another century. Constantine was responsible, however, for a truly dramatic break from Roman traditions. To carry out his idea that unity could be reinforced through the influence of the Christian church, he founded a Christian city, Constantinople, and proclaimed it the new capital city of the empire. When he died in A.D. 337, baptized at last in his final hours, one suspects that he actually did believe that the Christian God had chosen him to lead Rome on a new path of glory.

WORD STUDY XIII

Latin and the Romance Languages

Although Latin has influenced the development of many languages (including English, of course), there are five modern languages that are so universally derived from Latin as to be called "Romance" (i.e., Roman) languages. These languages are Italian, French, Spanish, Portuguese, and Rumanian. The following examples show clearly the relationship of the Romance languages to Latin:

Latin	French	Italian	Spanish	Portuguese	Rumanian
arbor, *tree*	arbre	albero	árbol	árvore	arbore
dulcis, *sweet*	doux	dolce	dulce	doce	dulce

Rome's conquering legions brought Latin to lands as far apart as Britain and Egypt. In those places with well-established civilizations, such as Egypt, Latin did not displace the native languages; when the Romans left, Latin left with them. However, in areas such as Gaul (France) where civilization in Roman times was relatively primitive, Latin took hold and became the language of the people. The Romans also sent many colonists to these less-developed and less-populated provinces, further ensuring the dominance of Latin as the accepted tongue in these lands.

In the evolution of provincial Latin into the Romance languages, these major developments (as well as many others) took place:

1. In general, the importance of word endings (inflection) in classical Latin was greatly reduced in the Romance languages. Nouns were usually reduced to two forms: a singular and a plural, e.g., the French *homme, hommes*, from the Latin **hominem**; and endings such as those of the comparative and superlative of adjectives were often replaced by words meaning "more" and "most," e.g., the Latin **dīligentior** became in Italian, *più diligente*. (*Più* is derived from the Latin **plūs**.)

2. The definite article developed from the demonstrative pronoun and adjective **ille**. For example, the Latin **ille lupus** became "the wolf" in each of the Romance languages, as follows:

French	Italian	Spanish	Portuguese	Rumanian
le loup	il lupo	el lobo	o lobo	lupul*

(*The article is attached as a suffix in Rumanian.)

3. Pronunciation developed separately in each language, diverging greatly from that of classical Latin, e.g., the Latin word **caelum** (*c* pronounced *k*) became *cielo* in Italian (*c* pronounced *ch*), and *ciel* in French (*c* pronounced *s*).

Exercise 1

Next to each number below are words of equivalent meaning from each of three Romance languages. Give the Latin word from which each trio of Romance language words is derived and give the English meaning. Consult an Italian, Spanish, or French dictionary, as needed:

Italian	Spanish	French	Latin	Meaning
		Nouns		
1. acqua	agua	eau	_____	_____
2. amico	amigo	ami	_____	_____
3. libro	libro	livre	_____	_____
4. lingua	lengua	langue	_____	_____
5. madre	madre	mère	_____	_____
6. ora	hora	heure	_____	_____
7. pane	pan	pain	_____	_____
8. tempo	tiempo	temps	_____	_____
9. terra	tierra	terre	_____	_____
		Verbs		
10. abitare	habitar	habiter	_____	_____
11. amare	amar	aimer	_____	_____
12. dormire	dormir	dormir	_____	_____
13. scrivere	escribir	écrire	_____	_____
		Adjectives		
14. buono	bueno	bon	_____	_____
15. breve	breve	bref	_____	_____
16. fàcile	fácil	facile	_____	_____
17. male	malo	mal	_____	_____
		Numbers		
18. quattro	cuatro	quatre	_____	_____
19. sette	siete	sept	_____	_____
20. dieci	diez	dix	_____	_____

Exercise 2

In which of the following places is French spoken? In which is Spanish spoken? In which is Portuguese spoken? Consult an encyclopedia as needed:

1. Brazil
2. Haiti
3. Guatemala
4. Belgium
5. Madagascar
6. Angola
7. Quebec
8. Argentina
9. Switzerland
10. Mexico

CHAPTER 52

PAPIRIUS PRAETEXTATUS

Now that Marcus has assumed the **toga virīlis**, Cornelius will begin to consider his public career. In the early Republic, boys began their training for public life when they were much younger than Marcus is now. In those days fathers took their sons with them while they carried out their public duties. This story shows that Papirius, though still wearing the **toga praetexta**, had already learned how to be discreet.

Mōs anteā senātōribus Rōmae fuit in Cūriam cum praetextātīs fīliīs introīre. Ōlim in senātū rēs maior agēbātur et in diem posterum prōlāta est. Placuit nē quis eam rem ēnūntiāret. Māter Papīriī, puerī quī cum parente suō in Cūriā fuerat, rogāvit fīlium quid in senātū patrēs ēgissent. Puer tamen respondit nōn licēre eam rem ēnūntiāre. Eō magis mulier audīre cupiēbat; silentium puerī animum eius adeō incitāvit ut vehementius 5 quaereret.

Tum puer, mātre urgente, prūdēns cōnsilium cēpit. Dīxit āctum esse in senātū utrum ūnus vir duās uxōrēs habēret an ūna uxor duōs virōs. Hoc ubi illa audīvit, domō trepidāns ēgressa est. Ad cēterās mātrōnās rem pertulit.

Vēnit ad senātum postrīdiē mātrōnārum caterva. Lacrimantēs atque obsecrantēs 10 ōrāvērunt ut ūna uxor duōs virōs habēret potius quam ut ūnus vir duās uxōrēs. Senātōrēs ingredientēs in Cūriam mīrābantur quid mātrōnae vellent.

(continued)

1 **mōs, mōris,** m., *custom;* pl., *character*	7 **dīxit āctum esse,** *he said that there had been a debate*
2 **posterus, -a, -um,** *next, following*	**utrum...an...,** conj., *whether...or...*
placuit, *it was decided*	8 **habēret,** *should have*
nē quis, *that no one*	**trepidāns, trepidantis,** *in a panic*
3 **ēnūntiō, -āre, -āvī, -ātus,** *to reveal, divulge*	10 **caterva, -ae,** f., *crowd*
4 **patrēs, patrum,** m. pl., *senators*	11 **potius quam,** *rather than*
eō magis, adv., *all the more*	

2 **agō, agere, ēgī, āctus,** *to do, drive;* here, *to discuss, debate*
prōferō, prōferre, prōtulī, prōlātus, irreg., *to carry forward, continue*
7 **urgeō, urgēre, ursī,** *to press, insist*

Exercise 52a
Respondē Latīnē:

1. Quī mōs senātōribus Rōmae fuit?
2. Quālis rēs in senātū agēbātur?
3. Quid senātōribus placuit?
4. Quid māter Papīrium rogāvit?

5. Quid puer respondit?
6. Quid mulier vehementius faciēbat?
7. Quid puer prūdēns dīxit?
8. Quid māter fēcit?

Puer Papīrius in medium prōgressus nārrāvit quid māter audīre cupīvisset et quid ipse mātrī dīxisset. Senātus fidem atque ingenium puerī laudāvit ac cōnsultum fēcit nē posteā puerī cum patribus in Cūriam introīrent praeter illum ūnum Papīrium. Puerō 15 posteā cognōmen honōris causā Praetextātus datum est quod tantam prūdentiam praebuerat.

14 **fidēs, fideī,** f., *good faith, reliability, trust*
   ingenium, -ī, n., *intelligence, ingenuity*
   cōnsultum, -ī, n., *decree*
16 **cognōmen, cognōminis,** n., *surname (third or fourth name of a Roman)*

honōris causā, *for the sake of an honor, as an honor*
17 **praebeō, -ēre, -uī, -itus,** *to display, show*

Respondē Latīnē:
1. Quid Papīrius senātōribus nārrāvit?
2. Quod cōnsultum senātus fēcit?
3. Cūr cognōmen Papīriō datum est?

BUILDING THE MEANING
Impersonal Verbs I

You have seen the following impersonal verbal phrases and impersonal verbs since early in this course (for discussion, see Chapter 20):

1. **necesse est,** *it is necessary*
   Nōbīs **necesse est** statim discēdere. (9:13–14)
   To leave immediately is necessary for us.
   It is necessary *for us to leave immediately.*

2. **licet, licēre, licuit** + dat., *it is allowed*
   Vōbīs **licet** hīc cēnāre. (cf. 20:8)
   To dine here is allowed for you.
   It is allowed *for you to dine here.*
   You are allowed to dine here.
   You may dine here.

The underlined infinitives are the subjects of the impersonals, but other translations, as suggested above, make better English.

You have seen **licet** used in the infinitive:

Puer tamen respondit nōn **licēre** eam rem ēnūntiāre. (52:4)
The boy replied that it was not permitted to reveal the matter.

Here is another verb that may be used impersonally:

3. **placeō, placēre, placuī-** + dat., *to please*

This verb can be used with a noun as its subject:

Placuitne tibi <u>cēna</u>, Gaī? (34h:3)
***Did** <u>the dinner</u> **please** you, Gaius?*
Did you like the dinner, Gaius?

Or it may be used with an impersonal subject (expressed or unexpressed):

"Quīntus Valerius vult tē in mātrimōnium dūcere, <u>id quod</u> nōbīs **placet.**
Placetne tibi, Cornēlia?" "Mihi quoque **placet**," respondit. (50:17–21)
*"Quintus Valerius wishes to marry you, <u>that which</u> **is pleasing** to us. **Is it pleasing** to
you, Cornelia?" **"It is** also **pleasing** to me," she replied.*

This verb is often used impersonally in the perfect tense, meaning not *it pleased*
but *it was decided*, with a clause in the subjunctive as its subject:

Placuit <u>nē quis eam rem ēnūntiāret.</u> (52:2–3)
<u>*That no one should reveal the matter*</u> ***was decided.***
It was decided <u>*that no one should reveal the matter*</u>.

You have seen these other impersonal verbs:

4. **decet, decēre, decuit**, *it is becoming, fitting; should*

Nōn **decet** <u>patrem dēspondēre fīliam</u>, īnsciā mātre. (50:15–16)
<u>*That a father betroth his daughter*</u> *without the mother knowing* **is** not ***fitting.***
It is not ***fitting*** <u>*that a father betroth his daughter*</u> *without the mother knowing.*
*A father **should** not betroth his daughter without the mother knowing.*

Here the accusative and infinitive serve as the subject of the impersonal verb.

5. **oportet, oportēre, oportuit**, *it is fitting; ought*

<u>Festīnāre tē</u> **oportet.** (50:9)
<u>*That you hurry*</u> **is fitting.**
It is fitting <u>*that you hurry*</u>.
You ought to hurry.

6. **taedet, taedēre, taesum est**, *it bores, makes one* (acc.) *tired of something* (gen.)

Mē **taedet** sōlitūdinis. (50:2)
It tires *me of loneliness.*
I am tired of/bored with loneliness.

Exercise 52b
Read aloud and translate:

1. Papīriō nōn licuit rem ēnūntiāre.
2. Papīriī respōnsum mātrī nōn placuit.
3. Papīriō tamen necesse erat rem cēlāre.
4. Puerō nōn decuit rem mātrī ēnūntiāre.
5. Mātrem taesum est silentiī Papīriī.
6. "Loquī tē oportet," inquit māter.
7. Papīriō placuit ut aliam rem mātrī nārrāret.

Exercise 52c
Read aloud and translate. Identify the type of subordinate clause in each sentence:

1. Senātōrēs Papīriō imperāvērunt nē rem ēnūntiāret.
2. Māter Papīriī rogāvit fīlium quid ā senātōribus āctum esset.
3. Puer respondit sē eam rem nōn ēnūntiātūrum esse.
4. Silentium puerī mātrem adeō incitāvit ut vehementius quaereret.
5. Cum māter respōnsum audīvisset, domō ēgressa est.
6. Māter mātrōnās hortāta est ut ad senātum postrīdiē īrent.
7. Trepidantēs ōrāvērunt ut ūna uxor duōs virōs habēret potius quam ut ūnus vir duās uxōrēs.
8. Senātōrēs mīrābantur cūr mātrōnae hoc dīcerent.
9. Papīrius ēnūntiāvit quid ipse mātrī dīxisset.
10. Ingenium puerī senātōrēs adeō incitāvit ut eī cognōmen dederint.

mōs maiōrum *literally, "the custom of the ancestors," inherited custom, tradition*
mōs prō lēge *A long established custom has the force of law.*
mōre suō *in one's own way*
nūllō mōre *without precedent, unparalleled*

Mōribus antīquīs rēs stat Rōmāna virīsque. *On customs and men of olden times the Roman state stands firm.* (Ennius)
Ō tempora! Ō mōrēs! *How times and customs have changed!*
(Cicero, *Orations against Catiline* I.2)

ROMAN RELIGION

In Chapter 51 you saw how important it was for Marcus to dedicate his **bulla** and **toga praetexta** at the shrine of the household gods (**larārium**). In order to understand this ritual and the rites that will take place at Cornelia's wedding in the next chapter, you need to know something about Roman religion.

When Romans said they believed in gods, they were saying that gods were every-where at work in the ordinary events of nature. Their religious activity therefore consist-ed of trying to make these unseen forces work for them rather than against them. Sometimes they gave them names and fashioned images of them, such as Mars, Jupiter, and Venus, whom they visualized in human form, godlike in power but otherwise all too human. Sometimes they gave them names but no precise form, such as Vesta, goddess of the hearth, and the peasant-farmer gods, Pomona (fruit), Robigus (blight), and Ceres (growth). This idea that each god had a particular domain was worked out in great detail. For example, since the security of a house depended on the security of its door, there was thought to be a god (Janus Patulcius) in charge of opening doors and another (Janus Clusivius) to see that they were properly closed.

Melitene, priestess of the Mother of the Gods. Roman marble bust, consecrated A.D. 162
Louvre, Paris, France

Sacrifice to Apollo

Detail from "Landscape with the Father of Psyche Sacrificing to Apollo," oil on canvas by Claude Lorrain, National Trust, Fairhaven

Religious observances that could harness the power of these beings were prayer and sacrifice. These could be offered together, or prayer could be used to ask for something, and a sacrifice made if the request were granted. For instance, we have the inscription **servus vōvit, līber solvit** (*a slave made the vow, a free man carried it out*), showing that the slave had promised a gift to a god if he became free and that he had kept his promise when he got his freedom.

Essentially, a sacrifice had to embody life in some form, since life is energy, and divine energy is necessary to answer the prayer. Animals were therefore generally used for sacrifice, but small cakes, flour mixed with salt, flowers, honey, cheese, fruit, wine, and milk were all employed, especially in domestic rites, at the **larārium** in the **ātrium**, for example. In fact, it was thought that these gifts kept up the vitality of the gods, enabling them to put forth the power required to grant the request. Accordingly, when an animal was sacrificed, the most vital parts (the heart, liver, entrails, etc.) were burnt upon the altar, and the rest of the carcass, fortunately the more appetizing part, was eaten at the time by those present at the sacrifice. The sacrificial procedure was as follows: Suppliants chose the deity appropriate to the request they had in mind and went along to that god's temple with a sacrifice, which had to be the proper animal for the god in question. For instance, black animals were correct for the underworld gods, white animals for gods in the upper world, and no one would have dreamed of offering a male animal to a female deity, or vice versa. While the rite was in progress, a flute player played to drown out any ill-omened sounds. If the flute player stopped playing or a mistake was made in the ceremony, the whole process had to be repeated from the beginning!

The sacrifice took place on a large altar in front of the temple in the open air. The temple itself, consisting of a walled chamber surrounded by a colonnade, contained no seats and only a small altar on which incense was burned. It was not used for religious services but for housing the image of the god, which was made on the grandest scale and of the most precious materials. Often the only light in the building fell upon the statue from the doorway, so that the worshiper, who came in from the blinding sun to the half-gloom of the shrine, would indeed feel the presence of the god.

A worshiper making a vow would advance to the image and fasten to its legs waxen tablets inscribed with prayers and details of the promised sacrifice. Then, standing erect, and with arms outstretched to the god, the worshiper reverently prayed aloud.

In addition, the Romans, like the Etruscans, laid great stress upon augury, the "science" of "taking the omens." They would not contemplate taking any important step until it was clear from the omens that the gods were in favor of it.

First of all, they would offer a sacrifice to some appropriate god or gods. For example, for an important family event, they would offer a sacrifice to their household gods, called the **Larēs** and **Penātēs**, at the family shrine in the **ātrium**; someone planning to go on a journey might offer a sacrifice to Mercury, a soldier going into battle a sacrifice to Mars or Mithras, and a young man in love an offering to Venus or Fortuna.

At home, the sacrifice could be small cakes, honey, cheese, or fruit, which would be burned upon the altar. At a temple, an animal such as a pig, a sheep, or a bull (or all three, the **suovetaurīlia**) would be sacrificed.

In the latter case, once the animal had been killed, the vital organs—heart, liver, and intestines—were inspected by the **haruspicēs**, who claimed to be able to tell from the spots or marks on these organs whether the omens were favorable or not. If the omens were bad, the ordinary Roman simply put off the undertaking to another day. More sceptical Romans usually dismissed all this as mumbo-jumbo and, in fact, the Elder Cato said, "How can one **haruspex** look at another without laughing?" Yet Julius Caesar, though a confessed atheist, held the office of Pontifex Maximus, the chief priest who was in charge of all public religious observances.

The most popular form of augury, **auspicium** (*taking the auspices*), can be described quite accurately as "bird watching" (from **avis**, *bird*, and **spectāre**, *to watch*). The **auspex** based his predictions upon the number of birds seen at a particular time, the direction of flight, and so on. Astrology, dreams, thunder and lightning, and strange events of any kind were all taken very seriously by those engaged in augury.

There was no creed in which people were expected to believe. For ideas of this kind we have to turn to Stoic and Epicurean philosophy, and for religion in our sense to the Eastern cults of Isis and Mithras, Isis being originally an Egyptian goddess and Mithras a Persian god.

The Romans continued to worship the **Larēs** and **Penātēs** in their own homes and the great gods in the temples of their cities, and, since the emperor stood for the continuity of household and city and wielded so much power, he too began to be worshiped as a god.

Many legends about auguries surround the early kings of Rome.
"Tarquin the Elder Consulting Attus Nevius the Augur," oil on canvas by Sebastiano Ricci, Sotheby's, London

In A.D. 80 the Romans regarded Christianity as eccentric superstition. They could hardly have foreseen that a little over two centuries later it would oust other religions and, though it was the religion of the common man, that it would make a convert of the emperor himself.

CORNELIA'S WEDDING

In spite of the unromantic pre-arrangements, the wedding itself was celebrated with great festivity by the families and guests. The second half of June was considered to be the luckiest time for a wedding.

On the evening before her marriage, the girl dedicated her toys to the household gods and her **toga praetexta** to the goddess Fortuna Virginalis in the city, just as a boy dedicated his **toga praetexta** and **bulla** at the coming-of-age ceremony. At the same time, she received her **mundus muliebris**—the jewelry, perfumes, toilet articles, and attire of the grown-up woman.

On her wedding day, the bride wore a white tunic (**tunica alba**) and white shoes. Her hair was specially styled for the occasion with a yellow hairnet (**rēticulum**), and over it she wore a bright orange veil (**flammeum**). Her attendant was a married woman (**prōnuba**). The bride's house, where the wedding ceremony (**nūptiae**) was performed, was also decorated for the occasion.

The bride and her family and friends assembled in the **ātrium** and received the bridegroom and his guests. The ceremony began with a sacrifice, usually of a pig, the entrails of which were carefully examined by the **auspex** to make sure that the omens were favorable. If they were unfavorable, the marriage was postponed. The ceremony also included the signing of the marriage contract (**tabulās nūptiālēs obsignāre**) by ten witnesses, the joining of the couple's right hands (**dextrās iungere**) by the **prōnuba**, and the repetition of the formula **Ubi tū Gaius, ego Gaia** by the bride. Then the guests all shouted, "Good luck!" (**Fēlīciter!**).

The ceremony was followed by a banquet, and then, after nightfall, the couple prepared to go to their new home. The bridegroom pretended to carry off the bride by force just as the Romans once carried off the Sabine women. Then the bride and groom were escorted home by a procession of guests (**dēductiō**) carrying torches (**taedae**) and singing songs to Hymen, god of marriage. Some guests threw nuts (**nucēs**) to children for luck. On arrival at the house, the bride was carried over the threshold (**super līmen tollere**) to avoid an unlucky stumble.

Ubi diēs nūptiālis vēnit, omnēs mātūrē surrēxērunt. Aurēlia Marcum Sextumque hortābātur ut festīnārent. Ancillae hūc illūc concursābant ut omnia parārent.

Flāvia et Vīnia, māter eius, iam diū aderant. Mox adveniēbant cēterī amīcī et propinquī. Appropinquantēs laetī vīdērunt iānuam et postēs vittīs et corōnīs myrtī laurīque ōrnātōs esse. Domum ingressī in ātrium ductī sunt ubi Cornēlia, tunicā albā 5 indūta, flammeum gerēns, eōs exspectābat. Paulō post clāmor rīsusque maximus audītus est. Valerius cum propinquīs amīcīsque suīs intrābat.

Cornēlia cum prōnubā ad āram stābat. Sacrīs rīte parātīs, auspex prōcessit ut porcum sacrificāret. Cum exta īnspexisset, "Ōmina," inquit, "bona sunt." Deinde tabulae nūptiālēs obsignātae sunt. Vīnia prōnuba dextrās Valeriī et Cornēliae iūnxit. Valeriō 10 rogantī, "Quid nōmen tibi est?" Cornēlia, "Ubi tū Gaius, ego Gaia," respondit. Quō factō, cūnctī, "Fēlīciter!" exclāmābant.

Cēnā iam parātā, omnēs convīvae accubuērunt, atque optimam post cēnam cōnsecūta est commissātiō hilaritātis plēna.

Iam advesperāscēbat. Cornēlia ad mātrem haerēbat; Valerius simulābat sē eam ē 15 manibus mātris vī abripere. Mox illa domum novam multīs comitantibus dēdūcēbātur. Praecēdēbant quīnque puerī quī taedās ārdentēs ferēbant; subsequēbantur cēterī rīdentēs et cantantēs; nucēs ad līberōs, quī undique concurrerant, coniciēbant. Cum domum vēnissent, nova nūpta super līmen sublāta est nē lāberētur.

"Quam fēlīx est Cornēlia!" exclāmāvit Flāvia. 20

4 **vitta, -ae,** f., *ribbon*	**rīte,** adv., *properly*
myrtus, -ī, f., *myrtle*	**auspex, auspicis,** m., *augur, officiating*
5 **laurus, -ī,** f., *bay (tree), laurel*	*priest*
ōrnō, -āre, -āvī, -ātus, *to decorate*	9 **exta, -ōrum,** n. pl., *the inner organs of*
8 **āra, -ae,** f., *altar*	*sacrificial animals (heart, lungs, liver)*
sacra, -ōrum, n. pl., *religious rites,*	10 **dextra, -ae,** f., *right hand*
sacrifice	19 **nova nūpta, -ae,** f., *bride*
	nē lāberētur, *so she wouldn't stumble*

10 **iungō, iungere, iūnxī, iūnctus,** *to join*
17 **ārdeō, ārdēre, ārsī, ārsūrus,** *to burn, blaze*

Exercise 53a
Respondē Latīnē:

1. Cūr ancillae hūc illūc concursābant?
2. Quandō clāmor rīsusque maximus audītus est?
3. Quandō prōcessit auspex?
4. Cūr auspex prōcessit?
5. Quid Valerius rogāvit cum dextrae iūnctae essent?
6. Quid Cornēlia respondit?
7. Quid Valerius simulābat?
8. Cūr nova nūpta super līmen sublāta est?

BUILDING THE MEANING
Purpose Clauses

In addition to the uses of the subjunctive described in Chapter 43 (causal and circumstantial clauses and indirect questions), Chapter 50 (result), and Chapter 51 (indirect commands), the subjunctive is used with **ut** to express *purpose*. Here, it is usually most naturally translated as *to* or *so that*. The corresponding negative, **nē**, can be translated in various ways, e.g., *lest, so that…not, in case, to avoid,* or *to prevent*:

> Ancillae hūc illūc concursābant **ut** omnia **parārent**. (53:2)
> *The slave-women were running about here and there to prepare everything.*

> Super līmen sublāta est **nē lāberētur**. (53:19)
> *She was carried over the threshold so she wouldn't stumble/to avoid stumbling.*

The imperfect subjunctive is used in secondary sequence (as in the examples above). The present subjunctive is used in primary sequence (as below):

> Ancillae hūc illūc concursant **ut** omnia **parent**.
> *The slave-women are running about here and there to prepare everything.*

> Super līmen tollētur **nē lābātur**.
> *She will be carried over the threshold to avoid stumbling.*

Exercise 53b

Read aloud and translate each sentence, identify the tenses of all verbs, and determine whether the subordinate clauses are in primary or secondary sequence:

1. Multī amīcī convēnērunt ut novae nūptae grātulārentur.
2. Iānitor baculum habet ut eōs quī neque amīcī neque propinquī sint repellat.
3. Marcus ante larārium stābat ut bullam Laribus cōnsecrāret.
4. Cavēte nē cadātis, amīcī!
5. Ancilla in cubiculum festīnāvit ut Cornēliae speculum daret.
6. Servus vestīmenta custōdit nē quis ea surripiat.
7. Flāvia Rōmam veniet ut Cornēliam adiuvet.
8. Eucleidēs per viās festīnāvit nē ā praedōnibus caperētur.
9. Pater Sextī Rōmam redībit ut fīlium sēcum domum dūcat.
10. Marcus ad Tabulārium dēductus est ut nōmen eius in tabulīs pūblicīs īnscrīberētur.

Exercise 53c

There is much evidence to show that husbands and wives loved each other and lived as happily as if they had themselves chosen each other. When a bride repeated the words **Ubi tū Gaius, ego Gaia** at the wedding ceremony, she was promising to be a faithful wife. The following story, adapted from Pliny (*Letters* III.16), tells us how Arria, during the illness of her husband, concealed the death of her son from him to avoid aggravating his illness.

Read the paragraph aloud and translate it:

> Aegrōtābat Caecina Paetus, marītus Arriae; aegrōtābat et fīlius, uterque mortiferē, ut vidēbātur. Fīlius dēcessit, puer eximiā pulchritūdine et parentibus cārissimus. Huic Arria ita fūnus parāvit, ita dūxit exsequiās ut ignōrāret marītus. Praetereā cum cubiculum eius intrāverat, simulābat vīvere fīlium atque etiam convalēscere; ac Paetō saepe interrogantī quid ageret puer, respondēbat, "Bene quiēvit; libenter cibum sūmpsit." Deinde cum lacrimae prōrumperent, ē cubiculō ēgrediēbātur. Tum sē dolōrī dabat. Tandem siccīs iam oculīs, vultū iam compositō redībat; atque dum marītus aegrōtābat, sīc lacrimās retinēbat, dolōrem operiēbat.   5

1 **marītus, -ī,** m., *husband*
2 **mortiferē,** adv., *mortally, critically*
   eximius, -a, -um, *outstanding*
3 **cārus, -a, -um,** *dear, beloved*
   fūnus, fūneris, n., *funeral*

dūxit exsequiās, *(she) carried out the funeral rites*
4 **cum...intrāverat,** *whenever she entered*
5 **quid ageret,** *how he was*
7 **siccus, -a, -um,** *dry*

2 **dēcēdō, dēcēdere, dēcessī, dēcessūrus,** *to die*
8 **operiō, operīre, operuī, opertus,** *to hide, cover*

Exercise 53d

Using story 53 as a guide, give the Latin for the following. Use subordinate clauses with the subjunctive in each sentence:

1. When the pig had been sacrificed, the nuptial tablets were signed.
2. Vinia went forward to join the right hands of Valerius and Cornelia.
3. The cook went into the kitchen to prepare dinner.
4. Cornelia was clinging to Aurelia lest she be snatched away by Valerius.
5. The bride was carried across the threshold with such great care that she did not stumble.

Exercise 53e

The following is part of a longer poem by Catullus (c. 84–54 B.C.). It is to be sung as the bride is accompanied on the evening of her wedding from her father's house to her new home. The bride's name is Aurunculeia. In the first two stanzas she is told to dry her tears. After all, she is very beautiful!

Read the stanzas and translate them:

> Flēre dēsine! Nōn tibi, Au-
> runculeia, perīculum est
> nē qua fēmina pulchrior
> clārum ab Ōceanō diem
>   vīderit venientem.   5
>
> Tālis in variō solet
> dīvitis dominī hortulō
> stāre flōs hyacinthinus.
> Sed morāris! Abit diēs!
>   Prōdeās, nova nūpta!   10

At last the chorus see the bright veil of the bride appearing. It is time for the hymn and the distribution of nuts:

> Tollite, ō puerī, facēs!
> Flammeum videō venīre.
> Īte, concinite in modum
> "Iō Hymēn Hymenaee iō,
>   iō Hymēn Hymenaee!"   15
>
> Da nucēs puerīs, iners
> concubīne: satis diū
> lūsistī nucibus. Lubet
> iam servīre Talassiō.
>   Concubīne, nucēs da!   20

—Catullus LXI. 86–95, 121–125, and 131–135

1 **nōn...perīculum est nē qua,** *there is no danger that any*
4 **clārus, -a, -um,** *bright*
   Ōceanus, -ī, m., *Ocean*
6 **varius, -a, -um,** *different, varied, many-hued*
7 **hortulus, -ī,** m., *small garden*
11 **fax, facis,** f., *wedding-torch*
13 **modus, -ī,** m., *way, method;* here, *rhythmic/harmonious manner*

14 **Iō!**: a ritual exclamation; the *-i* is consonantal, and the word is pronounced as one syllable

Hymēn!: an exclamation chanted at weddings; later thought of as the god of weddings

Hymenaee! = **Hymēn!**

16 **iners, inertis,** *lazy*
17 **concubīnus, -ī,** m., *bridegroom*
19 **serviō, -īre, -īvī, -itūrus** + dat., *to serve*
Talassius, -ī, m., *Talassius (god of marriage)*

1 **fleō, flēre, flēvī, flētus,** *to weep, cry*
dēsinō, dēsinere, dēsiī, dēsitus, *to stop*
10 **prōdeō, prōdīre, prōdiī, prōditūrus,** irreg., *to come forth*
The present subjunctive **prōdeās** expresses a command.
13 **concinō, concinere, concinuī,** *to sing together*
18 **lubet = libet, libēre, libuit** or **libitum est,** *it is pleasing to someone* (dat.) *to do something* (infin.). Supply **tibi.**

Aurelius Hermia and his wife, a freedwoman

Exercise 53f

The culmination of Arria's devotion is described in the following story of her death, also told in the letter of Pliny (III.16) from which the passage in Exercise 53c is adapted.

Read this portion of the letter:

> Many years later Scribonianus in Illyria took up arms against the emperor Claudius, and Paetus took part in the revolt. Scribonianus was killed, and Paetus was captured and put on board a ship to be taken to Rome. When he was about to go on board, Arria pleaded with the soldiers to be allowed to go with him. "Surely a man of senatorial rank is entitled to have some slaves to prepare his food, dress him, and put on his shoes? I will do all of these tasks on my own." Her request was refused, however. She therefore hired a small fishing boat and followed the larger vessel. When they reached Rome, Paetus was condemned to death, but he was told that he might take his own life, if he wished. At that point, Arria, who had no desire to go on living after the death of her husband, drew a dagger, plunged it into her breast, drew it out, and, as she held it out to her husband, uttered the immortal words, **Paete, nōn dolet** ("*Paetus, it does not hurt*").

Martial wrote the following epigram on Arria's death. Read it aloud and translate it:

> Casta suō gladium cum trāderet Arria Paetō
>   quem dē vīsceribus trāxerat ipsa suīs,
> "Crēde mihī, vulnus quod fēcī nōn dolet," inquit.
>   "Sed quod tū faciēs, hoc mihi, Paete, dolet."
>
> —Martial, *Epigrams* I.13

1 **castus, -a, -um,** *virtuous, chaste*
2 **dē,** prep. + abl., *down from, concerning, about*; here, *from*
  viscera, viscerum, n. pl., *vital organs*
4 **quod,** (*the one*) *that*

ADDITIONAL READING:
The Romans Speak for Themselves: Book II: "The Wedding of Cato and Marcia," pages 73–80.

A SAD OCCASION

When a death occurred in a Roman family, it was the custom to display grief. Tears and lamentation were expected, and it was usual, for female mourners at least, to beat the breast (**pectus plangere**) and go about with torn clothing (**scissā veste**) and dishevelled hair (**capillīs solūtīs**). Some families even hired professional mourners to do this for them.

In the case of an important family, like the Cornelii in our story, the actual funeral procession (**pompa**) was a very elaborate affair. After the body had lain in state, feet toward the door, in the **ātrium** of the house surrounded by lamps (**lucernae**) and candles (**candēlae**), there would be a procession through the city to the Forum and then on to the family tomb. For the procession, the deceased was placed on a litter with face uncovered. Musicians playing pipes, horns, and trumpets headed the procession, which would include torchbearers, professional mourners, and singers of dirges (**nēniae**), as well as members of the mourning family and household (including freedmen and slaves), friends, and buffoons, who would jestingly mock the dead person. Also in the procession would be actors wearing masks of the dead person's ancestors and appropriate clothing and, in the case of a magistrate or ex-magistrate, public attendants (**līctōrēs**) carrying the symbols of office, bundles of rods (**fascēs**).

A halt was made in the Forum where a speech of praise (**laudātiō**) was made in honor of the deceased.

At the family tomb outside the walls, the body was usually placed on a funeral pyre (**rogus**), which was set alight by a member of the family after some of the deceased's possessions had been placed on it. Flowers and spices were also thrown on the fire.

After the body had been cremated, the ashes were cooled with wine and were collected with the bones in an urn and placed in the family tomb. The last farewell was then uttered, and after nine days of mourning a food offering was made at the tomb to the spirit of the dead man (**mānēs**).

Slaves and the very poor, who could not afford even to hire bearers to carry the bier, were usually buried in public cemeteries in simple coffins. Some, however, would join one of the guilds or societies that were formed to ensure a respectable funeral for their members and spare them the indignity of being flung into a common grave. The poor were buried on the day they died, and their funerals, like those of children, usually took place after dark with a minimum of ceremony. Death among children was common, both in the early vulnerable years and in later childhood, as is proved by many inscriptions found on tombstones in various parts of the Roman world.

Mēnse Iūliō tantus erat calor in urbe ut omnēs ad vīllam īre vellent. Gaius Cornēlius igitur omnia parāre coepit ut Baiās īrent. Antequam profectī sunt, accidit rēs trīstissima.

Cornēlius, ut solēbat, cum Titō frātre ad balneās ierat. Per tōtam domum erat silentium. Subitō audītae sunt vōcēs atque clāmor. Cornēlius servōs hortābātur ut 5 lectīcam in domum maximā cum cūrā ferrent. Aurēlia, vōcibus audītīs, in ātrium irrūpit. "Quid factum est, Gāī? Cūr servōs iubēs lectīcam in domum ferre?" Cui Cornēlius, "Titus noster aliquid malī accēpit. Frīgidāriī pavīmentum tam lēve et lūbricum erat ut ille lāpsus ceciderit. Putō eum coxam frēgisse. Medicus statim est arcessendus."

Multōs diēs Titus in lectō iacēbat. Prīmō convalēscere vidēbātur; mox tamen fīēbat 10 īnfirmior, nam in febrem subitō inciderat. In diēs morbus ingravēscēbat.

Tandem tam īnfirmus erat ut vix loquī posset. Haud multō post ē vītā excessit. Cornēlius maximō dolōre affectus est. Tōta domus sē dolōrī dedit. Aurēlia et Cornēlia et omnēs ancillae, scissā veste capillīsque solūtīs, pectora plangēbant. Corpus Titī in ātriō in lectō fūnebrī positum est. Circum lectum ardēbant lucernae et candēlae. 15

Postrīdiē corpus Titī summō honōre ēlātum est. Praecēdēbant tībīcinēs, cornicinēs, tubicinēs. In pompā erant virī taedās tenentēs, mulierēs nēniās cantantēs, āctōrēs imāginēs et vestīmenta maiōrum gerentēs, mīmī, līctōrēs fascēs ferentēs, familiārēs, amīcī plōrantēs.

(continued)

5 **hortor, -ārī, -ātus sum,** *to encourage, urge*
8 **lēvis, -is, -e,** *smooth*
9 **coxa, -ae,** f., *hipbone*
est arcessendus, *must be sent for*
11 **febris, febris,** gen. pl., **febrium,** f., *fever*
morbus, -ī, m., *illness*
15 **fūnebris, -is, -e,** *funeral*

16 **tībīcen, tībīcinis,** m., *piper*
18 **imāgō, imāginis,** f., *likeness, mask*
maiōrēs, maiōrum, m. pl., *ancestors*
mīmus, -ī, m., *actor of mime, buffoon*
familiārēs, familiārium, m. pl., *members of the household*
19 **plōrō, -āre, -āvī, -ātus,** *to lament, mourn*

9 **frangō, frangere, frēgī, frāctus,** *to break*
11 **ingravēscō, ingravēscere,** *to grow worse*
14 **scindō, scindere, scidī, scissus,** *to cut, split, carve, tear*
solvō, solvere, solvī, solūtus, *to loosen, untie, dishevel*

Exercise 54a
Respondē Latīnē:

1. Quō erant Cornēliī itūrī?
2. Quālis rēs accidit?
3. Quō ierant Cornēlius et Titus?
4. Quid Cornēlius servōs hortābātur ut facerent?
5. Quis in ātrium irrūpit?
6. Cūr Titus cecidit?
7. Quid Cornēlius eum frēgisse putat?
8. Quis arcessendus est?
9. Cūr Titus īnfirmior fīēbat?
10. Quam īnfirmus fīēbat Titus?
11. Quōmodo affectus est Cornēlius?
12. Quid faciēbant Aurēlia et Cornēlia et omnēs ancillae?
13. Quī in pompā fūnebrī erant?

Cum in Forum vēnissent, Gaius Cornēlius prōcessit ut frātrem mortuum laudāret. 20
Commemorāvit quālis vir Titus fuisset, quot merita in prīncipem cīvēsque contulisset.

Quō factō, corpus Titī ad sepulcra Viae Flāminiae in pompā lātum est. Ibi rogus
exstrūctus erat. In rogum impositum est corpus et super corpus vestēs atque ōrnāmenta.
Appropinquāvit Gaius Cornēlius taedam manū tenēns. Quam taedam oculīs āversīs in
rogum iniēcit. 25

Exsequiīs cōnfectīs, Cornēliī trīstēs domum regressī sunt. Multa dē Titō loquēbantur.
Commemorābant quam hilaris fuisset, quantum līberōs amāvisset. "Maximē," inquiunt,
"nōs omnēs eum dēsīderābimus."

21 **commemorō, -āre, -āvī, -ātus,** *to*
   mention, comment on, recount
   merita cōnferre, *to render services (to)*

22 **Via Flāminia, -ae,** f., *Via Flaminia (a
road from Rome leading through the
Campus Martius and north to
Ariminum on the Adriatic Sea)*

27 **hilaris, -is, -e,** *cheerful*

23 **exstruō, exstruere, exstrūxī, exstrūctus,** *to build*

Respondē Latīnē:

1. Quid Cornēlius in Forō fēcit?
2. Ubi rogus exstrūctus erat?
3. Quō īnstrūmentō Cornēlius rogum accendit?
4. Quālis vir fuerat Titus?

   accendō, accendere, accendī, accēnsus, *to set on fire*

BUILDING THE MEANING
Translating *ut*

You have now met the following uses of **ut**:

A. With an indicative verb:

Semper sum, **ut** vidēs, negōtiōsus. (47:3)
As you see, I am always busy.

Sextus, **ut** lupum cōnspexit, arborem ascendit.
***When** Sextus caught sight of the wolf, he climbed the tree.*

Clue: **ut** followed by an indicative verb should be translated by *as* or *when*.

B. With a subjunctive verb:

    1. To indicate *result*:

        Tam īnfirmus erat **ut** vix loquī posset. (54:12)
        *He was **so** weak **that** he could scarcely speak.*

        Clue: a word like **tam, tantus, tālis, tot,** or **adeō** suggests that the translation will be *so…that*.

    2. In an *indirect command*:

        Cornēlius servōs hortābātur **ut** lectīcam maximā cum cūrā ferrent. (54:5–6)
        Cornelius was urging the slaves to carry the litter very carefully.

        Ōrāvērunt **ut** ūna uxor duōs virōs habēret. (52:11)
        *They begged **that** one wife should have two husbands.*

        Clue: the **ut** clause depends on a verb of *telling, ordering, begging, urging, persuading,* etc.

    3. To indicate *purpose*:

        Gaius Cornēlius prōcessit **ut** frātrem mortuum laudāret. (54:20)
        Gaius Cornelius came forward to praise his dead brother.

        This type of **ut** clause is very common after verbs that suggest that someone went somewhere *to do* something.

Exercise 54b

Read aloud and translate each of the following sentences, and then identify each use of **ut** and explain the sequence of tenses for all subjunctives:

  1. Magister Sextō imperāvit ut domum statim redīret.
  2. Sextus, ut imperāverat magister, domum statim rediit.
  3. Marcus nōs rogat ut sēcum ad Campum Mārtium eāmus.
  4. Titus tam īnfirmus erat ut surgere nōn posset.
  5. Amīcō meō persuāsī ut mēcum ad Circum venīret.
  6. Cum Titus mortuus esset, Marcus et Sextus tam trīstēs erant ut lacrimārent.
  7. Servō imperāvistī ut pānem emeret.
  8. Cornēliī ex urbe Rōmā discēdent ut Baiās eant.
  9. In balneīs diū morābāmur ut cum amīcīs colloquerēmur.
10. Eucleidēs, "Ut fēriātī estis," inquit, "vōs moneō ut multōs librōs legātis."

Exercise 54c
Complete the following sentences and explain the use of **ut** in each:

1. Cornēlius Cornēliae praecēpit ut…
2. Tantus erat terror in urbe ut…
3. Marcus, ut tū…, est fīlius senātōris.
4. Iānitor servīs imperāvit ut…
5. In urbem dēscendit ut…
6. Aurēlia tam īrāta erat ut…
7. Puerī, ut vōcem patris…, in tablīnum intrāvērunt.
8. Senātōrēs nūntium mīsērunt ut…
9. Sextus adeō ēsuriēbat ut…
10. Eucleidēs, ut nōs omnēs…, est ērudītissimus.

Exercise 54d
Using story 54 as a guide, give the Latin for the following. Use **ut** clauses in each sentence:

1. There is such great heat in the city that the Cornelii wish to go to Baiae.
2. Cornelius, as he is accustomed, goes to the baths with Titus.
3. Cornelius urges the slaves to carry the litter into the house with great care.
4. Cornelius orders a doctor to be summoned.
5. Cornelius approaches to throw a torch onto the pyre.

Funeral procession of a warrior
*Engraving by Joseph Charles
Barrow, Victoria and Albert Museum,
London, England*

ROMAN FUNERALS

The following account of Roman funerals was given by Polybius, a historian of the second century B.C.:

> Whenever an important citizen dies, they have a funeral procession, in which his body is carried into the Forum to the Rostra, sometimes upright so as to be conspicuous, less often in a reclining position. There, surrounded by the whole populace, a grown-up son mounts the rostrum and delivers a speech about the virtues and achievements of the deceased. As a result, the majority of those present are so deeply affected that the loss seems not merely a private one affecting the relatives only, but a public loss involving everyone.
>
> Then, after he is buried with the usual ceremonies, they place a likeness of the deceased in a part of the house where everyone can readily see it, and they enclose it in a little wooden shrine. This likeness is a mask that reproduces with remarkable faithfulness the features and complexion of the deceased.
>
> On the death of any important member of the family, these likenesses are taken to the Forum, worn by those members of the family who seem most nearly to resemble them in height and bearing. These people wear togas with a purple border if the deceased was a consul or praetor, totally purple if he was a censor, and edged with gold if he had celebrated a triumph or had any similar distinction. They all ride in chariots preceded by the **fascēs**, axes, and other emblems appropriate to the official positions held by each during his life; and when they arrive at the Rostra, they all sit down in their proper order on chairs of ivory.
>
> It would be difficult to imagine a sight more inspiring to an ambitious young man than to see the likenesses of men who had once been famous for their goodness all together and as if alive and breathing. What sight could be finer than this?
>
> Besides, the person who makes the speech over the deceased, after speaking of the deceased himself, goes on to tell of the successful exploits of the other ancestors whose likenesses are present, beginning from the earliest. In this way, by constantly refreshing their memories about the fame of good men, the glory of those who performed noble deeds becomes immortal, and the fame of those who served their country well is passed on to future generations.
>
> —Polybius, *Histories* VI.3

TWO LAWS CONCERNING BURIAL

Law of the XII Tables:

> Hominem mortuum in urbe nē sepelītō nēve ūritō.
> *Let no one bury or burn a dead man in the city.*

Law of the Colony of Julia Genetiva in Spain:

> No person shall bring a dead person or bury one or burn one inside the boundaries of the town or the area marked around by the plough or build a monument to a dead person there. Any person breaking this law shall be fined 5,000 sesterces.

THE CRIER'S WORDS AT A CEREMONIAL FUNERAL

_____*, a citizen, has died; it is now time for those for whom it is convenient to go to his funeral. _____* is being brought from his house for burial.

(*name of deceased)

EPITAPHS

Roman tombs ranged from the very simple to the extremely elaborate. There was usually an inscription on the tomb, and many of these have survived. The following five are in some cases slightly modified.

(i)
Pontia Prīma hīc est sita. Nōlī violāre!

situs, -a, -um, *located, situated, buried*
violō, -āre, -āvī, -ātus, *to do harm*

(ii)
Est hoc monumentum Marcī Vergileī Eurysacis pīstōris redēmptōris appāritōris.

pīstor, pīstōris, m., *baker*
redēmptor, redēmptōris, m., *contractor*
appāritor, appāritōris, m., *gate-keeper, public servant*

(iii)

Carfinia Marcī līberta vīxit annōs XX. Iūcunda suīs, grātissima amīcīs, omnibus officiōsa fuit.

iūcundus, -a, -um, *pleasant, delightful*
grātus, -a, -um + dat., *loved (by), pleasing (to), dear (to)*
officiōsus, -a, -um + dat., *ready to serve, obliging*

(iv)

Dīs mānibus. C. Tullius Hesper āram fēcit sibi ubi ossa sua coniciantur. Quae sī quis violāverit aut inde exēmerit, optō eī ut cum dolōre corporis longō tempore vīvat et, cum mortuus fuerit, īnferī eum nōn recipiant.

dīs mānibus, *to the spirits of the dead*
os, ossis, n., *bone*
optō, -āre, -āvī, -ātus, *to wish*

    eximō, eximere, exēmī, exēmptus, *to remove*

(v)

Hospes, quod dīcō paullum est; adstā ac perlege.
Hīc est sepulcrum haud pulchrum pulchrae fēminae:
nōmen parentēs nōminārunt Claudiam.
Suum marītum corde dīlēxit suō:
nātōs duōs creāvit: hōrum alterum   5
in terrā linquit, alium sub terrā locat.
Sermōne lepidō, tum autem incessū commodō,
domum servāvit. Lānam fēcit. Dīxī. Abī.

1 **paul(l)us, -a, -um,** *little, small*	7 **sermō, sermōnis,** m., *conversation, talk*
3 **nōminārunt = nōmināvērunt**	**lepidus, -a, -um,** *charming*
4 **cor, cordis,** n., *heart*	**incessus, -ūs,** m., *bearing, walk(ing)*
5 **nātus, -ī,** m., *son*	**commodus, -a, -um,** *pleasant*

    4 **dīligō, dīligere, dīlēxī, dīlēctus,** *to love, have special regard for*
    6 **linquō, linquere, līquī,** *to leave*

Exercise 54e

The poet Catullus was very devoted to his brother, who died far away from home in Asia Minor. Catullus visited the tomb and wrote these lines. He does not tell us what he sees for his brother beyond the grave. He merely seeks comfort from the age-old Roman ritual for the dead.

Read aloud and translate:

> Multās per gentēs et multa per aequora vectus,
>   adveniō hās miserās, frāter, ad īnferiās,
> ut tē postrēmō dōnārem mūnere mortis
>   et mūtam nēquīquam alloquerer cinerem.
> Quandōquidem fortūna mihī tētē abstulit ipsum,   5
>   heu miser indignē frāter adēmpte mihi,
> nunc tamen intereā haec, prīscō quae mōre parentum
>   trādita sunt trīstī mūnere ad īnferiās,
> accipe frāternō multum mānantia flētū,
>   atque in perpetuum, frāter, avē atque valē!   10

1   **gens, gentis,** gen. pl., **gentium,** f., *family, clan;* pl., *peoples*
    aequor, aequoris, n., *sea*
    vectus, -a, -um, *having been carried, having traveled*
2   **īnferiae, -ārum,** f. pl., *offerings and rites in honor of the dead at the tomb*
3   **dōnō, -āre, -āvī, -ātus,** *to give; to present somebody* (acc.) *with something* (abl.)
    mūnus, mūneris, n., *gladiatorial show;* here, *gift, service*
4   **mūtus, -a, -um,** *silent*
    nēquīquam, adv., *in vain*

    cinis, cineris, m., *ashes, dust (of the cremated body)*
5   **quandōquidem,** adv., *since*
    tētē = emphatic **tē**
6   **indignē,** adv., *undeservedly*
7   **prīscus, -a, -um,** *of olden times, ancient*
    prīscō...mōre, *by the ancient custom*
8   **trīstī mūnere,** *as a sad service (to the dead)*
    ad īnferiās, *for (these) rites in honor of the dead*
9   **mānō, -āre, -āvī,** *to flow*
    flētus, -ūs, m., *weeping, tears*
10 **in perpetuum,** *forever*

1   **vehō, vehere, vexī, vectus,** *to carry;* pass., *to be carried, travel*
4   **alloquor, alloquī, allocūtus sum,** *to speak to, address*

Exercise 54f

Read and translate these humorous epigrams of Martial:

(i)
Doctor and Undertaker: Same Trade

Nūper erat medicus, nunc est vispillo Diaulus:
    quod vispillo facit, fēcerat et medicus.

—I.47

vispillō, vispillōnis, m., *undertaker*

(ii)
Symmachus Takes the Students Around

Languēbam: sed tū comitātus prōtinus ad mē
    vēnistī centum, Symmache, discipulīs.
Centum mē tetigēre manūs aquilōne gelātae;
    nōn habuī febrem, Symmache: nunc habeō.

—V.9

languēo, -ēre, *to be ill in bed*
comitātus, -a, -um, *accompanied*
prōtinus, adv., *immediately*
tangō, tangere, tetigī, tāctus, *to touch*
    tetigēre = tetigērunt
aquilōne gelātae, *chilled by the north wind*

(iii)
Hermocrates, Who Cures All

Lōtus nōbīscum est, hilaris cēnāvit, et īdem
    inventus māne est mortuus Andragorās.
Tam subitae mortis causam, Faustīne, requīris?
    In somnīs medicum vīderat Hermocratem!

—VI.53

lōtus = lautus, perfect passive participle of **lavō**
    lōtus est, *he bathed*
subitus, -a, -um, *sudden*

    requīrō, requīrere, requīsīvī, requīsītus,
        to ask, inquire

(iv)
Epitaph with a Difference!

Sit tibi terra levis, mollīque tegāris harēnā
    nē tua nōn possint ēruere ossa canēs!

—IX.29.11–12

sit, *may (it) be*
levis, -is, -e, *light*
mollis, -is, -e, *soft*
tegāris, *may you be covered*
harēna, -ae, f., *sand*
nē...nōn possint, *so that (they) may not be unable*

    ēruo, ēruere, ēruī, ērutus, *to dig up*

Review XII:
Chapters 50-54

Exercise XIIa: Subjunctives

Give the present, perfect, imperfect, and pluperfect active and passive subjunctives of the following verbs in the first person plural:

1. amō
2. moneō
3. dūcō
4. cōnspiciō
5. inveniō

Exercise XIIb: Subjunctives

Give the present, perfect, imperfect, and pluperfect subjunctives of the following deponent verbs in the third person plural:

1. moror
2. vereor
3. loquor
4. ingredior
5. experior

Exercise XIIc: Subjunctives

Give the present, perfect, imperfect, and pluperfect subjunctives of the following irregular verbs in the second person plural:

1. sum
2. possum
3. volō
4. nōlō
5. mālō
6. eō
7. ferō
8. fīō

Exercise XIId: Translation and Identification

Read aloud and translate. Identify each result clause, indirect command, purpose clause, and indirect question:

1. Cornēlia tam dēfessa est ut paene lacrimet.
2. Cornēlius Sextum monuit nē iterum in lūdō tam ignāvus esset.
3. Iānitor eīs imperat ut statim abeant.

4. Matrōnae ad senātum lacrimantēs vēnērunt ut senātōribus persuādērent.
5. Servus in aquam dēsilit nē fūr effugiat.
6. Eucleidēs puerīs persuāsit ut vēra dīcerent.
7. Cornēlia nescit cūr pater sē adesse in tablīnō iusserit.
8. Puerōs rogāvit ut extrā tablīnum manērent.
9. Gaius puerōs monet nē ē cubiculō exeant.
10. Ancillae in cubiculum festīnant ut crīnēs Aurēliae cūrent.
11. Servus arborem ascendit nē caperētur.
12. Ille liber est tālis ut Aurēlia eum legere nōlit.

Exercise XIIe: Translation and Identification

Read aloud and translate. Identify the tense and voice of each verb in the subjunctive and tell whether each subordinate clause is in primary or secondary sequence:

1. Tanta multitūdō ad domum convenit ut omnibus intrāre nōn liceat.
2. Tam longum erat iter ut Valerius dēfessus esset.
3. Cornēlius Valerium rogat quid in itinere factum sit.
4. Sextus Marcum rogat ut sibi nārret quid in amphitheātrō āctum sit.
5. Cīvēs in palaestram excēdunt ut sē exerceant.
6. Aenēās ad Hesperiam nāvigābat ut urbem novam conderet.
7. Servus casam pīrātārum celerrimē petīvit ut dominum servāret.
8. Grammaticus Sextum rogat unde Aenēās nāvigāverit.
9. Praedōnēs tam celeriter currunt ut Eucleidem facile cōnsequantur.
10. Tot et tanta erant incendia ut cīvēs aedificia servāre nōn possent.
11. Tanta tempestās coorta est ut mīlitēs nāvem cōnscendere vix possent.
12. Eucleidēs Sextō imperat nē pūpam laedat.

Exercise XIIf: Impersonal Verbs

Read aloud and translate:

1. Gaiō et Aurēliae placuit ut Valerius Cornēliam in mātrimōnium dūceret.
2. Valeriō placet Cornēliam in mātrimōnium dūcere.
3. Hodiē Marcō togam virīlem gerere licet.
4. Sextō nōn iam decet togam virīlem gerere.
5. Cornēliam diē nūptiālī tunicam albam gerere oportet.
6. Nunc Cornēlia ūnā cum Valeriō vīvit. Valdē occupāta est; eam nōn iam taedet sōlitūdinis.

Exercise XIIg

Read the following passage and answer the questions below in English.

CONSTANTINE

Annō MXLVI A.U.C. imperium Rōmānum multās per prōvinciās patēbat. Eō tempore tot gentēs, tot nātiōnēs regēbant Rōmānī ut placuerit summum imperium inter quattuor imperātōrēs, duōs Augustōs et duōs Caesarēs, dīvidī. Inde alter Augustus Nīcomēdīae regēbat, alter Mediōlānī. Duodecim post annīs Galērius, ut Augustus, imperium Nīcomēdīae, Cōnstantius, alter Augustus, Trēverīs imperium obtinēbat.   5

Cōnstantiī fīlius erat Cōnstantīnus, iuvenis summī ingeniī et reī mīlitāris perītissimus. Galērius autem, cum tōtō imperiō Rōmānō potīrī vellet, Cōnstantīnum sēcum Nīcomēdīae dētinēbat nē iuvenis ille mīlitibus patris grātus fieret. Cōnstantīnus tamen, cum cognōvisset patrem iam in Britanniā bellum gerentem morbō affectum esse, ā custōdibus effūgit, atque summā celeritāte in Britanniam festīnāvit. Patrī occurrit   10
Eborācī. Haud multō post Cōnstantius mortuus est.

Tum Cōnstantīnus ut Augustus ā mīlitibus salūtātus est. Cum autem multī eī invidērent, imperium armīs cōnfirmandum erat. Dum per Italiam iter Rōmam cum mīlitibus facit, vīdit Cōnstantīnus signum mīrum: in caelō appāruit crux flammea et super crucem haec verba: IN HOC SIGNO VINCES. Quō vīsō, Cōnstantīnus statim mīlitibus   15
imperāvit ut signum crucis scūtīs galeīsque impōnerent. Deinde proeliō ad Rōmam ad pontem Mulvium factō hostēs vīcit. Quam propter victōriam tam grātus fuit Cōnstantīnus ut semper posteā crucem prō signō suō retinēret atque paucīs post mēnsibus annō MLXVI A.U.C. ēdictum Mediōlānī prōnūntiāverit nē Chrīstiānī diūtius vexārentur. Ipse autem nōndum Chrīstiānus factus est.   20

Itaque Cōnstantīnus post victōriam Mulviānam in potestāte redēgit illam partem imperiī Rōmānī ad occidentem sitam; alteram quoque partem, quae ā Liciniō regēbātur, bellō capere in animō habēbat. Putābat enim imperium Rōmānum ab ūnō prīncipe regī dēbēre. Itaque post ūndecim annōs maximum exercitum contrā Licinium dūxit. Liciniō multīs proeliīs victō, Cōnstantīnus summō imperiō potītus prīnceps sōlus rēgnābat.   25

Iam intellegēbat Cōnstantīnus Byzantium, nōn Rōmam, orbis terrārum caput esse dēbēre. Cum enim mercātōrēs iter ad orientem iam saepe facerent, Byzantium aptius ad mercātūram quam Rōma situm erat. Sēdem igitur imperiī Rōmā Byzantium mōvit, quō in locō aedificāvit urbem novam et pulcherrimam quam ā suō nōmine Cōnstantīnopolem nōminārī iussit. Haud multō antequam mortuus est, Cōnstantīnus ipse Chrīstiānus   30
factus est.

1 **imperium, -ī,** n., *empire, power*
   pateō, -ēre, -uī, *to extend*
2 **summus, -a, -um,** *highest, supreme*
4 **Nīcomēdīa, -ae,** f., *Nicomedia (a city in Bithynia)*
5 **Trēverī, -ōrum,** m. pl., *Treveri (the modern city of Trier)*

6 **rēs mīlitāris, reī mīlitāris,** f., *military affairs*
7 **perītus, -a, -um** + gen., *skilled (in), expert (in)*
   potior, -īrī, -ītus sum + abl., *to obtain, seize*
9 **bellum gerere,** *to wage war*

11 **Eborācum, -ī,** n., *York (in Britain)*
13 **cōnfirmō, -āre, -āvī, -ātus,** *to strengthen, make secure*
   cōnfirmandum erat, *had to be...*
14 **crux, crucis,** f., *cross*
16 **scūtum, -ī,** n., *shield*
   galea, -ae, f., *helmet*
   proelium, -ī, n., *battle*
17 **hostis, hostis,** gen. pl., **hostium,** m., *enemy*
   grātus, -a, -um + dat., *loved (by), pleasing (to), dear (to); here, grateful, thankful*
18 **prō,** prep. + abl., *as*
19 **ēdictum, -ī,** n., *edict*
   prōnūntiō, -āre, -āvī, -ātus, *to give out, proclaim*

21 **potestās, potestātis,** f., *control, power*
22 **occidēns, occidentis,** m., *the west*
24 **exercitus, -ūs,** m., *army*
25 **rēgnō, -āre, -āvī, -ātus,** *to rule*
26 **Byzantium, -ī,** n., *Byzantium (the modern Constantinople)*
   orbis, orbis, gen. pl., **orbium,** m., *circle*
     orbis terrārum, *the circle of the lands, the whole earth*
27 **oriēns, orientis,** m., *the east, the orient*
   aptus, -a, -um + **ad** + acc., *suitable (for), favorable (to)*
28 **mercātūra, -ae,** f., *trade, trading*
   sēdēs, sēdis, gen. pl., **sēdium,** f., *seat*

2 **regō, regere, rēxī, rēctus,** *to rule*
5 **obtineō, obtinēre, obtinuī, obtentus,** *to hold*
8 **dētineō, dētinēre, dētinuī, dētentus,** *to detain, hold as a prisoner*
13 **invideō, invidēre, invīdī, invīsus** + dat., *to envy, be jealous of*
21 **redigō, redigere, redēgī, redāctus,** *to bring*
   in potestātem redigere, *to bring under the control/power (of)*

1. In what year, according to our reckoning, does our story begin?
2. What decision was made?
3. Who were the two Augusti in A.D. 305?
4. Where and by whom was Constantius' son being held?
5. What did he do?
6. How did he become Augustus?
7. Why did he have to take up arms?
8. What did he see when marching to Rome?
9. What order did Constantine then give?
10. Where did he conquer his enemies?
11. What two things did he do that showed his gratitude for his victory?
12. Why did he wish to conquer the other half of the Empire?
13 What new city did he found and why?
14. What did he do before he died?

THE FUTURE LIVES OF OUR CHARACTERS

Unfortunately for Gaius Cornelius, the Emperor Titus, whose favor he had enjoyed, died in September, A.D. 81. Distrustful of his brother Domitian's ambition, Titus had not given him any active role in government, and Domitian, who became emperor on September 14, was in turn distrustful of anyone Titus had favored. After a rebellion by Antonius Saturninus, governor of the province of Upper Germany, failed in A.D. 89, Domitian was relentless in punishing anyone who had participated or seemed to have participated in the rebellion. Cornelius was fortunate in having only to give up his estate at Baiae.

Domitian was assassinated on September 18, A.D. 96, by a conspiracy led by his own wife and two praetorian prefects, and the next emperor, Nerva, recalled those who had been exiled by Domitian and tried to undo the damage Domitian had caused. He therefore rewarded and honored a number of able senators, whom Domitian had ignored or exiled, including Cornelius, by appointing them to serve as consul for one month. Nerva returned the estate at Baiae to Cornelius and helped him be named by the Senate to be proconsular governor in Africa for A.D. 98. Upon his return to Rome, Cornelius from time to time served in a number of positions such as curator to prevent flooding by the Tiber (**cūrātor rīpārum Tiberis**). He died in A.D. 112, at age seventy-two.

Aurelia also had some property of her own taken by Domitian, but it was restored to her by Nerva. She accompanied Cornelius to Africa and upon his death lived with Marcus. Wishing to assist her native town of Narnia in Umbria (where Nerva also had been born), she endowed a school for orphan girls, where they learned to read and write, were trained in a trade, and were given a dowry upon reaching age fifteen. She died in A.D. 123, at age seventy-six.

Because of Domitian's dislike of Gaius Cornelius, Marcus' early career suffered. He served for three years as officer of an auxiliary infantry unit (**praefectus cohortis peditum**) in Lower Germany, due to the influence of Valerius' father. Upon returning to Rome, he began to plead cases in the civil court at Rome. In A.D. 92, Marcus married a distant cousin, Cornelia Hispulla, and they eventually had three daughters and two sons. Again, through the influence of the Valerii, he served from time to time on the staff of various governors of the provinces of Bithynia and Asia, until Nerva's accession.

Marcus' career advanced steadily under Nerva and his excellent successor, Trajan. Marcus was appointed in A.D. 97 as an official in charge of keeping the streets clean (**quattuorvir viīs in urbe pūrgandīs**) and in the next year became quaestor at age forty-three. Four years later, he was elected praetor, and two years later he became governor (**lēgātus**) of Further Spain. His appointment as a consul designate for A.D. 113 was made just before

Roman soldiers destroying a German camp

his father died; Marcus was very happy that his father knew of this honor to the family. His last honor, before his accidental death in A.D. 120, was to be appointed augur.

Quintus Valerius, age twenty-six when he married Cornelia, was already well started on his political career. He had served as officer of an auxiliary infantry unit and as officer of a legion (**tribūnus legiōnis**) in Upper Germany, and as an official in charge of the mint (**triumvir monētālis**) in Rome. Just prior to his return to Rome for the marriage, he had been on the staff of the governor of Bithynia. In A.D. 83, he and Cornelia rejoiced at the birth of the first of their three sons, and the next year he became quaestor. From A.D. 85 to 87, he furthered his military experience in Lower Germany as officer of an auxiliary cavalry unit (**praefectus ālae equitum**); because of Sextus' ties with the Cornelius family, Valerius took Sextus along.

Upon his return to Rome, Valerius resumed his career as a lawyer in Rome's courts and held the position of **praetor urbānus** before Domitian, who favored Valerius despite his marriage ties with the Cornelii, appointed him as administrator (**prōcūrātor**) of his imperial estates in Bithynia in A.D. 95. Under Nerva, who admired Valerius both for his ability and his loyalty to the Cornelii, he served as governor of Galatia. In all his posts outside Rome, Cornelia accompanied him, but she particularly enjoyed Ancyra, the capital of Galatia. After a lesiurely sight-seeing trip back to Rome, Valerius and Cornelia collaborated in writing a history of Galatia and Bithynia. They lived long enough to see their great-grandchildren and died within two days of each other in A.D. 135.

When Sextus arrived in Lower Germany, Valerius helped him become one of the 120 young men of equestrian rank attached to a legion as an aide-de-camp to learn military leadership. In three years' time Sextus became an officer of an auxiliary infantry unit and gradually advanced through the ranks. His unit, the **āla Gallōrum et Thrācum,** was transferred to Britain in the early years of Trajan's reign. Sextus enjoyed military life. He held the rank of **tribūnus legiōnis** when he bravely died at age forty-nine trying to rally his panicked *Legio IX* stationed at York (**Eboracum**) during a native revolt early in Hadrian's reign.

When Domitian seized the villa at Baiae, he sold a number of slaves, including Davus. The Cornelii were unable to find out what happened to Davus, but they freed his daughter. After Sextus rejoined his own father, Eucleides became Gaius' secretary and steward. He accompanied Cornelius to Africa but fell ill with a fever and died there.

Roman Britain

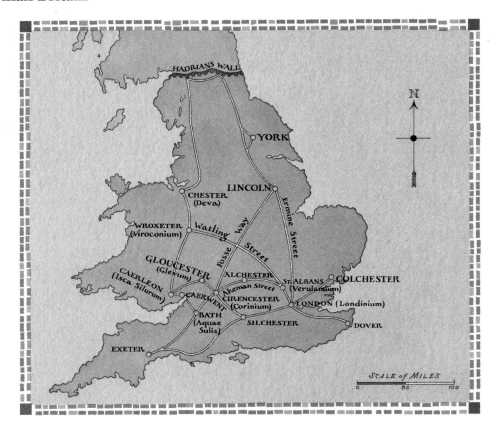

The sons of Lucius the legionary participated in the Roman invasion of Britain in A.D. 43 under the Emperor Claudius and helped establish a Roman presence in Britain. The *Legio XX* suppressed the wild cult of the Druids, helped defeat Boudicca the rebellious queen of the native tribe of the Iceni, established a base at Virconium and built towns and roads to link the towns together. Under the legate Agricola, the *Legio XX* campaigned in the far north against the Pictish tribes and defeated Calgacus, chief of the Caledonians. After retreating from the north, Roman legions at the behest of the Emperor Hadrian built a wall across the island of Britain, eight feet thick, sixteen feet high, and seventy-five miles long with a **castra** for an auxiliary cohort every six miles and a fortress (**castellus**) every mile. But then the empire was divided into two halves, and the strength of the legions declined. Eventually the legions were withdrawn from Britain to protect Italy and Rome itself from barbarian attacks.

At the beginning of the fifth century A.D., the Alemanni and other barbarian hordes were massing on the Rhine, Alaric the Visigoth was threatening Rome, and Flavius Stilicho, the Roman general and ruler of the Western Empire, needed reinforcements. He recalled the *Legio XX* from Britain. Under the capable leadership of Stilicho, the *Legio XX* defeated Alaric in a battle fought Easter Sunday, A.D. 403, at Pollentia, Italy. The legion was probably later posted to the frontier along the Rhine. In A.D. 406, the Alemanni and other tribes massed on the eastern bank of the river. That winter the river froze and on New Year's day, A.D. 407, the hordes crossed, destroying everything and everyone in their path. The *Legio XX* disappears from history, probably destroyed in that battle.

In 410 Alaric the Visigoth sacked Rome; in 455 Gaeseric the Vandal sacked the city again. In 476 Odoacer the German deposed the last Roman Emperor of the West, Romulus Augustulus. Odoacer was in turn overthrown by Theodoric the Ostrogoth in 493, who established an Ostrogothic kingdom in Italy, ushering in the Middle Ages.

THE MULTICULTURAL TRADITION

In the streets of Rome or in any of the cities and towns of the empire, one would meet people from all areas of the Roman world, which, by the time of the Cornelii, encompassed a variety of European, Mid-Eastern, and African lands and peoples (see map below). While some of the inhabitants of these lands had gained Roman citizenship and the right to wear the toga, most had not, and their various native costumes and languages must have made the streets and forums of Rome a fascinating, ever-changing scene. The very household of Cornelius reflected the multicultural Roman Empire. Eucleides, of course, was a Greek, Davus a Briton captured in Boudicca's rebellion. To judge from their names, Syria, Phrygia, and Geta were originally from Syria, Phrygia (a region in modern Turkey), and Thrace (roughly modern Bulgaria).

The Roman Empire, A.D. 80

THE ANCIENT MULTICULTURAL TRADITION

Multiculturalism was a basic aspect of ancient Mediterranean life. Rome, like other ancient civilizations, owed much of its culture to civilizations that preceded it, including Eygpt, Greece, Persia (modern Iran), Palestine, North Africa (northern parts of modern Morocco, Algeria, and Libya), and perhaps even India. The Roman alphabet, for instance, came from the Etruscans, who had modified the Greek alphabet, and the Greeks in turn had modified the alphabet of the Phoenicians (a maritime culture inhabiting the coast of Syria and Lebanon). The papyrus scrolls the **grammaticus** Palaemon read from were an Egyptian invention.

Rome also borrowed freely from its various provinces, and through trade cultural exchanges became easier than ever before. From the provinces of Gaul, Germany, and Britain, for instance, the Romans and the peoples of the empire adopted various kinds of warm, water-proof cloaks, such as the **cucullus,** and soldiers' warm pants, **brācae.** The bright plaids that Helge and her friends wove proved so popular that weavers in the eastern provinces began to imitate them. The Romans brought to Italy and to their European provinces the cherry and the peach (**persica,** *Persian fruit*) among other Oriental, Arabic, and African foods and spices. The culture of imperial Rome was such an amalgam of cultures that "Roman" signifies a great deal more than "pertaining to the people of the city of Rome."

For example, many of Rome's most famous literary figures were neither born in Rome themselves, nor were they even of Roman/Italian descent. Vergil, Rome's "national poet laureate" was born of a father who had a small farm near Mantua in northern Italy. His **cognōmen**, Maro, suggests that his family was of Celtic descent, perhaps from the Gauls who ravaged Italy and even sacked Rome in 390 B.C. The satiric poet Martial was from Spain, as was the philosopher Seneca, tutor of the Emperor Nero. And, of course, the Romans, tutored by the Greeks, were well read in the works of ancient Greece, from the philosophers, poets, and lofty dramatists to the immensely popular fable-teller, Aesop.

The Greek philosopher, Socrates
Marble statue, British Museum, London

Likewise, beginning with the Emperor Trajan, a number of emperors were not born in Rome or even in Italy. Trajan and Hadrian, for example, were born in the Roman colony Italica, near Seville, Spain. Septimius Severus, emperor from A.D. 193–211, was born in North Africa near Leptis Magna in Libya, and the Emperor Constantine in the province of **Moesia superior** (modern West-Central Balkans).

Much of the strength and vitality of the empire was due to the willingness of its various inhabitants to adopt, adapt, and develop ideas, inventions, customs, religions, and philosophies from other provinces and a willingness to tolerate differences. If it is true that in the eastern Mediterranean an earlier melding of cultures called "Hellenistic" was inherited by the Romans when they conquered this area, it was the Romans who spread multiculturalism out of the Mediterranean basin into northern Europe and, in turn, enabled the northern European cultures to influence those of the Mediterranean more strongly than they had before. And it was only the Romans who became willing to extend their citizenship to those of other tribes and nations. The Emperor Claudius, who was born in Lugdunum (Lyons) in Gaul, enrolled some Gallic nobles in the Senate, opened the public magistracies to all Roman citizens in Gaul, and began to extend a limited form of citizenship to urban communities in Romanized provinces. Under the Flavian emperors this policy of granting citizenship was systematized and expanded until finally the Emperor Caracalla (also born in Lugdunum) in A.D. 212 conferred Roman citizenship on all free residents of the empire who had not yet received it. Such a willingness to extend citizenship found support and reinforcement in the tradition of the "unity of mankind" of the Hellenistic Stoic philosophy, which was embraced by many prominent Romans.

Roman depicted as Egyptian pharoah

Egyptian marble bust, Louvre, Paris

AVENUES OF MULTICULTURAL INFLUENCE

In antiquity one culture might receive and absorb cultural influences from another in several ways. One way—but not the main way—was through conquest of a town or nation and the enslavement of the conquered inhabitants. (The hero ancestor of the Romans, Aeneas, and his band of Trojans, is one example of a people fleeing death and enslavement by defeat in war.) Often, however, such military conquest might result in the enslavement of only a small percentage of the conquered population (if at all). Instead, the majority of the conquered people and territory would become a source of economic advantage to the victors through payment of money (taxes) or of raw goods. The troubles in Africa, over which Cornelius was recalled to the Senate in Rome, originated because of this kind of economic exploitation of defeated peoples.

More frequently, however, societies in the ancient world came into contact through expansion of trading relationships along new land, and, even more often, along new sea routes. Many times such trading ventures were primarily seeking more abundant supplies of minerals, food stuffs, or other raw materials, but, as merchants traveled to new places, they also came across new materials, technologies, and luxury goods.

Warship

Slavery as an Avenue of Multicultural Influence

Such merchants also engaged in the trade of slaves. A person might become a slave in various ways in addition to being enslaved as a result of defeat in war. Areas and periods of political unrest saw increased piracy: individual pirate ships might land on an unprotected coastal estate, while flotillas of pirate ships might have enough manpower to raid an unsuspecting town and take away many inhabitants. Illegal kidnapping continued despite any measures a city or town might take. Parents who felt they could not raise an additional child would "expose" the child. Anyone who found the child could raise it as a family member or as a slave. It was also legal in many societies to sell a child into slavery or to sell oneself to raise money to pay off a debt. Slaves also

Merchant ship

had children, who were automatically slaves. Even such "hereditary" slaves, however, could earn or be awarded freedom.

Slaves could be members of any race or any culture. Slaves from societies such as existed in the Near East were often skilled at some craft and were especially in demand by owners of workshops making pottery, weapons, jewelry, and woven goods. Slaves not so skilled were used as agricultural laborers. If they proved talented at learning the master's language and were obedient, they might become domestic servants, such as maids, grooms, gardeners, and, in time, overseers of slaves. Those Greek slaves who were educated and literate were particularly prized by the Roman elite as tutors, doctors, secretary-accountants, and teachers. Slaves from northern provinces were usually untrained in any skill in demand by Mediterranean cultures and often proved (or were regarded as) very stubborn but physically strong and so were often used in situations where strength was required. The Athenians, for example, used enslaved Scythian archers as a kind of security force in Athens; among the Romans, male barbarian slaves were often placed in the training schools for gladiators or used as personal bodyguards by emperors. People showed off their wealth and social status by giving slaves specialized duties and by having numerous slaves attend them in the street, Forum, and law courts. State or local governments also owned slaves who did the manual labor required for street repair and the building of walls, sewers, and aqueducts. Slavery was so basic a part of ancient societies that even freedmen would own slaves, and a slave like Davus, before his own captivity, might have owned a slave or two himself.

The cultural influence a slave might have could be considerable. The earliest author in Roman literature, known to us as L. Livius Andronicus, had become a slave after the Romans took the Greek city Tarentum in 272 B.C. His Roman master established him in Rome as a teacher of Greek; when manumitted the freed slave took his master's name. Not only did Andronicus translate Homer's *Odyssey* into Latin (this became almost immediately one of the standard texts read in Roman schools), but he became the first author-actor in Rome, adapting Greek comedies to Roman taste. Doubtless these comedies were read by the later playwright, P. Terentius Afer (190?–159 B.C.), himself a slave, brought to Rome from North Africa. His **cognōmen** suggests that his family might have been from some Berber tribe conquered by the Carthaginians; he came to Rome as a slave in the house of Terentius Lucanus, a Senator. Having learned Latin, his intelligence, African origin, and skill as a comic writer brought him to the notice of Scipio Africanus the Younger and his literary circle. Though Terence died young, his six surviving plays have for centuries continued to influence playwrights of the world, including Shakespeare and Molière. The great Roman poet Horace (65–8 B.C.) was the son of a freedman father who is thought to have been a public slave owned by a town. Horace's poetic genius and insightful observations about human nature not only gained him the patronage of Augustus himself, but also endure to this day for their wit and accuracy.

MULTICULTURAL ORIGINS OF MEDICINE

The whole discipline and art of medicine is a legacy of cross-cultural origin that passed to and through Rome. The **medicus** treating Titus before he died relied on a wide range of drugs, ointments, and salves that evolved out of the medical treatments of the Mesopotamians, Egyptians, and Hebrews, as well as the Greeks. His close observation of the symptoms of Titus' fatal illness derived from the principles established by the Greek physician, Hippocrates, whose analytic, scientific observation of disease earned him the title "Father of Medicine." The physician Galen began his practice at a training school for gladiators in Pergamum (modern Turkey) and later went to Rome to teach medicine and become the personal physician of the emperor Commodus. Galen's main work on therapy, *Ars magna*, was used by physicians until the last century. Most medical books in the empire, however, were written in Greek, and after the fall of the empire the Jewish physicians living in the Mediterranean countries now ruled by the Arabs were the

"Visit of a sick child to the temple of Asclepius"
Oil on canvas by John William Waterhouse, The Fine Art Society, London

main translators in the East of the Greek texts into Syriac and Arabic and, much later, in the West from Arabic into Latin for European doctors. In fact, one of the most important medical centers, especially for surgery, was Spain under Arabic (Moorish) rule because Arabic and Jewish doctors there had access to Greco-Roman texts in both Greek and Latin. In former Roman Gaul, however, the Greek medical texts were not available, and medical practice and knowledge regressed with the decline of imperial Roman culture, so that Charlemagne, emperor of the Holy Roman Empire, had to request help from the Caliph (ruler) of Bagdad (modern Iran) in improving the knowledge of his doctors. The continued importance of imperial Roman medical knowledge for the modern European, American, and Arabic cultures is reflected in today's scientific and medical vocabulary, which is ninety percent or more drawn from Greek and Latin roots.

Asclepius, son of Apollo, god of medicine

MULTICULTURAL SPREAD OF THE LATIN LANGUAGE

Like medical knowledge and other aspects of imperial Roman culture, the survival of Latin varied from province to province. The Latin used by the common people of Rome was quite different from the Latin used by the wealthy, aristocratic elite. Widely spoken throughout the European provinces by common Roman citizens (called in Latin **vulgus**), vulgar Latin gradually developed into the various Romance languages of French, Spanish, Portuguese, Italian, Catalan, Romansch, and Rumanian. Even though subsequent invasions by various barbarian peoples brought new languages into these provinces, Latin remained the basic language, though undergoing local changes in grammar and pronunciation over time.

In the Germanic territory, Germanic dialects, rather than Latin, predominated as the basis of communication, but these dialects absorbed Latin vocabulary. For example, the German word *Pfund* ("pound") is derived from the Latin **pondus** (*weight*), and the German noun for innkeeper, *Kaufmann*, is a compound of the German word *Mann* ("man") and the Latin noun **caupō** (*innkeeper*). English developed from Germanic dialects and was strongly influenced by Latin over the centuries. The use today of English as a worldwide language continues to sustain and spread elements of Latin to every corner of the world.

MULTICULTURAL SPREAD OF ROMAN LAW

The discipline of law has also gone through very interesting multicultural transformations while perpetuating Rome's legacy. The system of Roman law, a reasoned, consistent body of practices resolving the inevitable conflicts arising in daily life, was one of the benefits perceived by the peoples whom the Romans conquered. In general, the written Roman code of law remained an important basis for law of various countries, though beginning in the eleventh century it began to be interpreted, developed, and adapted to existing conditions. For example, "Roman-Dutch" law, as developed and adapted by jurists of the Netherlands, is used not only in the Netherlands but also in countries once part of the Dutch Empire, such as South Africa and Ceylon.

The barbarians who invaded Roman Germany, Gaul, and Spain (Visigoths, Burgundians, and Franks) generally wished to maintain the existing Roman administrative system, including its law. In Gaul, men of Roman descent remained under Roman law, but the barbarian invaders had the right to be tried by the customs of the tribe they belonged to. In imitation of the Roman code of law these barbarian customs were also written down and codified, assimilating some of the Roman law in the process. Over the centuries France continued to use this adaptation of Roman law for situations affecting the individual, tenure of real property, order of inheritance, and system of mortgages but used common or "customary" law for other legal problems until the French Revolution instituted a very radical system of law. Finding this system too radical, the emperor Napoleon decided to systematize French law, and he united in the Napoleonic *Code Civile* what in Roman law and in customary law was now best suited to France in its new conditions. Given the political and cultural importance of France in the 1800s, which paralleled the Roman Empire, this civil code became the model for countries reforming their legal codes or new countries instituting a legal code. The Canadian province of Quebec uses a French-derived law code built largely on Roman law, and the state of Louisiana (acquired by purchase from Napoleon in 1803) continues to use a civil code deriving from both the modified Roman law that was in effect when Spain owned this territory and from the Napoleonic code.

Lictor

Likewise in Germany during the Middle Ages, both Roman law and tribal customary law were in force, Roman law being applied in cases where it was not excluded by contrary local (customary) provisions. This situation changed when, in 1900, a common code for the whole German empire was adopted. A different situation occurred in Spain, where, under the Romans, Roman magistrates were expected to defer to the established law of the district (**mūnicipium**). This municipal system of law, along with Roman law, was continued by the Visigothic and the Arabic kingdoms of Spain and became part of the Spanish legal system when Spain came to be ruled by its own kings. As part of Napoleon's empire, Spain, too, adopted the Napoleonic Code.

Roman culture did not survive extensively in what is now the United Kingdom (Great Britain) after the Angles, Saxons, and Jutes invaded that region in the 400s. Roman culture had not been planted as deeply there as on the continent. So many Roman Britons fled to Gaul that the area they settled was named after them, Brittany. Nonetheless, Roman law influenced Anglo-Saxon tribal law indirectly through the Church. The Anglo-Saxon law of property was modified by Roman legal conceptions concerning ownership, donations, wills, and rights of women. After the Norman Conquest this modification continued as Britain was opened to contact with France and Italy. Today, in both England and the United States, Roman law is the source of doctrines, principles, and rules, some of which—for example, the law of gifts—remain virtually unchanged from the days of Rome.

TRACING THE SPREAD OF ROMAN INFLUENCE

The way the Roman inheritance was passed down among the cultures of the former provinces of the Roman Empire is a fascinating process. Consider, for example, how the Roman legacy traveled via **Hispānia** (modern Spain). The earliest inhabitants of **Hispānia** were **Hiberēs**, who migrated from northern Africa, and Celts, who entered the region by crossing the Pyrenees. In the 800s B.C., they began trading with the Phoenicians, who were an ancient maritime culture spread over southwest Asia and the eastern Mediterranean. The peoples of **Hispānia** thus came into contact with the cultures of the eastern Mediterranean and the Orient, who brought them new foods, such as wine and olive oil in exchange for gold and metals. Later, when the Greeks settled colonies on Spain's coasts in the 500s B.C., they introduced the natives to the use of coinage. When Spain became part of the Roman Empire, after the Second Punic War, the Romans established many **colōniae** of Roman citizens there who helped develop the two Spanish provinces into two of the most prosperous of Roman lands. Some of the emperors and writers who came from **Hispānia** to become leading Romans were mentioned above and included the philosopher Seneca, the satiric poet Martial, and the Emperors Trajan and Hadrian.

After the fall of the Roman Empire, Spain was ultimately taken over by Arabs who invaded from Morocco in A.D. 711. These Moroccan Arabs (Moors) brought to Spain their own adaptations of Roman imperial culture. When the Arabs began invading the former eastern provinces of Rome and taking over their cities, they were impressed, among other things, by the buildings and architecture. These they adapted to their own use. Building walls among the colonnaded avenues of the former classical cities, the Arabs created their

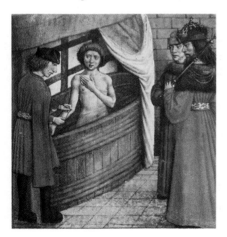

characteristic linear markets (*suqs*). The Arabs found they also enjoyed baths and kept the entire Roman bath complex save for the **tepidārium;** as it was for the Romans, bathing became for the Arabs a social occasion, and the bath complex of the Caliph's palace included a state room. The palaces kept the axial arrangement of Roman palaces. Imperial Roman cer-

Seneca, who suffered all his life from serious ill health, spoke out against the murderous entertainment staged in the Colosseum. A medieval artist depicts him here in a medicinal bath, attended by doctors.

"Seneca Bleeding in Bath," Roman de la Rosa, British Library, London, England

emony was adapted as well: the axis of the Caliph's main palace led to a triple arched facade and entrance gate. The entrance ceremony of the Caliph was inspired by the **adventus** (*arrival*) ceremony of the Roman emperor.

ROMAN ARCHITECTURE IN AMERICA

When the Spaniards came to the two American continents, they in turn brought their adaptations of Roman imperial architecture. Behind the typical layout of the cities that they established it is easy to discern the basic Roman plan. The center of a Spanish city was the rectangular plaza (from Latin **platea**, *wide street*, which itself is from the Greek *plateia*, "wide"), which corresponded to the **forum**, the center of a Roman town. Four principal streets led to the plaza from the north, south, east, and west, analogous to the main Roman streets, the **cardō maximus** and **decumānus maximus**. Like the Roman streets, these four principal streets were lined with arcades and shops.

But it is due to a most curious twist of history that the style of many of the public and governmental buildings of the United States is based on Roman imperial architecture. Former provinces of the Roman Empire had evolved into modern European nations, each with its own architectural "look" and style for their governmental buildings. By the time of the American Revolution, European public buildings were not constructed in a Roman style. Thomas Jefferson, who was himself an architect, argued that his new country should not use the architectural style then current in Britain and Europe. He was instrumental in developing the American Federal style of architecture, which was used for the Capitol Building in Washington, D.C., state capitols, public museums, and non-public buildings such as banks. A basic model for that style was a small Roman temple, the Maison Carrée in Nîmes, France, with which Jefferson had become entranced while he was ambassador to France. Jefferson also designed the campus of the University of Virginia to recreate a Roman villa with linked porticos, enclosed spaces, and pillared buildings. For his own home of Monticello, Jefferson drew on the Pantheon in Rome. The Pantheon also inspired the president of the Girard Trust of Philadelphia when he made a tour of Europe early in this century. Upon his return, he ordered that his new bank building be modeled on this second century A.D. Roman temple.

CONCLUSION

Acquiring facility with the Latin language and familiarity with Roman culture is actually, then, a starting point for lifelong enrichment along multicultural lines. With this learning we reach far back into history and keep contact with a fascinating, vital process of the world's development and our own. Our food and our drink, our clothing and our embellishments, our sports and our games, our literature and all our arts, our medicine and our law, the buildings and libraries and schools of our society, our political and military theories, our philosophies and our sciences, our history and our languages—all of these are an inherited, shared legacy, that we continuously modify, add to, and use in the real, living world with all its variety and all its common ground.

Philosophy (literally "love of wisdom") is a multicultural legacy from antiquity.

Woodcut by Albrecht Dürer

FORMS

The following charts show the forms of typical Latin nouns, adjectives, pronouns, and verbs. As an aid in pronunciation, markings of long vowels and of accents are included.

I. Nouns

Number Case	1st Declension	2nd Declension				3rd Declension		
	Fem.	Masc.	Masc.	Masc.	Neut.	Masc.	Fem.	Neut.
Singular								
Nominative	puéll*a*	sérv*us*	púer	áger	bácul*um*	páter	vōx	nómen
Genitive	puéll*ae*	sérv*ī*	púer*ī*	ágr*ī*	bácul*ī*	pátr*is*	vóc*is*	nómin*is*
Dative	puéll*ae*	sérv*ō*	púer*ō*	ágr*ō*	bácul*ō*	pátr*ī*	vóc*ī*	nómin*ī*
Accusative	puéll*am*	sérv*um*	púer*um*	ágr*um*	bácul*um*	pátr*em*	vóc*em*	nómen
Ablative	puéll*ā*	sérv*ō*	púer*ō*	ágr*ō*	bácul*ō*	pátr*e*	vóc*e*	nómin*e*
Vocative	puéll*a*	sérv*e*	púer	áger	bácul*um*	páter	vōx	nómen
Plural								
Nominative	puéll*ae*	sérv*ī*	púer*ī*	ágr*ī*	bácul*a*	pátr*ēs*	vóc*ēs*	nómin*a*
Genitive	puell*árum*	serv*órum*	puer*órum*	agr*órum*	bacul*órum*	pátr*um*	vóc*um*	nómin*um*
Dative	puéll*īs*	sérv*īs*	púer*īs*	ágr*īs*	bácul*īs*	pátr*ibus*	vóc*ibus*	nómín*ibus*
Accusative	puéll*ās*	sérv*ōs*	púer*ōs*	ágr*ōs*	bácul*a*	pátr*ēs*	vóc*ēs*	nómin*a*
Ablative	puéll*īs*	sérv*īs*	púer*īs*	ágr*īs*	bácul*īs*	pátr*ibus*	vóc*ibus*	nómín*ibus*
Vocative	puéll*ae*	sérv*ī*	púer*ī*	ágr*ī*	bácul*a*	pátr*ēs*	vóc*ēs*	nómin*a*

Number Case	4th Declension		5th Declension	
	Masc.	Neut.	Masc.	Fem.
Singular				
Nominative	árc*us*	gén*ū*	dí*ēs*	r*ēs*
Genitive	árc*ūs*	gén*ūs*	di*éī*	r*éī*
Dative	árc*uī*	gén*ū*	di*éī*	r*éī*
Accusative	árc*um*	gén*ū*	dí*em*	r*em*
Ablative	árc*ū*	gén*ū*	dí*ē*	r*ē*
Vocative	árc*us*	gén*ū*	dí*ēs*	r*ēs*
Plural				
Nominative	árc*ūs*	gén*ua*	dí*ēs*	r*ēs*
Genitive	árc*uum*	gén*uum*	di*érum*	r*érum*
Dative	árc*ibus*	gén*ibus*	di*ébus*	r*ébus*
Accusative	árc*ūs*	gén*ua*	dí*ēs*	r*ēs*
Ablative	árc*ibus*	gén*ibus*	di*ébus*	r*ébus*
Vocative	árc*ūs*	gén*ua*	dí*ēs*	r*ēs*

II. Adjectives

Number Case	1st and 2nd Declension			3rd Declension		
	Masc.	Fem.	Neut.	Masc.	Fem.	Neut.
Singular						
Nominative	mágn*us*	mágn*a*	mágn*um*	ómn*is*	ómn*is*	ómn*e*
Genitive	mágn*ī*	mágn*ae*	mágn*ī*	ómn*is*	ómn*is*	ómn*is*
Dative	mágn*ō*	mágn*ae*	mágn*ō*	ómn*ī*	ómn*ī*	ómn*ī*
Accusative	mágn*um*	mágn*am*	mágn*um*	ómn*em*	ómn*em*	ómn*e*
Ablative	mágn*ō*	mágn*ā*	mágn*ō*	ómn*ī*	ómn*ī*	ómn*ī*
Vocative	mágn*e*	mágn*a*	mágn*um*	ómn*is*	ómn*is*	ómn*e*
Plural						
Nominative	mágn*ī*	mágn*ae*	mágn*a*	ómn*ēs*	ómn*ēs*	ómn*ia*
Genitive	magn*órum*	magn*árum*	magn*órum*	ómn*ium*	ómn*ium*	ómn*ium*
Dative	mágn*īs*	mágn*īs*	mágn*īs*	ómn*ibus*	ómn*ibus*	ómn*ibus*
Accusative	mágn*ōs*	mágn*ās*	mágn*a*	ómn*ēs*	ómn*ēs*	ómn*ia*
Ablative	mágn*īs*	mágn*īs*	mágn*īs*	ómn*ibus*	ómn*ibus*	ómn*ibus*
Vocative	mágn*ī*	mágn*ae*	mágn*a*	ómn*ēs*	ómn*ēs*	ómn*ia*

III. Comparative Adjectives

Number Case	Masc.	Fem.	Neut.
Singular			
Nominative	púlchrior	púlchrior	púlchrius
Genitive	pulchriór*is*	pulchriór*is*	pulchriór*is*
Dative	pulchriór*ī*	pulchriór*ī*	pulchriór*ī*
Accusative	pulchriór*em*	pulchriór*em*	púlchrius
Ablative	pulchriór*e*	pulchriór*e*	pulchriór*e*
Vocative	púlchrior	púlchrior	púlchrius
Plural			
Nominative	pulchriór*ēs*	pulchriór*ēs*	pulchriór*a*
Genitive	pulchriór*um*	pulchriór*um*	pulchriór*um*
Dative	pulchriór*ibus*	pulchriór*ibus*	pulchriór*ibus*
Accusative	pulchriór*ēs*	pulchriór*ēs*	pulchriór*a*
Ablative	pulchriór*ibus*	pulchriór*ibus*	pulchriór*ibus*
Vocative	pulchriór*ēs*	pulchriór*ēs*	pulchriór*a*

Adjectives have *positive*, *comparative*, and *superlative* forms. You can usually recognize the comparative by the letters **-ior(-)** and the superlative by **-issimus**, **-errimus**, or **-illimus**:

ignávus, -a, -um, *lazy*	ignávior, ignávius	ignāvíssimus, -a, -um
púlcher, púlchra, púlchrum, *beautiful*	púlchrior, púlchrius	pulchérrimus, -a, -um
fácilis, -is, -e, *easy*	facílior, facílius	facíllimus, -a, -um

Some very common adjectives are irregular in the comparative and superlative:

Positive	Comparative	Superlative
bónus, -a, -um, *good*	mélior, mélius, *better*	óptimus, -a, -um, *best*
málus, -a, -um, *bad*	péior, péius, *worse*	péssimus, -a, -um, *worst*
mágnus, -a, -um, *big*	máior, máius, *bigger*	máximus, -a, -um, *biggest*
párvus, -a, -um, *small*	mínor, mínus, *smaller*	mínimus, -a, -um, *smallest*
múltus, -a, -um, *much*	plūs,* *more*	plúrimus, -a, -um, *most, very much*
múltī, -ae, -a, *many*	plúrēs, plúra, *more*	plúrimī, -ae, -a, *most, very many*

*Note that **plūs** is not an adjective but a neuter substantive, usually found with a partitive genitive, e.g., Titus **plūs vīnī** bibit. *Titus drank **more (of the) wine**.*

IV.   Present Participles

Number Case	Masc.	Fem.	Neut.
Singular			
Nominative	párāns	párāns	párāns
Genitive	parántis	parántis	parántis
Dative	parántī	parántī	parántī
Accusative	parántem	parántem	párāns
Ablative	paránt ī/e	paránt ī/e	paránt ī/e
Plural			
Nominative	parántēs	parántēs	parántia
Genitive	parántium	parántium	parántium
Dative	parántibus	parántibus	parántibus
Accusative	parántēs	parántēs	parántia
Ablative	parántibus	parántibus	parántibus

V. Numbers

Case	Masc.	Fem.	Neut.	Masc.	Fem.	Neut.	Masc.	Fem.	Neut.
Nom.	únus	úna	únum	dúo	dúae	dúo	trēs	trēs	tría
Gen.	ūníus	ūníus	ūníus	duórum	duárum	duórum	tríum	tríum	tríum
Dat.	únī	únī	únī	duóbus	duábus	duóbus	tríbus	tríbus	tríbus
Acc.	únum	únam	únum	dúōs	dúās	dúo	trēs	trēs	tría
Abl.	únō	únā	únō	duóbus	duábus	duóbus	tríbus	tríbus	tríbus

	Cardinal	**Ordinal**
I	únus, -a, -um, *one*	prímus, -a, -um, *first*
II	dúo, -ae, -o, *two*	secúndus, -a, -um, *second*
III	trēs, trēs, tría, *three*	tértius, -a, -um, *third*
IV	quáttuor, *four*	quártus, -a, -um
V	quínque, *five*	quíntus, -a, -um
VI	sex, *six*	séxtus, -a, -um
VII	séptem, *seven*	séptimus, -a, -um
VIII	óctō, *eight*	octávus, -a, -um
IX	nóvem, *nine*	nónus, -a, -um
X	décem, *ten*	décimus, -a, -um
XI	úndecim, *eleven*	ūndécimus, -a, -um
XII	duódecim, *twelve*	duodécimus, -a, -um
XIII	trédecim, *thirteen*	tértius décimus, -a, -um
XIV	quattuórdecim, *fourteen*	quártus décimus, -a, -um
XV	quíndecim, *fifteen*	quíntus décimus, -a, -um
XVI	sédecim, *sixteen*	séxtus décimus, -a, -um
XVII	septéndecim, *seventeen*	séptimus décimus, -a, -um
XVIII	duodēvīgíntī, *eighteen,*	duodēvīcésimus, -a, -um
XIX	ūndēvīgíntī, *nineteen,*	ūndēvīcésimus, -a, -um
XX	vīgíntī, *twenty*	vīcésimus, -a, -um
L	quīnquāgíntā, *fifty*	quīnquāgésimus, -a, -um
C	céntum, *a hundred*	centésimus, -a, -um
D	quīngéntī, -ae, -a, *five hundred*	quīngentésimus, -a, -um
M	mílle, *a thousand*	mīllésimus, -a, -um

N.B. The cardinal numbers from **quattuor** to **centum** do not change their form to indicate case and gender.

VI. Personal Pronouns

Number Case	1st Declension	2nd Declension	3rd Declension		
			Masc.	Fem.	Neut.
Singular					
Nominative	égo	tū	is	éa	id
Genitive	méī	túī	éius	éius	éius
Dative	míhi	tíbi	éī	éī	éī
Accusative	mē	tē	éum	éam	id
Ablative	mē	tē	éō	éā	éō
Plural					
Nominative	nōs	vōs	éī	éae	éa
Genitive	nóstrī	véstrī	eórum	eárum	eórum
	nóstrum	véstrum			
Dative	nóbīs	vóbīs	éīs	éīs	éīs
Accusative	nōs	vōs	éōs	éās	éa
Ablative	nóbīs	vóbīs	éīs	éīs	éīs

Note: The forms of **is, ea, id** may also serve as demonstrative adjectives.

VII. Reflexive Pronoun

Singular	
Nominative	——
Genitive	súī
Dative	síbi
Accusative	sē
Ablative	sē
Plural	
Nominative	——
Genitive	súī
Dative	síbi
Accusative	sē
Ablative	sē

VIII. Relative Pronoun

	Masc.	Fem.	Neut.
Singular			
Nominative	quī	quae	quod
Genitive	cúius	cúius	cúius
Dative	cui	cui	cui
Accusative	quem	quam	quod
Ablative	quō	quā	quō
Plural			
Nominative	quī	quae	quae
Genitive	quórum	quárum	quórum
Dative	quíbus	quíbus	quíbus
Accusative	quōs	quās	quae
Ablative	quíbus	quíbus	quíbus

IX. Interrogative Pronoun

Number Case	Masc.	Fem.	Neut.
Singular			
Nominative	quis	quis	quid
Genitive	cúius	cúius	cúius
Dative	cui	cui	cui
Accusative	quem	quem	quid
Ablative	quō	quō	quō
Plural	Same as the plural of the relative pronoun above.		

X. Indefinite Adjective

Number Case	Masc.	Fem.	Neut.
Singular			
Nominative	quídam	quaédam	quóddam
Genitive	cuiúsdam	cuiúsdam	cuiúsdam
Dative	cúidam	cúidam	cúidam
Accusative	quéndam	quándam	quóddam
Ablative	quódam	quádam	quódam
Plural			
Nominative	quídam	quaédam	quaédam
Genitive	quōrúndam	quārúndam	quōrúndam
Dative	quibúsdam	quibúsdam	quibúsdam
Accusative	quósdam	quásdam	quaédam
Ablative	quibúsdam	quibúsdam	quibúsdam

XI. Demonstrative Adjectives and Pronouns

Number Case	Masc.	Fem.	Neut.	Masc.	Fem.	Neut.
Singular						
Nominative	hic	haec	hoc	ílle	ílla	íllud
Genitive	húius	húius	húius	illíus	illíus	illíus
Dative	húic	húic	húic	íllī	íllī	íllī
Accusative	hunc	hanc	hoc	íllum	íllam	íllud
Ablative	hōc	hāc	hōc	íllō	íllā	íllō
Plural						
Nominative	hī	hae	haec	íllī	íllae	ílla
Genitive	hórum	hárum	hórum	illórum	illárum	illórum
Dative	hīs	hīs	hīs	íllīs	íllīs	íllīs
Accusative	hōs	hās	haec	íllōs	íllās	ílla
Ablative	hīs	hīs	hīs	íllīs	íllīs	íllīs

Number Case	Masculine	Feminine	Neuter
Singular			
Nominative	ípse	ípsa	ípsum
Genitive	ipsíus	ipsíus	ipsíus
Dative	ípsī	ípsī	ípsī
Accusative	ípsum	ípsam	ípsum
Ablative	ípsō	ípsā	ípsō
Plural			
Nominative	ípsī	ípsae	ípsa
Genitive	ipsórum	ipsárum	ipsórum
Dative	ípsīs	ípsīs	ípsīs
Accusative	ípsōs	ípsās	ípsa
Ablative	ípsīs	ípsīs	ípsīs

Number Case	Masc.	Fem.	Neut.	Masc.	Fem.	Neut.
Singular						
Nominative	is	éa	id	ídem	éadem	ídem
Genitive	éius	éius	éius	eiúsdem	eiúsdem	eiúsdem
Dative	éī	éī	éī	eídem	eídem	eídem
Accusative	éum	éam	id	eúndem	eándem	ídem
Ablative	éō	éā	éō	eódem	eádem	eódem
Plural						
Nominative	éī	éae	éa	eídem	eaédem	éadem
Genitive	eórum	eárum	eórum	eōrúndem	eārúndem	eōrúndem
Dative	éīs	éīs	éīs	eísdem	eísdem	eísdem
Accusative	éōs	éās	éa	eósdem	eásdem	éadem
Ablative	éīs	éīs	éīs	eísdem	eísdem	eísdem

XII. Adverbs

Latin adverbs may be formed from adjectives of the 1st and 2nd declensions by adding *-ē* to the base of the adjective, e.g., **strēnuē**, *strenuously*, from **strēnuus, -a, -um**. To form an adverb from a 3rd declension adjective, add *-iter* to the base of the adjective or *-er* to bases ending in **-nt-**, e.g., <u>**breviter**</u>, *briefly*, from **brevis, -is, -e**, and <u>**prūdenter**</u>, *wisely*, from **prūdēns, prūdentis**.

láetē, *happily*	laét**ius**	laet**íssimē**
fēlíc**iter**, *luckily*	fēlíc**ius**	fēlīc**íssimē**
celér**iter**, *quickly*	celér**ius**	celér**rimē**
prūdént**er**, *wisely*	prūdént**ius**	prūdent**íssimē**

Note the following as well:

díū, *for a long time*	diút**ius**	diūt**íssimē**
saépe, *often*	saép**ius**	saep**íssimē**
sérō, *late*	sér**ius**	sēr**íssimē**

Some adverbs are irregular:

béne, *well*	mélius, *better*	óptimē, *best*
mále, *badly*	péius, *worse*	péssimē, *worst*
fácile, *easily*	facílius	facíllimē
magnópere, *greatly*	mágis, *more*	máximē, *most*
paúlum, *little*	mínus, *less*	mínimē, *least*
múltum, *much*	plūs, *more*	plúrimum, *most*

XIII. Regular Verbs Active: Infinitive, Imperative, Indicative

			1st Conjugation	2nd Conjugation	3rd Conjugation		4th Conjugation
Infinitive			par*áre*	hab*ére*	mítt*ere*	iác*ere (-iō)*	aud*íre*
Imperative			pár*ā*	háb*ē*	mítt*e*	iác*e*	aúd*ī*
			par*áte*	hab*éte*	mítt*ite*	iác*ite*	aud*íte*
Present	Singular	1	pár*ō*	hábe*ō*	mítt*ō*	iáci*ō*	aúdi*ō*
		2	pár*ās*	háb*ēs*	mítt*is*	iác*is*	aúd*īs*
		3	pár*at*	hábe*t*	mítt*it*	iác*it*	aúd*it*
	Plural	1	par*ámus*	habé*mus*	mítt*imus*	iác*imus*	audí*mus*
		2	par*átis*	habé*tis*	mítt*itis*	iác*itis*	audí*tis*
		3	pár*ant*	hábe*nt*	mítt*unt*	iáci*unt*	aúdi*unt*
Imperfect	Singular	1	par*ábam*	habé*bam*	mitté*bam*	iacié*bam*	audié*bam*
		2	par*ábās*	habé*bās*	mitté*bās*	iacié*bās*	audié*bās*
		3	par*ábat*	habé*bat*	mitté*bat*	iacié*bat*	audié*bat*
	Plural	1	parā*bámus*	habē*bámus*	mittē*bámus*	iaciē*bámus*	audiē*bámus*
		2	parā*bátis*	habē*bátis*	mittē*bátis*	iaciē*bátis*	audiē*bátis*
		3	par*ábant*	habé*bant*	mitté*bant*	iacié*bant*	audié*bant*
Future	Singular	1	par*ábō*	habé*bō*	mítt*am*	iáci*am*	aúdi*am*
		2	par*ábis*	habé*bis*	mítt*ēs*	iáci*ēs*	aúdi*ēs*
		3	par*ábit*	habé*bit*	mítt*et*	jáci*et*	aúdi*et*
	Plural	1	parā*bimus*	habē*bimus*	mitt*émus*	iaci*émus*	audi*émus*
		2	par*ábitis*	habé*bitis*	mitt*étis*	iaci*étis*	audi*étis*
		3	par*ábunt*	habé*bunt*	mítt*ent*	iáci*ent*	aúdi*ent*
Perfect	Singular	1	par*ávī*	háb*uī*	mís*ī*	iéc*ī*	audí*vī*
		2	par*ávistī*	hab*ístī*	mis*ístī*	iec*ístī*	audī*vístī*
		3	par*ávit*	háb*uit*	mís*it*	iéc*it*	audí*vit*
	Plural	1	par*ávimus*	hab*úimus*	mís*imus*	iéc*imus*	audí*vimus*
		2	par*ávistis*	hab*ústis*	mis*ístis*	iec*ístis*	audī*vístis*
		3	par*avérunt*	hab*uérunt*	mis*érunt*	iec*érunt*	audī*vérunt*
Pluperfect	Singular	1	par*áveram*	hab*úeram*	mís*eram*	iéc*eram*	audí*veram*
		2	par*áverās*	hab*úerās*	mís*erās*	iéc*erās*	audí*verās*
		3	par*áverat*	hab*úerat*	mís*erat*	iéc*erat*	audí*verat*
	Plural	1	parāv*erámus*	habu*erámus*	mis*erámus*	iec*erámus*	audīv*erámus*
		2	parāv*erátis*	habu*erátis*	mis*erátis*	iec*erátis*	audīv*erátis*
		3	par*áverant*	hab*úerant*	mís*erant*	iéc*erant*	audí*verant*
Future Perfect	Singular	1	par*áverō*	hab*úerō*	mís*erō*	iéc*erō*	audí*verō*
		2	par*áveris*	hab*úeris*	mís*eris*	iéc*eris*	audí*veris*
		3	par*áverit*	hab*úerit*	mís*erit*	iéc*erit*	audí*verit*
	Plural	1	parāv*érimus*	habu*érimus*	mis*érimus*	iec*érimus*	audīv*érimus*
		2	parāv*éritis*	habu*éritis*	mis*éritis*	iec*éritis*	audīv*éritis*
		3	par*áverint*	hab*úerint*	mís*erint*	iéc*erint*	audí*verint*

XIV. Regular Verbs Passive: Infinitive, Imperative, Indicative

			1st Conjugation	2nd Conjugation	3rd Conjugation		4th Conjugation
Present	Infinitive	1	port*árī*	mov*érī*	mítt*ī*	iác*ī*	aud*írī*
	Imperative	1	port*áre*	mov*ére*	mítt*ere*	iác*ere*	aud*íre*
		2	port*áminī*	mov*éminī*	mítt*iminī*	iac*íminī*	aud*íminī*
	Singular	1	pórto*r*	móveo*r*	mítto*r*	iácio*r*	aúdio*r*
		2	port*áris*	mov*éris*	mítte*ris*	iáce*ris*	aud*íris*
		3	port*átur*	mov*étur*	mítti*tur*	iáci*tur*	aud*ítur*
	Plural	1	port*ámur*	mov*émur*	mítti*mur*	iáci*mur*	aud*ímur*
		2	port*áminī*	mov*éminī*	mittí*minī*	iací*minī*	aud*íminī*
		3	port*ántur*	mov*éntur*	mittú*ntur*	iaci*úntur*	audi*úntur*
Imperfect	Singular	1	port*ábar*	mov*ébar*	mitt*ébar*	iaci*ébar*	audi*ébar*
		2	port*ábáris*	mov*ébáris*	mitt*ébáris*	iaci*ébáris*	audi*ébáris*
		3	port*ábátur*	mov*ébátur*	mitt*ébátur*	iaci*ébátur*	audi*ébátur*
	Plural	1	port*ábámur*	mov*ébámur*	mitt*ébámur*	iaci*ébámur*	audi*ébámur*
		2	port*ábáminī*	mov*ébáminī*	mitt*ébáminī*	iaci*ébáminī*	audi*ébáminī*
		3	port*ábántur*	mov*ébántur*	mitt*ébántur*	iaci*ébántur*	audi*ébántur*
Future	Singular	1	port*ábor*	mov*ébor*	mítt*ar*	iáci*ar*	aúdi*ar*
		2	port*áberis*	mov*éberis*	mitt*éris*	iaci*éris*	audi*éris*
		3	port*ábitur*	mov*ébitur*	mitt*étur*	iaci*étur*	audi*étur*
	Plural	1	port*ábimur*	mov*ébimur*	mitt*émur*	iaci*émur*	audi*émur*
		2	port*ábíminī*	mov*ébíminī*	mitt*éminī*	iaci*éminī*	audi*éminī*
		3	port*ábúntur*	mov*ébúntur*	mitt*éntur*	iaci*éntur*	audi*éntur*

		Perfect Passive		Pluperfect Passive		Future Perfect Passive	
Singular	1	portátus, -a	sum	portátus, -a	éram	portátus, -a	érō
	2	portátus, -a	es	portátus, -a	érās	portátus, -a	éris
	3	portátus, -a, -um	est	portátus, -a, -um	érat	portátus, -a, -um	érit
Plural	1	portátī, -ae	súmus	portátī, -ae	erámus	portátī, -ae	érimus
	2	portátī, -ae	éstis	portátī, -ae	erátis	portátī, -ae	éritis
	3	portátī, -ae, -a	sunt	portátī, -ae, -a	érant	portátī, -ae, -a	érunt

XV. Regular Verbs Active: Subjunctive

			1st Conjugation	2nd Conjugation	3rd Conjugation		4th Conjugation
Present	Singular	1	pórt*em*	móve*am*	mítt*am*	iáci*am*	aúdi*am*
		2	pórt*ēs*	móve*ās*	mítt*ās*	iáci*ās*	aúdi*ās*
		3	pórt*et*	móve*at*	mítt*at*	iáci*at*	aúdi*at*
	Plural	1	port*émus*	move*ámus*	mitt*ámus*	iaci*ámus*	audi*ámus*
		2	port*étis*	move*átis*	mitt*átis*	iac*átis*	audi*átis*
		3	pórt*ent*	móve*ant*	mítt*ant*	iáci*ant*	aúdi*ant*
Imperfect	Singular	1	portár*em*	movér*em*	mítter*em*	iácer*em*	audír*em*
		2	portár*ēs*	movér*ēs*	mítter*ēs*	iácer*ēs*	audír*ēs*
		3	portár*et*	movér*et*	mítter*et*	iácer*et*	audír*et*
	Plural	1	portár*émus*	movér*émus*	mitter*émus*	iacer*émus*	audír*émus*
		2	portár*étis*	movér*étis*	mitter*étis*	iacer*étis*	audír*étis*
		3	portár*ent*	movér*ent*	mítter*ent*	iácer*ent*	audír*ent*
Perfect	Singular	1	portáv*erim*	móv*erim*	mís*erim*	iéc*erim*	audív*erim*
		2	portáv*eris*	móv*eris*	mís*eris*	iéc*eris*	audív*eris*
		3	portáv*erit*	móv*erit*	mís*erit*	iéc*erit*	audív*erit*
	Plural	1	portáv*érimus*	móv*érimus*	mís*érimus*	iéc*érimus*	audív*érimus*
		2	portáv*éritis*	móv*éritis*	mís*éritis*	iéc*éritis*	audív*éritis*
		3	portáv*erint*	móv*erint*	mís*erint*	iéc*erint*	audív*erint*
Pluperfect	Singular	1	portávíss*em*	mōvíss*em*	misíss*em*	iēcíss*em*	audivíss*em*
		2	portávíss*ēs*	mōvíss*ēs*	misíss*ēs*	iēcíss*ēs*	audivíss*ēs*
		3	portávíss*et*	mōvíss*et*	misíss*et*	iēcíss*et*	audivíss*et*
	Plural	1	portávissé*mus*	mōvissé*mus*	misissé*mus*	iēcissé*mus*	audivissé*mus*
		2	portávissé*tis*	mōvissé*tis*	misissé*tis*	iēcissé*tis*	audivissé*tis*
		3	portávíss*ent*	mōvíss*ent*	misíss*ent*	iēcíss*ent*	audivíss*ent*

XVI. Regular Verbs Passive: Subjunctive

			1st Conjugation	2nd Conjugation	3rd Conjugation		4th Conjugation
Present	Singular	1	pórt*er*	móve*ar*	mítt*ar*	iáci*ar*	aúdi*ar*
		2	port*éris*	move*áris*	mitt*áris*	iaci*áris*	audi*áris*
		3	port*étur*	move*átur*	mitt*átur*	iaci*átur*	audi*átur*
	Plural	1	port*émur*	move*ámur*	mitt*ámur*	iaci*ámur*	audi*ámur*
		2	port*éminī*	move*áminī*	mitt*áminī*	iaci*áminī*	audi*áminī*
		3	port*éntur*	move*ántur*	mitt*ántur*	iaci*ántur*	audi*ántur*
Imperfect	Singular	1	portáre*r*	movére*r*	mítter*er*	iácer*er*	audíre*r*
		2	portáré*ris*	movéré*ris*	mitteré*ris*	iaceré*ris*	audiré*ris*
		3	portáré*tur*	movéré*tur*	mitteré*tur*	iaceré*tur*	audiré*tur*
	Plural	1	portáré*mur*	movéré*mur*	mitteré*mur*	iaceré*mur*	audiré*mur*
		2	portáré*minī*	movéré*minī*	mitteré*minī*	iaceré*minī*	audiré*minī*
		3	portáré*ntur*	movéré*ntur*	mitteré*ntur*	iaceré*ntur*	audiré*ntur*
Perfect		1	portátus sim etc.	mótus sim etc.	míssus sim etc.	iáctus sim etc.	audítus sim etc.
Pluperfect		1	portátus éssem etc.	mótus éssem etc.	míssus éssem etc.	iáctus éssem etc.	audítus éssem etc.

XVII. Deponent Verbs: Infinitive, Imperative, Indicative

			1st Conjugation	2nd Conjugation	3rd Conjugation		4th Conjugation
Present Infinitive			cōn*árī*	ver*érī*	lóqu*ī*	régred*ī*	exper*írī*
Imperative			cōn*áre*	ver*ére*	lóqu*ere*	regréd*ere*	exper*íre*
			cōn*áminī*	ver*éminī*	loqu*íminī*	regred*íminī*	exper*íminī*
Present	Singular	1	cōn*or*	vére*or*	lóqu*or*	regréd*ior*	expéri*or*
		2	cōn*áris*	ver*éris*	lóqu*eris*	regréd*eris*	exper*íris*
		3	cōn*átur*	ver*étur*	lóqu*itur*	regréd*itur*	exper*ítur*
	Plural	1	cōn*ámur*	ver*émur*	lóqu*imur*	regréd*imur*	exper*ímur*
		2	cōn*áminī*	ver*éminī*	loqu*íminī*	regred*íminī*	exper*íminī*
		3	cōn*ántur*	ver*éntur*	loqu*úntur*	regredi*úntur*	experi*úntur*
Imperfect	Singular	1	cōn*ábar*	ver*ébar*	loqu*ébar*	regredi*ébar*	experi*ébar*
		2	cōn*abáris*	ver*ebáris*	loqu*ēbáris*	regredi*ēbáris*	experi*ēbáris*
		3	cōn*abátur*	ver*ebátur*	loqu*ēbátur*	regredi*ēbátur*	experi*ēbátur*
Future	Singular	1	cōn*ábor*	ver*ábor*	lóqu*ar*	regréd*iar*	expéri*ar*
		2	cōn*áberis*	ver*éberis*	loqu*éris*	regredi*éris*	experi*éris*
		3	cōn*ábitur*	ver*ébitur*	loqu*étur*	regredi*étur*	experi*étur*
Perfect		1	cōnátus sum	véritus sum	locútus sum	regréssus sum	expértus sum
Pluperfect		1	cōnátus éram	véritus éram	locútus éram	regréssus éram	expértus éram
Future Perfect		1	cōnátus érō	véritus érō	locútus érō	regréssus érō	expértus érō

XVIII. Deponent Verbs: Subjunctive

			1st Conjugation	2nd Conjugation	3rd Conjugation		4th Conjugation
Present	Singular	1	cón*er*	vére*ar*	lóqu*ar*	regréd*iar*	expéri*ar*
		2	cōn*éris*	vere*áris*	loqu*áris*	regredi*áris*	experi*áris*
		3	cōn*étur*	vere*átur*	loqu*átur*	regredi*átur*	experi*átur*
	Plural	1	cōn*émur*	vere*ámur*	loqu*ámur*	regredi*ámur*	experi*ámur*
		2	cōn*éminī*	vere*áminī*	loqu*áminī*	regredi*áminī*	experi*áminī*
		3	cōn*éntur*	vere*ántur*	loqu*ántur*	regredi*ántur*	experi*ántur*
Imperfect	Singular	1	cōn*árer*	ver*érer*	lóqu*erer*	regréd*erer*	exper*írer*
		2	cōn*aréris*	ver*eréris*	loqu*eréris*	regred*eréris*	exper*īréris*
		3	cōn*arétur*	ver*erétur*	loqu*erétur*	regred*erétur*	exper*īrétur*
	Plural	1	cōn*arémur*	ver*erémur*	loqu*erémur*	regred*erémur*	exper*īrémur*
		2	cōn*aréminī*	ver*eréminī*	loqu*eréminī*	regred*eréminī*	exper*īréminī*
		3	cōn*aréntur*	ver*eréntur*	loqu*eréntur*	regred*eréntur*	exper*īréntur*
Perfect		1	cōnátus sim etc.	véritus sim etc.	locútus sim etc.	regréssus sim etc.	expértus sim etc.
Pluperfect		1	cōnátus éssem etc.	véritus éssem etc.	locútus éssem etc.	regréssus éssem etc.	expértus éssem etc.

XIX. Irregular Verbs: Infinitive, Imperative, Indicative

Infinitive			ésse	pósse	vélle	nólle	málle
Imperative			es	——	——	nólī	——
			éste			nōlíte	
Present	Singular	1	sum	póssum	vólō	nólō	málō
		2	es	pótes	vīs	nōn vīs	mávīs
		3	est	pótest	vult	nōn vult	mávult
	Plural	1	súmus	póssumus	vólumus	nólumus	málumus
		2	éstis	potéstis	vúltis	nōn vúltis	māvúltis
		3	sunt	póssunt	vólunt	nólunt	málunt
Imperfect	Singular	1	éram	póteram	volébam	nōlébam	mālébam
		2	erās	póterās	volébās	nōlébās	mālébās
		3	érat	póterat	volébat	nōlébat	mālébat
	Plural	1	erámus	poterámus	volēbámus	nōlēbámus	mālēbámus
		2	erátis	poterátis	volēbátis	nōlēbátis	mālēbátis
		3	érant	póterant	volébant	nōlébant	mālébant
Future	Singular	1	érō	póterō	vólam	nólam	málam
		2	éris	póteris	vólēs	nólēs	málēs
		3	érit	póterit	vólet	nólet	málet
	Plural	1	érimus	potérimus	volémus	nōlémus	mālémus
		2	éritis	potéritis	volétis	nōlétis	mālétis
		3	érunt	póterunt	vólent	nólent	málent

Infinitive			férre	férrī	fíerī	íre
Imperative			fer	férre	——	ī
			férte	feríminī	——	íte
Present	Singular	1	férō	féror	fíō	éō
		2	fers	férris	fis	īs
		3	fert	fértur	fit	it
	Plural	1	férimus	férimur	fímus	ímus
		2	fértis	feríminī	fítis	ítis
		3	férunt	ferúntur	fíunt	éunt
Imperfect	Singular	1	ferébam	ferébar	fiébam	íbam
		2	ferébās	ferēbáris	fiébās	íbās
		3	ferébat	ferēbátur	fiébat	íbat
	Plural	1	ferēbámus	ferēbámur	fiēbámus	ībámus
		2	ferēbátis	ferēbáminī	fiēbátis	ībátis
		3	ferébant	ferēbántur	fiébant	íbant
Future	Singular	1	féram	férar	fíam	íbō
		2	férēs	feréris	fíēs	íbis
		3	féret	ferétur	fíet	íbit
	Plural	1	ferémus	ferémur	fiémus	íbimus
		2	ferétis	feréminī	fiétis	íbitis
		3	férent	feréntur	fíent	íbunt

XX. Irregular Verbs: Perfect, Pluperfect, Future Pefect Indicative

Full charts are not supplied for these forms because (except for the perfect of **eō**, for which see below) they are not irregular in any way. They are made in the same way as the perfect, pluperfect, and future perfect tenses of regular verbs, by adding the perfect, pluperfect and future perfect endings to the perfect stem. The perfect stem is found by dropping the *-ī* from the third principal part. The first three principal parts of the irregular verbs are as follows:

> sum, esse, <u>fu*ī*</u>
> possum, posse, <u>potu*ī*</u>
> volō, velle, <u>volu*ī*</u>
> nōlō, nōlle, <u>nōlu*ī*</u>
> mālō, mālle, <u>mālu*ī*</u>
> ferō, ferre, <u>tul*ī*</u>
> eō, īre, <u>i*ī*</u> or <u>īv*ī*</u>

Examples:

> Perfect: fuistī, voluērunt, tulimus
> Pluperfect: fueram, potuerant, nōluerāmus
> Future Perfect: fuerō, volueris, tulerimus

The perfect forms of **eō** made from the stem **i-** are as follows:

> Singular: iī, īstī, iit
> Plural: iimus, īstis, iērunt

Note that the stem vowel (**i-**) contracts with the *-i* of the endings *-istī* and *-istis* to give **ī-** (**īstī, īstis**). Thus also the perfect infinitive: **īsse** (for **iisse**).

The perfect forms of **eō** made from the stem **īv-** are regular, as follows:

> Singular: īvī, īvistī, īvit
> Plural: īvimus, īvistis, īvērunt

XXI. Irregular Verbs: Subjunctive

Present	Singular	1	s*im*	póss*im*	vél*im*	nól*im*	mál*im*
		2	s*īs*	póss*īs*	vél*īs*	nól*īs*	mál*īs*
		3	s*it*	póss*it*	vél*it*	nól*it*	mál*it*
	Plural	1	s*ímus*	poss*ímus*	vel*ímus*	nōl*ímus*	māl*ímus*
		2	s*ítis*	poss*ítis*	vel*ítis*	nōl*ítis*	māl*ítis*
		3	s*int*	póss*int*	vél*int*	nōl*int*	mál*int*
Imperfect	Singular	1	éss*em*	póss*em*	véll*em*	nóll*em*	máll*em*
		2	éss*ēs*	póss*ēs*	véll*ēs*	nóll*ēs*	máll*ēs*
		3	éss*et*	póss*et*	véll*et*	nóll*et*	máll*et*
	Plural	1	ess*émus*	poss*émus*	vell*émus*	nōll*émus*	māll*émus*
		2	ess*étis*	poss*étis*	vell*étis*	nōll*étis*	māll*étis*
		3	éss*ent*	póss*ent*	véll*ent*	nóll*ent*	máll*ent*
Perfect	Singular	1	fú*erim*	potú*erim*	volú*erim*	nōlú*erim*	mālú*erim*
		2	fú*eris*	potú*eris*	volú*eris*	nōlú*eris*	mālú*eris*
		3	fú*erit*	potú*erit*	volú*erit*	nōlú*erit*	mālú*erit*
	Plural	1	fu*érimus*	potu*érimus*	volu*érimus*	nōlu*érimus*	mālu*érimus*
		2	fu*éritis*	potu*éritis*	volu*éritis*	nōlu*éritis*	mālu*éritis*
		3	fú*erint*	potú*erint*	volú*erint*	nōlú*erint*	mālú*erint*
Pluperfect	Singular	1	fuíss*em*	potuíss*em*	voluíss*em*	nōluíss*em*	māluíss*em*
		2	fuíss*ēs*	posuíss*ēs*	voluíss*ēs*	nōluíss*ēs*	māluíss*ēs*
		3	fuíss*et*	potuíss*et*	voluíss*et*	nōluíss*et*	māluíss*et*
	Plural	1	fuiss*émus*	potuiss*émus*	voluiss*émus*	nōluiss*émus*	māluiss*émus*
		2	fuiss*étis*	potuiss*étis*	voluiss*étis*	nōluiss*étis*	māluiss*étis*
		3	fuíss*ent*	potuíss*ent*	voluíss*ent*	nōluíss*ent*	māluíss*ent*

Present	Singular	1	fér*am*	fér*ar*	fí*am*	é*am*
		2	fér*ās*	fer*áris*	fí*ās*	é*ās*
		3	fér*at*	fer*átur*	fí*at*	é*at*
	Plural	1	fer*ámus*	fer*ámur*	fi*ámus*	e*ámus*
		2	fer*átis*	fer*áminī*	fi*átis*	e*átis*
		3	fér*ant*	fer*ántur*	fí*ant*	é*ant*
Imperfect	Singular	1	férr*em*	férr*er*	fíer*em*	ír*em*
		2	férr*ēs*	ferr*éris*	fíer*ēs*	ír*ēs*
		3	férr*et*	ferr*étur*	fíer*et*	ír*et*
	Plural	1	ferr*émus*	ferr*émur*	fier*émus*	īr*émus*
		2	ferr*étis*	ferr*éminī*	fier*étis*	īr*étis*
		3	férr*ent*	ferr*éntur*	fíer*ent*	ír*ent*
Perfect	Singular	1	túl*erim*	látus sim	fáctus sim	í*erim*
		2	túl*eris*	látus sīs	fáctus sīs	í*eris*
		3	túl*erit*	látus sit	fáctus sit	í*erit*
	Plural	1	tul*érimus*	látī símus	fáctī símus	i*érimus*
		2	tul*éritis*	látī sítis	fáctī sítis	i*éritis*
		3	túl*erint*	látī sint	fáctī sint	í*erint*
Pluperfect	Singular	1	tulíss*em*	látus éssem	fáctus éssem	íss*em*
		2	tulíss*ēs*	látus éssēs	fáctus éssēs	íss*ēs*
		3	tulíss*et*	látus ésset	fáctus ésset	íss*et*
	Plural	1	tuliss*émus*	látī essémus	fáctī essémus	īss*émus*
		2	tuliss*étis*	látī essétis	fáctī essétis	īss*étis*
		3	tulíss*ent*	látī éssent	fáctī éssent	íss*ent*

Note: the perfect subjunctive of **eō** may be **ierim**, etc., as above, or **īverim**.
The pluperfect subjunctive of **eō** may be **īssem**, etc., as above, or **īvissem**.

XXII.　Participles of Non-deponent Verbs

		Active	Passive
Present	1	párāns, parántis	
	2	hábēns, habéntis	
	3	míttēns, mitténtis	
	-iō	iáciēns, iaciéntis	
	4	aúdiēns, audiéntis	
Perfect	1		parátus, -a, -um
	2		hábitus, -a, -um
	3		míssus, -a, -um
	-iō		iáctus, -a, -um
	4		audítus, -a, -um
Future	1	parātū́rus, -a, -um	
	2	habitū́rus, -a, -um	
	3	missū́rus, -a, -um	
	-iō	iactū́rus, -a, -um	
	4	audītū́rus, -a, -um	

XXIII.　Participles of Deponent Verbs

Present Participle	1	cṓnāns, cōnántis
	2	vérēns, veréntis
	3	lóquēns, loquéntis
	-iō	ēgrédiēns, ēgrediéntis
	4	expériēns, experiéntis
Perfect Participle	1	cōnátus, -a, -um
	2	véritus, -a, -um
	3	locútus, -a, -um
	-iō	ēgréssus, -a, -um
	4	expértus, -a, -um
Future Participle	1	cōnātū́rus, -a, -um
	2	veritū́rus, -a, -um
	3	locūtū́rus, -a, -um
	-iō	ēgressū́rus, -a, -um
	4	expertū́rus, -a, -um

XXIV. Infinitives of Non-deponent Verbs

		Active	Passive
Present	1	paráre	parárī
	2	habére	habérī
	3	míttere	míttī
	-iō	iácere	iácī
	4	audíre	audírī
Perfect	1	parāvísse	parátus, -a, -um ésse
	2	habuísse	hábitus, -a, -um ésse
	3	mīsísse	míssus, -a, -um ésse
	-iō	iēcísse	iáctus, -a, -um ésse
	4	audīvísse	audítus, -a, -um ésse
Future	1	parātúrus, -a, -um ésse	
	2	habitúrus, -a, -um ésse	
	3	missúrus, -a, -um ésse	
	-iō	iactúrus, -a, -um ésse	
	4	audītúrus, -a, -um ésse	

XXV. Infinitives of Deponent Verbs

Present	1	cōnárī
	2	verérī
	3	lóquī
	-iō	égredī
	4	experírī
Perfect	1	cōnátus, -a, -um ésse
	2	véritus, -a, -um ésse
	3	locútus, -a, -um ésse
	-iō	ēgréssus, -a, -um ésse
	4	expértus, -a, -um ésse
Future	1	cōnātúrus, -a, -um ésse
	2	veritúrus, -a, -um ésse
	3	locūtúrus, -a, -um ésse
	-iō	ēgressúrus, -a, -um ésse
	4	expertúrus, -a, -um ésse

REFERENCE GRAMMAR

I. NOUNS

A. Nominative Case

1. Subject
A noun or pronoun in the nominative case may be the subject of a verb:

In pictūrā est **puella**.... (1:1)
*A **girl** is in the picture....*

2. Complement
A linking verb may be accompanied by a complement in the nominative case:

Cornēlia est **puella**.... (1:1)
*Cornelia is a **girl**....*

Cornēlia est **laeta**.... (1:2–3)
*Cornelia is **happy**....*

While the verb **esse** is the most common linking verb, the verbs in the following sentences are also classed as linking verbs and have complements in the nominative case:

"Quam **scelestus** ille caupō <u>vidētur</u>!" (21:22)
*"How **wicked** that innkeeper <u>seems</u>!"*

"'Nōn sine causā tū <u>vocāris</u> **Pseudolus**.'" (31:23)
*"'Not without reason <u>are you called</u> **Pseudolus**.'"*

"Quis <u>creābitur</u> **arbiter** bibendī?" (34:4)
*"Who <u>will be chosen</u> **master** of the drinking?"*

<u>Fit</u> in diēs **molestior**. (34h:16)
*"He <u>becomes</u> **more troublesome** every day."*

B. Genitive Case (see Book I-A, page 80)
The genitive case usually relates or attaches one noun to another.

1. Genitive of Possession

...vīlicus ipse <u>vīllam</u> **dominī** cūrat. (11:3)
*...the overseer himself looks after the <u>country house</u> **of the master**.*

2. Genitive with Adjectives
Words or phrases in the genitive case may be found with certain adjectives, especially those having to do with fullness:

Brevī tempore ārea est <u>plēna</u> **servōrum** et **ancillārum**.... (11:4)
*In a short time the threshing-floor is <u>full</u> **of slaves and slave-women**....*

3. Partitive Genitive
A word or phrase in the genitive case may indicate the whole of which something is a part (see Book I-B, page 95):

"Nihil **malī**," inquit. (21:7)
"*Nothing **of a bad thing**,*" he said.
"*Nothing bad*" or "*There is nothing wrong.*"

Crās satis **temporis** habēbimus. (23f:14)
*Tomorrow we will have enough **(of) time.***

With numbers and the words **paucī**, *a few*, **quīdam**, *a certain*, and **nūllus**, *no, no one*, the preposition **ex** or **dē** with the ablative is used:

ūnus ē **praedōnibus** (26:24)
*one **of the robbers***

The partitive genitive is used with superlative adjectives and adverbs (see Book II-A, pages 64 and 76):

Titus erat bibendī arbiter pessimus **omnium**. (34:24)
*Titus was the worst master of the drinking **of all.***

Hic puer optimē **omnium** scrībit. (35h:2)
*This boy writes best **of all.***

4. Genitive of Indefinite Value
The genitive case may be found in statements or questions of the general value of something (compare this with the ablative of price, below):

"'**Quantī**,' inquit Pseudolus, 'est illa perna?'" (31:7–8)
"'***How much**,' says Pseudolus, 'is that ham?'*"

C. Dative Case
1. Indirect Object of Transitive Verbs
A word or phrase in the dative case may indicate the indirect object of transitive verbs, especially verbs of "giving," "telling," or "showing" (see Book I-B, pages 52–53 and 55 and Exercise 22d):

...servī cistās Cornēliōrum **raedāriō** trādidērunt. (22:2)
*...the slaves handed the chests of the Cornelii over **to the coachman.***

2. Dative with Intransitive Verbs
Intransitive verbs and verbs that may be transitive but are used without a direct object may be accompanied by words or phrases in the dative case (see Book I-B, page 55):

Aulus **Septimō** clāmāvit. (21:8–9)
*Aulus shouted **to Septimus.***

3. Dative with Intransitive Compound Verbs
   Many intransitive compound verbs are accompanied by words or phrases in the dative case (see Book I-B, pages 78–79):

   Iam **urbī** appropinquābant. (22:12)
   *Already <u>they were coming near to/approaching</u> **the city**.*

4. Dative with Special Intransitive Verbs (see Book I-B, page 119)
   The dative case is used with special intransitive verbs such as **cōn-fīdere**, *to trust*, **favēre**, *to (give) favor (to)*, *to (give) support (to)*, **nocēre**, *to do harm (to)*, and **placēre**, *to please*:

   Ego **russātīs** <u>favēbō</u>. (27:25)
   *I <u>will give favor</u> **to the reds**.*
   *I <u>will favor</u> **the reds**.*

5. Dative with Impersonal Verbal Phrases and Impersonal Verbs
   The dative case is found with impersonal verbal phrases such as **necesse est** and with impersonal verbs (see Book I-B, page 56):

   "**Nōbīs** <u>necesse est</u> statim discēdere." (9:13–14)
   *"<u>It is necessary</u> **for us** to leave immediately."*

   "<u>Licet</u>ne **nōbīs**," inquit Marcus, "hīc cēnāre?" (20:7)
   *"<u>Is it allowed</u> **for us**," said Marcus, "to dine here?"*
   "May we dine here?"

6. Dative with Verbs of Taking Away or Depriving
   A word in the dative case sometimes denotes the person or thing from which something is taken:

   Mihi <u>est adēmptum</u> baculum.... (35:20)
   *(My) stick <u>was taken away</u> **from me**....*

7. Dative of Possession
   When found with a form of the verb **esse,** the dative case may indicate possession; the thing possessed is the subject of the clause and the person who possesses it is in the dative:

   ...servus quīdam **cui** nōmen <u>est</u> Pseudolus. (31:5–6)
   *...a certain slave, **to whom** the name <u>is</u> Pseudolus.*
   ...whose name is Pseudolus.
   ...who has the name Pseudolus.

8. Dative of Purpose
   A noun in the dative case may express purpose:

   Hanc pūpam fīliae Dāvī **dōnō** dabō. (46:19–20)
   *I will give this doll to the daughter of Davus **to serve as a gift**.*
   *I will give this doll **as a gift** to the daughter of Davus.*

9. Double Dative

Two datives may be used together in what is called the double dative construction. One of the datives is a dative of reference, denoting the person or thing concerned, and the other is a dative of purpose:

Omnēs **spectātōribus admīrātiōnī** fuērunt leōnēs. (49:1–2)
*All the lions were **a source of amazement with reference to the spectators**.*
*All the lions were **a source of amazement to the spectators**.*

10. Dative of Agent

With the passive periphrastic conjugation (see V. D, Gerundive or Future Passive Participle, below), consisting of the gerundive and a form of the verb **esse**, the person by whom the thing is to be done is regularly denoted by the dative, not by **ab** and the ablative:

"Nunc...domum **nōbīs** redeundum est." (48:20)
*"Now...there must be a returning home **by us**."*
"Now...we must return home."

D. Accusative Case

1. Direct Object

A word or phrase in the accusative case may be the direct object of a transitive verb (see Book I-A, pages 20 and 40–41):

Sextus...semper **Cornēliam** vexat. (4:1)
*Sextus...is always annoying **Cornelia**.*

2. Double or Predicate Accusative

Verbs of naming, electing, making, and asking often take two accusatives, the first the direct object and the second a predicate to that object:

Cēterōs...puerōs semper **facillima**, **mē** semper **difficillima** rogat. (40:18)

*He always (asks) **the other boys very easy things**, **me** he always asks **very difficult things**.*

3. Accusative with Prepositions

The accusative case is used with certain prepositions, especially those expressing motion toward or into or through (see Book I-A, page 64):

ad **vīllam**, *to/toward* **the country house** (2:7)
in **piscīnam**, *into* **the fishpond** (3:8)
per **agrōs**, *through* **the fields** (9:1)

Prepositional phrases with the accusative case may also indicate the vicinity in which someone or something is located:

prope **rīvum** (5:3)
near **the stream**
…iānitor <u>ad</u> **iānuam** vīllae dormit. (9:3)
…the doorkeeper sleeps <u>near/at</u> **the door** *of the country house.*

4. Accusative of Place to Which without a Preposition
With names of cities, towns, small islands, and the words **domus** and **rūs**, the idea of place to which is expressed by the accusative case without a preposition (see Book II-A, pages 118–120):

Rōmam festīnāvit.
He hurried **to Rome**.

Domum iit.
He went **home**.

Rūs proficīscitur.
He sets out **for the country**.

5. Accusative of Duration of Time
Words or phrases in the accusative case without a preposition may indicate duration of time (see Book II-A, page 121):

Iam **multōs diēs** in scaphā erāmus…. (42:38)
We had already been in the boat **for many days**….

6. Adverbial Accusative
A word in the accusative case may be used as an adverb:

Multum et diū clāmat lanius, sed Pseudolus **nihil** respondet. (31:25)
The butcher shouts **a lot** *and for a long time, but Pseudolus makes* **no** *reply.*

7. Exclamatory Accusative
The accusative case is used in exclamations:

"**Ō mē miseram!**" (9:18)   *"Poor me!"*

8. For the accusative and infinitive, see IX.D–F below.

E. Ablative Case
1. Ablative of Respect
A noun or phrase in the ablative may denote that with respect to which something is or is done:

In pictūrā est puella, **nōmine** Cornēlia. (1:1)
In the picture is a girl, Cornelia **with respect to her name**.
In the picture is a girl, Cornelia **by name/called** *Cornelia.*

2. Ablative of Time When
   A noun or phrase in the ablative case without a preposition may indicate time when:

   Etiam in pictūrā est vīlla rūstica ubi Cornēlia **aestāte** habitat. (1:2)
   *Also in the picture is the country house and farm where Cornelia lives **in summer**.*

3. Ablative of Time within Which
   A noun or phrase in the ablative case without a preposition may indicate time within which:

   Brevī tempore Cornēlia est dēfessa. (2:4–5)
   ***In/Within a short time** Cornelia is tired.*

4. Ablative of Instrument, Means, or Cause
   A word or phrase in the ablative case without a preposition may indicate the means by which, the instrument with which, or the cause on account of which an action is carried out or a person or thing is in a certain state (see Book I-A, page 91, Book I-B, page 79, and Book II-A, pages 34–35):

   Dāvus eum **tunicā** <u>arripit</u> et **baculō** <u>verberat</u>. (means, instrument, 12:17–18)
   *Davus <u>grabs hold of</u> him **by the tunic** and <u>beats</u> him **with his stick**.*

   Tuā culpā raeda <u>est in fossā</u>. (cause, 14:7)
   ***Because of your fault** the carriage <u>is in the ditch</u>.*
   It's your fault that the carriage is in the ditch.

   The ablative of instrument, means, or cause is often used with passive verbs (see Book II-A, page 35):

   …nam interdiū nihil intrā urbem **vehiculō** <u>portātur</u>. (29:3–4)
   *…for during the day nothing <u>is carried</u> **by a vehicle** within the city.*

5. Ablative of Agent
   If the action of a passive verb is carried out by a person, the ablative of agent is used, consisting of the preposition **ā** or **ab** with the ablative case (see Book II-A, page 35):

   …māter et fīlia **ā servīs** per urbem <u>ferēbantur</u>. (29:1–2)
   *…the mother and her daughter <u>were being carried</u> through the city **by slaves**.*

6. Ablative of Manner

A phrase consisting of a noun and adjective in the ablative case may be used with or without the preposition **cum** to indicate how something happens or is done (see Book II-A, page 34):

Tum venit Dāvus ipse et, "Tacēte, omnēs!" **magnā vōce/magnā cum vōce** <u>clāmat</u>. (11:6)
*Then Davus himself comes, and <u>he shouts</u> **in a loud voice**, "Be quiet, everyone!"*

The ablative of manner may consist of a single noun with **cum**:

Caupō iam **cum rīsū** <u>clāmāvit</u>.... (19:17)
*Now **with a laugh/jokingly** the innkeeper <u>shouted</u>....*

Occasionally the ablative of manner may consist of a noun in the ablative case without an accompanying adjective or **cum**:

Tum ego **silentiō** ingressus.... (42:34)
*Then I having entered **silently**....*

7. Ablative of Price

The ablative case is used to refer to the specific price of something (compare this with the genitive of indefinite value, above):

"Itaque tibi **decem dēnāriīs** eum vēndam." (31:17–18)
*"Therefore I will sell it to you **for ten denarii**."*

8. Ablative of Comparison

The ablative of comparison may be found with comparative adjectives and adverbs (see Book II-A, pages 72 and 76):

Mārtiālis **Eucleide** est multō <u>prūdentior</u>. (35d:4)
*Martial is much <u>wiser</u> **than** Eucleides.*

Sextus paulō <u>celerius</u> **Marcō** currere potest. (35h:4)
*Sextus can run a little <u>faster</u> **than** Marcus.*

9. Ablative of Degree of Difference

The ablative case is used to express the degree of difference with comparative adjectives, adverbs, and other words implying comparison (see Book II-A, pages 72 and 76):

"Quam libenter eum rūrsus vidēbō! Sānē tamen **multō** <u>libentius</u> tē vidēbō ubi tū Rōmam veniēs!" (36:10–11)
*"How gladly I will see him again! But of course I will see you **much** <u>more gladly/more gladly</u> **by much** when you come to Rome!"*

Multīs <u>post</u> **annīs**...pervēnit. (39c:3)
*"He arrived...**many years** <u>later/later</u> **by many years**.*

10. Ablative of Separation
   Verbs or adjectives implying separation are often accompanied by words or phrases in the ablative, sometimes with **ab** or **ex** and sometimes without a preposition, to express the thing from which something is separated or free:

   ...vir **vīnō** <u>abstinentissimus</u>! (34h:28)
   *...a man <u>most abstinent</u> **from wine**!*

11. Ablative with Prepositions
   The ablative case is used with certain prepositions, especially those expressing motion from or out of, place where, and accompaniment (see Book I-A, pages 64 and 90):

   <u>ab</u> **urbe**, <u>*from*</u> ***the city*** (13:12)   <u>in</u> **pictūrā**, <u>*in*</u> ***the picture*** (1:1)
   <u>ē</u> **silvā**, <u>*out of*</u> ***the woods*** (5:12)   <u>sub</u> **arbore**, <u>*under*</u> ***the tree*** (1:3)
   <u>ex</u> **agrīs**, <u>*out of*</u> ***the fields*** (2:7)   <u>cum</u> **canibus**, <u>*with*</u> ***dogs*** (12:9)

12. Ablative of Place from Which without a Preposition
   With names of cities, towns, small islands, and the words **domus** and **rūs**, the idea of place from which is expressed by the ablative case without a preposition (see Book II-A, page 119):

   Brundisiō...proficīscētur.... (36:8–9)
   *He will set out **from Brundisium**....*

   Domō/Rūre profectus est.
   *He set out **from home/from the country**.*

13. Ablative of Description
   A noun and adjective in the ablative case may be used without a preposition to describe another noun:

   [Vergilius] semper **īnfirmā** erat **valētūdine**. (39f:9–10)
   *[Vergil] was always **of weak health**.*

14. Ablative Absolute
   A noun (or pronoun) and a participle in the ablative case form an ablative absolute, an adverbial phrase separate from the rest of the sentence and often set off with commas (see Book II-B, page 15). Ablatives absolute are best translated in English with clauses introduced by *when*, *although*, *since*, or *if*.

   Titus..., **pecūniā datā**, in vestibulum ingressus est. (43:4)
   *Titus..., **<u>with his money having been given</u>**, entered the vestibule.*
   *...**<u>after paying his entrance fee</u>**,...*

   Fūre vestīmenta **surripiente**, Sextus in apodytērium ingrediēbātur.
   ***<u>While the thief was stealing</u>** the clothes, Sextus was entering the changing room.*

Since classical Latin has no present participle for the verb **esse,** ablatives absolute sometimes consist only of two nouns in the ablative case or a noun and an adjective:

Titō prīncipe....   **Sextō aegrō....**
Titus (being) Emperor....   *Sextus (being) sick....*
When Titus is (was) Emperor....   *Since Sextus is (was) sick....*

F. Vocative Case
The vocative case is used when addressing a person or persons directly (see Book I-A, page 56):

"Dēscende, **Sexte**!" (4:6)
*"Come down, **Sextus!**"*

"Abīte, **molestī**!" (3:8–9)
*"Go away, **pests!**"*

G. Locative Case
The locative case is used to indicate place where with names of cities, towns, small islands, and the words **domus** and **rūs** (see Book II-A, pages 119–120):

Rōmae *at Rome*, **Brundisiī** *at Brundisium*, **Carthāginī** *at Carthage*, **Baiīs** *at Baiae*, **domī** *at home*, and **rūrī** *in the country*

II. ADJECTIVES

A. Agreement
Adjectives agree with the nouns they modify in gender, number, and case (see Book I-B, pages 5–6)

B. Adjectives Translated as Adverbs
Adjectives may sometimes best be translated as adverbs:

Brevī tempore, ubi Marcus advenit, eum **laetae** excipiunt. (5:12–13)
*In a short time, when Marcus arrives, they welcome him **happily**.*

C. Adjectives as Substantives
Adjectives may be used as substantives, i.e., as nouns (see Book I-B, page 66):

"Abīte, **molestī**!" (3:8–9)
*"Go away, **pests!**"*

Multa et **mīra** vidēbunt puerī. (23:12)
*The boys will see **many** (and) **wonderful (things)**.*

D. Comparison of Adjectives
Adjectives occur in positive, comparative, and superlative degrees (see Book II-A, pages 64 and 65). For an example of a comparative adjective, see **prūdentior** in I.E.8 above, and for an example of a superlative adjective, see **pessimus** in I.B.3 above.

Instead of following the rules given in Book II-A, page 65, a few adjectives form their comparative and superlative degrees with the adverbs **magis** and **maximē**:

Paulātim igitur fīēbat **magis ēbrius?** (34h:21)
*Did he therefore gradually become **more drunk?***

Statim factus est **maximē ēbrius**…. (34h:22)
*Suddenly he became **very drunk**.*

Comparative adjectives may be used with **quam** or with the ablative case to express the comparison (see Book II-A, pages 64 and 72):

"Quis enim est prūdentior **quam** Gaius?" (34:7)
"Quis enim est prūdentior **Gaiō**?"
*"For who is wiser **than** Gaius?"*

Mārtiālis est multō prūdentior **quam** Eucleidēs.
Mārtiālis **Eucleide** est multō prūdentior. (35d:4)
*Martial is much wiser **than** Eucleides.*

Superlative adjectives may be used with the partitive genitive, see I.B.3 above.

III. ADVERBS

A. Adverbs may modify verbs, other adverbs, or adjectives (see Book I-A, pages 100–101):

Laeta est Flāvia quod Cornēlia **iam** in vīllā <u>habitat</u>. (1:5)
*Flavia is happy because Cornelia <u>is</u> **now** <u>living</u> in the country house.*

Scrībe **quam** <u>saepissimē</u>. (36:25)
*Write **as** <u>often</u> **as possible**.*

"**Valdē** <u>dēfessī</u>," respondit Cornēlius. (23:9)
*"**Very** <u>tired</u>," replied Cornelius.*

B. Comparison of Adverbs
Adverbs occur in positive, comparative, and superlative degrees (see Book II-A, pages 74–76). For an example of a comparative adverb, see **celerius** in I.E.8 above, and for an example of a superlative adverb, see **optimē** in I.B.3 above.

The comparative adverb may be used with **quam** or with the ablative case:

Nēmō celerius **quam** frāter meus currere potest. (35h:3)
*No one is able to run faster **than** my brother.*

Sextus celerius **Marcō** currere potest. (35h:4)
*Sextus is able to run faster **than** Marcus.*

The superlative adverb may be used with a partitive genitive, see I.B.3 above.

IV. VERBS

A. Function
Verbs may be divided into three types according to their function in the sentence or clause:
1. Linking verbs connect a subject with a predicate noun or adjective:

   Cornēlia **est** puella Rōmāna. (1:1)   *Cornelia **is** a Roman girl.*

   For other examples, see I.A.2 above.

2. Intransitive verbs describe actions that do not take direct objects:

   Cornēlia...in Italiā **habitat**. (1:1–2)   *Cornelia **lives** in Italy.*

3. Transitive verbs describe actions that take direct objects:

   Sextus...semper Cornēliam **vexat**. (4:1)
   *Sextus...always **annoys** Cornelia.*

B. Voice
1. Active and Passive
   Verbs may be either active or passive in voice. In the active voice the subject performs the action of the verb; in the passive voice the subject receives the action of the verb (see Book II-A, pages 23–24, 33, and 42–43):

   Incolae omnia **agunt**. (active, Book II-A, page 23)
   *The tenants **are doing** everything.*

   Ab incolīs omnia **aguntur**. (passive, Book II-A, page 23)
   *Everything **is being done** by the tenants.*

2. Deponent Verbs
   Some verbs, called deponent, are passive in form but active in meaning (see Book II-A, pages 98–100):

   Subitō **collāpsus est**. (34:22)   *Suddenly **he collapsed**.*

3. Semi-deponent Verbs
   Some verbs, such as **audeō**, **audēre**, **ausus sum**, have regular active forms with active meanings in the present, imperfect, and future tenses but have passive forms with active meanings in the perfect, pluperfect, and future perfect tenses (see Book II-A, pages 132–133):

   Tum Marcus arborem ascendit neque dēsilīre **ausus est**.
   (40:10–11)
   *Then Marcus climbed a tree and **did** not **dare** jump down.*

4. Impersonal Passive
   Verbs may be used impersonally in the passive, with an implied subject *it*, to place emphasis on the action itself rather than on any of the participants in it:

   Complūrēs hōrās ācriter **pugnābātur**.... (48:18)
   *For several hours **it was fought** fiercely....*
   ***The fight went on** fiercely for several hours....*

5. Impersonal Verbs
   See Book II-B, pages 116–117, and IX.c, Uses of the Infinitive, below.

C. Tenses of the Indicative
   1. Present
      The present tense describes an action or a state of being in present time (see Book I-A, page 73):

      In pictūrā **est** puella...quae in Italiā **habitat**. (1:1–2)
      *In the picture **is** a girl...who **lives** in Italy.*

   2. Vivid or Historic Present
      Sometimes a writer will switch to the present tense while describing past events; this is called the vivid or historic present and helps make the reader feel personally involved in the narrative (see Book II-A, page 23).

   3. Imperfect
      The imperfect tense (see Book I-A, page 106) describes a continuing, repeated, or habitual action or state of being in past time:

      Ego et Marcus **spectābāmus** cisium. (continuing action, 14:10)
      *Marcus and I **were watching** the carriage.*

      Cornēlius...Syrum identidem **iubēbat** equōs incitāre.
      (repeated action, 13:1–2)
      *Cornelius **kept ordering** Syrus again and again to spur on the horses.*

      Dāvus in Britanniā **habitābat**. (habitual action)
      *Davus **used to live** in Britain.*

The imperfect tense may also indicate the beginning of an action in past time (see Book I-A, page 107):

Equōs ad raedam nostram **dēvertēbat**. (14:11)
*He **began to turn** the horses **aside** in the direction of our carriage.*

The imperfect tense with **iam** and an expression of duration of time is often best translated in English with a pluperfect:

Iam <u>multōs diēs</u> in scaphā **erāmus** cum ā mercātōribus quibusdam inventī sumus. (42:38)
*We **had already been** in the boat <u>for many days</u> when we were found by certain merchants.*

4. Future
The future tense indicates an action that will take place at some time subsequent to the present (see Book I-B, page 67):

"Brevī tempore ad Portam Capēnam **adveniēmus**...." (22:26)
*"In a short time **we will arrive** at the Porta Capena...."*

5. Perfect System
The perfect, pluperfect, and future perfect tenses are formed from the perfect stem, which is derived from the third principal part of the verb.

a. The perfect tense refers to an action that happened or that someone did in past time or to an action completed as of present time (see Book I-B, pages 16–17):

Eō ipsō tempore ad iānuam caupōnae **appāruit** homō obēsus... (18:12)
*At that very moment a fat man **appeared** at the door of the inn....*

"Servī meī alium lectum tibi **parāvērunt**." (19:17–18)
*"My slaves **have prepared** another bed for you."*

b. The pluperfect tense describes an action that was completed prior to some other action in the past (see Book I-B, page 79):

Titus in itinere mōnstrāvit puerīs mīra aedificia quae prīncipēs in Palātīnō **aedificāverant**. (24:19–20)
*Along the way Titus showed the boys the wonderful buildings that the emperors **had built** on the Palatine.*

c. The future perfect tense describes an action that will have been completed before another action in future time begins (see Book I-B, page 84):

"Cum **intrāverimus**, tandem aurīgās ipsōs spectābimus." (26:17–18)
*"When we **enter/will have entered**, we will finally watch the charioteers themselves."*

D. Mood

1. Indicative Mood

    The term *indicative mood* refers to a set of verb forms that are used to express statements or questions of fact in main clauses and statements of fact in many subordinate clauses:

    "Cum **intrāverimus**, tandem aurīgās ipsōs **spectābimus**." (26:17–18)
    *"When **we enter/will have entered**, we **will** finally **watch** the charioteers themselves."*

2. Imperative Mood

    The imperative mood is used to express a command (see Book I-A, page 74):

    "**Abīte**, molestī!" (3:8–9)
    *"**Go away**, pests!"*

    A negative command is expressed by **nōlī/nōlīte** and the infinitive:

    "**Nōlī** servōs **excitāre**!" (9:9)
    *"**Don't wake up** the slaves!"*

3. Subjunctive Mood

    The term *subjunctive mood* refers to a set of verb forms that you have seen used in certain types of subordinate clauses: **cum** causal clauses, **cum** circumstantial clauses, indirect questions, result clauses, purpose clauses, and indirect commands (see below). This mood gets its name from the Latin elements **sub-**, *under*, and **iūnct-**, *joined*, because verbs in this mood are often found in subordinate clauses, i.e., clauses that are "joined under" the main clause. In such clauses the subjunctive is often not translated any differently from the way a verb in the corresponding tense of the indicative would be translated. (For examples, see below.)

4. Subjunctive in Main Clauses

    a. Hortatory Subjunctive

       The present subjunctive may be used in main clauses for a variety of purposes. One is to issue commands. When commands are addressed by speakers to themselves and those with them, we call them exhortations, and we label the subjunctive hortatory:

       "Nunc in palaestram **exeāmus**," inquit. (44:6)
       *"Now **let us go out** into the exercise-ground," he said.*

b. Potential Subjunctive
The subjunctive may be used in a main clause that stands by itself but implies a larger sentence in the form of a condition that would require the subjunctive:

"Ego nōn **crēdidissem** tot hominēs amphitheātrō continērī posse." (48d:4)
"I would not have believed that so many men could be held (in) the amphitheater."

The larger conditional sentence would have been: *If I had not seen it for myself, I would not have believed....*

V. PARTICIPLES

A. Present Participles (see Book II-A, pages 133–134)
1. Participles as Verbal Adjectives
Participles are verbal adjectives and may modify nouns:

Nunc cōnspicit <u>poētam</u> versūs **recitantem**. (29:5)
*Now she catches sight of a <u>poet</u> **reciting** verses.*

Since the participle is a verbal adjective, it may take a direct object of its own; in the sentence above **versūs** is the object of the participle **recitantem**.

2. Participles as Substantives
Present active participles are frequently used as substantives (nouns) (see Book II-A, page 134):

"Cavēte!" exclāmant **adstantēs**.... (29:9–10)
*"Watch out!" shout **the bystanders**....*

B. Perfect Participles as Adjectives
Perfect participles often modify the subject of the verb of the clause (see Book II-A, pages 50–51):

Itaque coquus **vocātus** ab omnibus laudātus est. (33:26)
*Therefore the cook, **having been summoned**, was praised by everyone.*
See Book II-A, page 51 for alternative translations.

...inde **regressus**...in hortō labōrābam. (40:6–7)
*...**having returned** from there...I worked in the garden.*

Perfect participles may also modify other elements in the sentence, for example, the direct object (see Book II-B, page 14):

Coquum vocātum omnēs laudāvērunt.
*They all praised <u>the cook</u> **who had been summoned**.*
When the cook had been summoned, they all praised him.

C. Future Active Participles

The future active participle, translated *going to*, *likely to*, *intending to*, *determined to*, *on the point of...-ing*, may modify a noun (see Book II-B, page 22):

Thisbē, iam moritūra, "Ō mē miseram!" clāmat. (45:25)
*Thisbe, now **about to die**, cries, "Poor me!"*

It may also be used in a verbal phrase with any tense of the verb **esse**; this is called the active periphrastic:

Marcum tamen mēcum **sum ductūrus**. (47:16–17)
*However, **I am intending to take** Marcus with me.*

D. Gerundive or Future Passive Participle

The gerundive is a verbal adjective that appears in all genders, numbers, and cases. It is future and passive in meaning and is often called a future passive participle. It will be formally introduced in Book III.

Sometimes it is used as a simple adjective:

"Minimē, ō puer **abominande**! Hesperia est Italia." (39:16)
*"No, **horrible** child! Hesperia is Italy."*

Sometimes it is used with some form of the verb **esse** to express obligation or necessity. This is called the passive periphrastic. In the following sentence **cōnficienda** is the gerundive of **cōnficere**.

"Nunc haec epistula **est cōnficienda**." (47:23)
*"Now this letter **must be finished**."*

VI. GERUNDS

The gerund is a neuter verbal noun that appears in the genitive, dative, accusative, and ablative singular only. It will be formally introduced in Book III. Gerunds are translated as verbal nouns in English:

"Quis creābitur arbiter **bibendī**?" (34:4)
*"Who will be made master **of the drinking**?"*

VII. SENTENCES

A. Agreement

The subject and verb of a sentence must agree in number; a singular subject takes a singular verb, and a plural subject, a plural verb:

Cornēlia est puella Rōmāna.... (1:1)
Cornelia is a Roman girl....

Cornēlia et Flāvia sunt puellae Rōmānae.... (2:1–2)
Cornelia and Flavia are Roman girls....

B. Questions
1. Questions may be introduced by many interrogative words:

   Quid facit Cornēlia?   ***What** is Cornelia doing?*

2. Questions may also be introduced by the particle **-ne** attached to the end of the first word (often the verb) of the question:

   Est**ne** puer ignāvus? (5:4)   *Is the boy cowardly?*

3. Questions that expect the answer "yes" are introduced with **nōnne**:

   "**Nōnne** cēnāre vultis?" (19:2)   *"**Surely** you want to eat, **don't you?**"*

C. Coordinating Conjunctions
Conjunctions are words that join together (Latin **con-,** *together* + **iungere,** *to join*) sentences or elements within a sentence. Coordinating conjunctions join elements that are simply added to one another and are of equal grammatical importance (Latin **co-,** *together, same* + **ōrdō,** *order, rank*):

Cornēlia sedet **et** legit. (1:3)
*Cornelia sits **and** reads.*

Etiam Sextus dormit **neque** Cornēliam vexat. (6:2)
*Even Sextus is sleeping **and** is **not** annoying Cornelia.*

Marcus **neque** ignāvus **neque** temerārius est. (5:5–6)
*Marcus is **neither** cowardly **nor** rash.*

Hodiē puellae nōn sedent **sed** in agrīs ambulant. (2:2–3)
*Today the girls are not sitting **but** are walking in the fields.*

Servī in vīllā sedent, **nam** dēfessī sunt. (8c:8)
*The slaves are sitting in the country house, **for** they are tired.*

Sextus est puer molestus quī semper Cornēliam vexat. Cornēlia **igitur** Sextum nōn amat. (4:1–2)
*Sextus is an annoying boy who always annoys Cornelia. Cornelia, **therefore**, does not like Sextus.*

VIII. SUBORDINATE CLAUSES
A clause is a group of words containing a verb. The following sentence contains two clauses, each of which is said to be a main clause because each could stand by itself as a complete sentence:

Rīdent Marcus et Cornēlia, sed nōn rīdet Sextus. (4:10–11)
Marcus and Cornelia laugh, but Sextus does not laugh.

Subordinate (Latin **sub-**, *below* + **ōrdō**, *order, rank*) clauses are clauses that are of less grammatical importance than the main clause in a sentence. They are sometimes called dependent (Latin **dē-**, *down from* + **pendēre**, *to hang*) clauses because they hang down from the main clause and cannot stand by themselves. They are joined to the main clause by pronouns, adverbs, or subordinating conjunctions.

A. Adjectival Subordinate Clauses with Verbs in the Indicative
   Subordinate clauses are modifiers. They may be descriptive, like adjectives, and modify nouns:

Cornēlia est puella Rōmāna **quae** in Italiā habitat. (1:1–2)
*Cornelia is a Roman girl, **who lives in Italy**.*

Etiam in pictūrā est vīlla rūstica **ubi** Cornēlia aestāte habitat. (1:2)
*Also in the picture is a country house and farm **where Cornelia lives in the summer**.*

The relative pronoun (**quī, quae, quod**) introduces relative clauses, as in the first example above, and agrees with its antecedent in number and gender; its case depends on its use in its own clause (see Book II-A, pages 4–5):

Deinde īrā commōtus servum petit ā **quō** porcus aufūgit. (29:11–12)
*Then in a rage he goes after the slave **from whom the pig escaped**.*

The relative pronoun **quō** is masculine and singular because of the gender and number of its antecedent, **servus**; it is ablative because of its use with the preposition **ā** in its own clause.

Omnia **quae** videt Cornēlia eam dēlectant. (29:5)
*Everything **that Cornelia sees** pleases her.*

The relative pronoun **quae** is neuter and plural because of the gender and number of its antecedent, **omnia**; it is accusative because of its use as the direct object of **videt** in its own clause.

"...īre ad mercātōrem quendam **cuius** taberna nōn procul abest...." (28:10)
*"...to go to a certain merchant **whose shop is not far away**...."*

The relative pronoun **cuius** is masculine and singular because of the gender and number of its antecedent, **mercātōrem quendam**; it is genitive because of its use as a possessive within its own clause *(whose shop)*.

B. Adverbial Subordinate Clauses with Verbs in the Indicative

In contrast to adjectival subordinate clauses described above, most subordinate clauses are adverbial, that is, they modify the verb of the main clause or the action of the main clause as a whole and are introduced by subordinating conjunctions that express ideas such as the following:

sī, condition:

> **Sī** <u>tū puer strēnuus es</u>, ascende arborem!
> ***If*** <u>*you are an energetic boy*</u>, *climb a tree!*

quamquam, concession:

> **Quamquam** <u>dominus abest</u>, necesse est nōbīs strēnuē labōrāre. (11:7)
> ***Although*** <u>*the master is away*</u>, *it is necessary for us to work hard.*

dum, **ubi**, **cum**, etc., time:

> **Dum** <u>Cornēlia legit</u>, Flāvia scrībit. (1:4–5)
> ***While*** <u>*Cornelia reads*</u>, *Flavia writes.*

> **Dum** <u>per viam ībant</u>, Aurēlia et Cornēlia spectābant rūstīcōs quī in agrīs labōrābant. (13:3–4)
> (**Dum** with the imperfect tense = *while/as long as.*)
> ***While/As long as*** *they were going along the road, Aurelia and Cornelia were looking at the peasants who were working in the fields.*

> **Dum** <u>puerī cibum dēvorant</u>, subitō intrāvit mīles quīdam. (20:13)
> ***While*** <u>*the boys were devouring*</u> *their food, a certain soldier suddenly entered.*
> (Here the present tense verb in the **dum** clause is to be translated with the English past tense that describes ongoing action.) (See Book I-B, page 27.)

> Puerī, <u>**ubi** clāmōrem audiunt</u>, statim ad puellās currunt. (5:10)
> *The boys,* <u>***when** they hear the shout*</u>, *immediately run to the girls.*

> Crās, <u>**ubi surgētis**</u>, puerī, clāmōrem et strepitum audiētis.
> *Tomorrow* <u>***when** you get up/will get up*</u>, *boys, you will hear shouting and noise.*

> **Cum** <u>intrāverimus</u>, tandem aurīgās ipsōs spectābimus. (26:17–18)
> ***When*** <u>*we enter/will have entered*</u>, *we will finally watch the charioteers themselves.*

> (While the verbs of the subordinate clauses are in the future, **surgētis**, and future perfect, **intrāverimus**, we translate them into English as presents; see Book I-B, page 84. The use of the tenses is more exact in Latin.)

quod, cause:

> Cornēlia est laeta **quod** iam in vīllā habitat. (1:2–3)
> *Cornelia is happy **because** she now lives in the country house.*

Conjunctions you have met that may introduce adverbial subordinate clauses with their verbs in the indicative are:

dum, *as long as* (15:1)
dum, *while* (20:13)
nisi, *if not, unless* (18:16)
postquam, *after* (21:10)
quamquam, *although* (11:7)
quod, *because* (1:3)
simulac, *as soon as* (24:1)
sī, *if* (5:1)
ubi, *when* (5:10)
ut, *as* (16:17)

C. Subordinate Clauses with Verbs in the Subjunctive
If a subordinate clause has its verb in the subjunctive, the tense of the subjunctive is determined by the following rules for the sequence of tenses (see Book II-B, pages 98–99):

When the verb in the main clause is in the present or a future tense (primary sequence), a present subjunctive in the subordinate clause indicates an action going on at the same time as (or after) that of the main verb, and a perfect subjunctive in the subordinate clause indicates an action that took place before that of the main verb.

When the verb in the main clause is in a past tense (secondary sequence), an imperfect subjunctive in the subordinate clause indicates an action going on at the same time as (or after) that of the main verb, and a pluperfect subjunctive indicates an action that took place before that of the main verb.

For examples, see Indirect Questions below.

Note that sometimes the perfect tense describes an action completed as of present time (e.g., *I have ordered*) instead of a simple past action (*I ordered*). In this case, primary sequence is followed:

"Dominus imperāvit ut iānua **claudātur**." (51c:10)
*"The master has ordered that the door **be closed**."*

Here the present instead of the imperfect subjunctive is used after the main verb in the perfect tense, because the perfect tense here clearly implies present time (*The master has ordered*).

D. Adverbial Subordinate Clauses with Verbs in the Subjunctive

1. **Cum** Causal Clauses

   Subordinate clauses that are introduced by the conjunction **cum** and have their verbs in the subjunctive may be **cum** causal clauses; **cum** is translated as *since* or *because*. Such clauses are adverbial and state the reason for the action of the main clause (see Book II-A, page 153):

   Magister nāvis, **cum** valdē **timēret**, suōs vetuit nōs adiuvāre. (42:17)
   *The captain of the ship, **since/because he was very frightened**, forbade his own men to help us.*

   Cum prīmā lūce **profectī essēmus**, iam dēfessī erāmus (43d:1).
   ***Since we had set** out at dawn, we were now tired.*

2. **Cum** Circumstantial Clauses

   Subordinate clauses that are introduced by the conjunction **cum** and have their verbs in the subjunctive may also be **cum** circumstantial clauses; **cum** is translated as *when*. Such clauses are adverbial and describe the circumstances that prevailed at the time of the action of the main clause (see Book II-A, page 153):

   Cum omnēs dormīrent, ego surrēxī. (42:30)
   ***When all were sleeping**, I got up.*

   Quō cum Titus **pervēnisset**, in vestibulum ingressus est. (43:4)
   ***When Titus had arrived** there, he entered the entrance hall.*

   Often only the context and sense will tell you whether **cum** is to be translated *since/because* or *when*.

3. Result Clauses

   The result of an action described in the main clause of a sentence may be expressed by an adverbial subordinate clause introduced by **ut** (positive) or **ut nōn** (negative); the present subjunctive is used in primary sequence and the imperfect subjunctive (or sometimes the perfect subjunctive) in secondary sequence. Result clauses are usually anticipated in the main clause by a word such as **adeō,** *so,* **sīc,** *thus, in this way,* **tālis,** *such,* **tam,** *so,* and **tantum,** *so, so much* (see Book II-B, pages 94–95 and 99 and the examples on the next page).

a. Primary sequence:

"Pater tantum temporis in tablīnō agit ut eum numquam videam." (50:3–4)
*"Father spends so much time in the study **that I never see him**."*

b. Secondary sequence with imperfect subjunctive, emphasizing the natural or logical connection between the main clause and the result (see Book II-B, page 99):

Cornēlia <u>adeō</u> perturbāta erat **ut** <u>vix loquī</u> **posset**. (50:20)
*Cornelia was <u>so</u> confused **that she was scarcely able to speak**.*

c. Secondary sequence with perfect subjunctive, emphasizing the fact that the result actually did take place:

Leō <u>tantus</u> et <u>tam</u> <u>ferōx</u> erat **ut** <u>servus metū exanimātus</u> **ceciderit.**
*The lion was **so large** and **so** fierce **that the slave fell down**, <u>paralyzed with fear</u>.*

d. Negative with **ut...nōn** (see Book II-B, page 95):

<u>Adeō</u> perturbāta est **ut** <u>loquī</u> **nōn possit.**
*She is <u>so</u> confused **that she cannot speak**.*

4. Purpose Clauses
The purpose for which the action described in the main clause of a sentence is undertaken may be expressed by an adverbial subordinate clause introduced by **ut** (positive) or **nē** (negative). Purpose clauses are sometimes translated with infinitives in English (see Book II-B, page 126):

Iānitor baculum habet **ut** <u>clientēs</u> **repellat**. (53b:2)
The doorkeeper has a stick <u>to drive off clients</u>.

Nova nūpta super līmen sublāta est **nē lāberētur**. (53:19)
*The bride was carried over the threshold **so she would not stumble**.*

E. Substantive Subordinate Clauses with Verbs in the Subjunctive
1. Indirect Questions (see Book II-A, pages 153–154 and Book II-B, pages 4–5 and 98)
Indirect questions are substantive or noun clauses that may serve as the object of the main verb of the sentence; their verbs are in the subjunctive. The examples on the next page illustrate the sequence of tenses (see C above) and show how direct questions become indirect:

Primary Sequence:

Direct question (present tense):

Cūr servae mē **neglegunt**?
*Why do the slave girls **neglect** me?*

Indirect question:

Nōn intellegō <u>cūr servae mē **neglegant**</u>.
*I do not understand <u>why the slaves girls **neglect** me</u>.*

Direct question (past tense):

Cūr servae mē **neglēxērunt**?
*Why **did** the slave girls **neglect** me?*

Indirect Question:

Nōn intellegō <u>cūr servae mē **neglēxerint**</u>.
*I do not understand <u>why the slave girls **neglected** me</u>.*

Secondary Sequence:

Direct question (present tense):

Cūr servae mē **neglegunt**?
*Why **do** the slave girls **neglect** me?*

Indirect question:

Nōn intellēxī <u>cūr servae mē **neglegerent**</u>.
*I didn't understand <u>why the slave girls **were neglecting** me</u>.*

Direct question (past tense):

Cūr servae mē **neglēxērunt**?
*Why **did** the slave girls **neglect** me?*

Indirect question:

Nōn intellēxī <u>cūr servae mē **neglēxissent**</u>.
*I didn't understand <u>why the slave girls **had neglected** me</u>.*

2. Telling to, Asking to: Indirect Commands
Direct requests or commands such as **In ātrium procēdite!** *Step forward into the atrium!* may be stated indirectly in substantive clauses introduced by **ut** for a positive command or **nē** for a negative command, with the verb in the subjunctive. Indirect commands are usually translated with infinitives in English (see Book II-B, pages 106–107):

Cornēlius convīvās omnēs invītat **ut in ātrium procēdant**. (51c:1)
*Cornelius invites all the guests **to go forward** into the atrium.*

Hī iānitōrem ōrābant **nē sē dīmitteret**. (51:11)
*These kept begging the doorkeeper **not to send** them away.*

IX. USES OF THE INFINITIVE

A. Complementary Infinitive
The meaning of verbs and verbal phrases such as **velle**, **nōlle**, **posse**, **parāre**, **solēre**, **timēre**, and **in animō habēre** is often completed by a complementary infinitive (see Book I-A, page 26):

Cūr Marcus arborēs **ascendere** <u>nōn vult</u>? (5:4)
Why <u>does Marcus not want</u> to climb trees?

B. Infinitive as Subject
The infinitive may be used as the subject of the verb **est**, with a neuter singular complement (see Book I-B, page 28):

"Etiam in caupōnā **pernoctāre** saepe <u>est</u> <u>perīculōsum</u>." (20:19)
*"**To spend the night** in an inn <u>is</u> also often <u>dangerous</u>."*
*"<u>It is</u> also often <u>dangerous</u> **to spend the night** in an inn."*

C. Infinitive with Impersonal Verbal Phrases and Impersonal Verbs
Impersonal verbal phrases and impersonal verbs are often used with infinitives (see Book I-B, page 28, and Book II-B, pages 116–117):

Nōbīs igitur <u>necesse est</u> statim **discēdere.** (9:13–14)
***To leave** immediately <u>is necessary</u> for us.*
*<u>It is necessary</u> for us **to leave** immediately.*

"<u>Licet</u>ne nōbīs," inquit Marcus, "hīc **cēnāre**?" (20:7)
*"<u>Is it allowed</u> for us," Marcus said, "**to dine** here?"*
"May we dine here?"

Strictly speaking, the infinitive is the subject of the impersonal verbal phrase or impersonal verb, but we usually supply *it* as the subject in English and translate the infinitive after the verb.

D. Accusative and Infinitive as Subject (see Book II-B, page 117)
An accusative and infinitive phrase may serve as the subject of an impersonal verb:

Nōn <u>decet</u> **patrem dēspondēre fīliam,** inscīā mātre. (50:15–16)
***That a father betroth his daughter** without the mother knowing <u>is not fitting</u>.*
*<u>It is</u> not <u>fitting</u> **that a father betroth his daughter** without the mother knowing.*
A father should not betroth his daughter without the mother knowing.

Festīnāre tē <u>oportet</u>. (50:9)
***That you hurry** <u>is fitting</u>.*
*<u>It is fitting</u> **that you hurry**.*
You ought to hurry.

E. Accusative and Infinitive as Object (see Book I-A, page 72, and Book I-B, page 28):

The verbs **docēre**, *to teach*, **iubēre**, *to order*, and **vetāre**, *to forbid*, are used with an accusative and infinitive as object:

> Aurēlia **Cornēliam** <u>docet</u> vīllam **cūrāre**. (6:11)
> *Aurelia teaches **Cornelia** (how) **to take care of** the country house.*

> **Ancillam** <u>iubet</u> aliās tunicās et stolās et pallās in cistam **pōnere**. (10:2)
> *<u>She orders</u> **the slave woman to put** other tunics and stolas and pallas into a chest.*

> Cūr pater meus **nōs exīre** <u>vetat</u>? (26:12)
> *Why <u>does</u> my father <u>forbid</u> **us to go out**?*

Note, however, that the verb **imperō**, *to order*, is used with the dative case and an indirect command:

> <u>Coquō</u> **imperāvit** <u>ut in ātrium venīret.</u>
> ***He ordered*** <u>*the cook*</u> <u>*to come into the atrium.*</u>

F. Accusative and Infinitive: Indirect Statement
A number of verbs of saying, hoping, thinking, perceiving, and feeling may be found with an accusative and infinitive construction (indirect statement). The tense of the infinitive in the indirect statement is the same as the tense of the verb in the original, direct statement.

When translating into English, the present infinitive in the indirect statement will be translated with the same tense as that of the verb in the main clause; a future infinitive will be translated to show action after that of the verb in the main clause; and a perfect infinitive will be translated to show time before that of the verb in the main clause.

The following examples show direct statements (active and passive, present, future, and perfect tenses) being changed into indirect statements:

1. Verb of main clause in **present** tense:

   a. Pater **est** crūdēlis.

   > Putō **patrem esse** <u>crūdēlem</u>. (46:3–4)
   > *I think <u>that **father is** cruel</u>.*

   Present infinitive replaces present indicative of the original statement (see Book II-B, pages 38–39). Note the agreement of **patrem** and **crūdēlem**.

b. Leōnēs in arēnam **immittuntur.**

Vidētisne **leōnēs** in arēnam **immittī**? (49e:8)
*Do you see that **the lions are being sent** into the arena?*

Present passive infinitive replaces present passive indicative of the original statement (see Book II-B, page 67).

c. Tū crās nōn **labōrābis.**

Prō certō habeō **tē** crās nōn **labōrātūrum esse.** (47:4)
*I am certain that **you will** not **work** tomorrow.*

Future active infinitive replaces future active indicative of the original statement (see page 62).

d. Hoc per iocum **dīxī.**

Nōnne sentīs **mē** per iocum hoc **dīxisse**? (47:9)
*Surely you realize that **I said** this as a joke, don't you?*

Perfect active infinitive replaces perfect active indicative of the original statement (see Book II-B, page 52).

e. Servus ā prīncipe **arcessītus est.**

Videō **servum** ā prīncipe **arcessītum esse.** (49e:18)
*I see that **the slave was summoned** by the emperor.*

Perfect passive infinitive replaces perfect passive indicative of the original statement (see Book II-B, page 67).

2. Verb of main clause in **past** tense:

a. Discēdere nōlō.

Respondit Titus **sē** discēdere **nōlle.** (48:23)
*Titus replied that **he did not want** to leave.*

Present active infinitive replaces present active indicative of the original statement (see Book II-B, pages 64–65).

b. Imperātor ā gladiātōribus **salūtātur.**

Vīdī **imperātōrem** ā gladiātōribus **salūtārī.** (48d:8–9)
*I saw **the emperor being greeted** by the gladiators.*

Present passive infinitive replaces present passive indicative of the original statement (see Book II-B, page 67).

c. Merīdiānī mox in arēnam **venient.**

Respondit Titus **merīdiānōs** mox in arēnam **ventūrōs esse**. (48:23–24)
*Titus replied that **the midday fighters would** soon **come into the arena**.*

Future active infinitive replaces future active indicative of the original statement (see Book II-B, pages 64–65).

d. Titus iam **cōnsēdit.**

Subitō vīdit **Titum** iam **cōnsēdisse**. (48:6)
*Suddenly he saw that **Titus had** already **taken his seat**.*

Perfect active infinitive replaces perfect active indicative of the direct statement (see Book II-B, pages 64–65).

e. Titus eō iam **ductus est**.

Vīdimus **Titum** eō iam **ductum esse**. (48d:6–7)
*We saw that **Titus had** already **been led** to that place.*

Perfect passive infinitive replaces perfect passive indicative of the original statement.

3. A reflexive pronoun or adjective in an indirect statement refers to the subject of the verb in the main clause that introduces the indirect statement (see Book II-B, page 53):

Puellae puerīs dīxērunt **sē** eōs adiūtūrās esse.
*The girls told the boys that **they** would help them.*

Puerī dīxērunt puellās **sē** adiūtūrās esse.
*The boys said that the girls would help **them**.*

LATIN TO ENGLISH VOCABULARY

Numbers in parentheses at the end of entries refer to the chapters in which the words appear in vocabulary entries or in Building the Meaning or Forms sections. Roman numerals refer to Review chapters.

A

ā or **ab**, prep. + abl., *from, by* (13, 29, 31)

ábeō, abíre, ábiī or **abívī, abitúrus**, irreg., *to go away* (3, 9)

abhínc, adv., *ago, previously* (25, 39)

abōminándus, -a, -um, *detestable, horrible* (39)

abrípiō, abrípere, abrípuī, abréptus, *to snatch away* (46)

ábstinēns, abstinéntis + abl., *refraining from* (34)

ábstulī (see **aúferō**)

ábsum, abésse, áfuī, āfutúrus, irreg., *to be away, be absent, be distant* (11, 25)

ac, conj., *and* (30)

   ídem ac, *the same as* (39)

accéndō, accéndere, accéndī, accénsus, *to set on fire* (54)

áccidit, accídere, áccidit, *it happens* (14, 26)

accípiō, accípere, accépī, accéptus, *to receive, get, welcome* (31)

accúmbō, accúmbere, accúbuī, accubitúrus, *to recline (at table)* (32)

accúrrō, accúrrere, accúrrī, accursúrus, *to run toward/up to* (29)

accúsō, -áre, -ávī, -átus, *to accuse* (21)

ácer, ácris, ácre, *keen* (34)

ácriter, adv., *fiercely* (48)

áctor, āctóris, m., *actor* (54)

ad, prep. + acc., *to, toward, at, near* (2, 9)

   ad témpus, *on time* (37)

áddō, áddere, áddidī, ádditus, *to add* (31)

addúcō, addúcere, addúxī, addúctus, *to lead on, bring* (29)

adémpte (from **adémptus**, see **ádimō**)

ádeō, adv., *so much, to such an extent* (50)

ádeō, adíre, ádiī, áditus, irreg., *to come to, approach*

adhúc, adv., *still, as yet* (5, 13)

ádimō, adímere, adémī, adémptus + dat., *to take away (from)* (35)

ádiuvō, adiuváre, adiúvī, adiútus, *to help* (6, 21)

admīrátiō, admīrātiónis, f., *amazement* (48)

   admīrātiónī ésse, *to be a source of amazement (to)* (49)

admíror, -árī, -átus sum, *to wonder (at)* (49)

admóveō, admovére, admóvī, admótus, *to move toward* (22)

adóptō, -áre, -ávī, -átus, *to adopt* (IX)

adórior, adorírī, adórtus sum, *to attack* (42)

ádstō, adstáre, ádstitī, *to stand near, stand by* (54)

   adstántēs, adstántium, m. pl., *bystanders* (29)

ádsum, adésse, ádfuī, adfutúrus, irreg., *to be present, be near* (26)

aduléscēns, adulēscéntis, m., *young man, youth* (36)

advéniō, adveníre, advénī, adventúrus, *to reach, arrive (at)* (5, 23)

advesperáscit, advesperáscere, advesperávit, *it gets dark* (17)

aedifícium, -ī, n., *building* (17)

aedíficō, -áre, -ávī, -átus, *to build* (24)

aéger, aégra, aégrum, *ill* (39)

aegrótō, -áre, -ávī, -ātúrus, *to be ill* (39)

Aenéās, Aenéae, m., *Aeneas (son of Venus and Anchises and legendary ancestor of the Romans)* (38)

Aenéis, Aenéidis, f., *the Aeneid* (38)

aéquor, aéquoris, n., *sea* (54)

aequóreus, -a, -um, *of/belonging to the sea* (48)

aéstās, aestátis, f., *summer* (1, 12)

aéstus, -ūs, m., *heat* (24, 25)

áfferō, afférre, áttulī, allátus, irreg., *to bring, bring to, bring in* (29, 32)

affíciō, affícere, affécī, afféctus, *to affect* (54)

   afféctus, -a, -um, *affected, overcome* (35)

África, -ae, f., *Africa* (38)

áger, ágrī, m., *field, territory, land* (2)

agnóscō, agnóscere, agnóvī, ágnitus, *to recognize* (18)

ágō, ágere, égī, áctus, *to do, drive; discuss, debate* (8, 14, 23, 52)

    Áge!/Ágite! *Come on!* (8)

    grátiās ágere + dat., *to thank* (26, 51)

    Quid ágis? *How are you?* (18)

áit, *he/she says, said* (50)

Albánus, -a, -um, *of Alba Longa (city founded by Aeneas' son, Ascanius)* (39)

albátus, -a, -um, *white* (27)

álbus, -a, -um, *white* (53)

áliās, adv., *at another time* (48)

áliquī, -ae, -a, *some* (38)

áliquis, áliquid, *someone, something* (25, 51)

    áliquid málī, *some harm* (46)

    nē quis (quis = áliquis), *that no one* (52)

    sī quis (quis = áliquis), *if anyone* (51)

áliter, adv., *otherwise* (26)

álius, ália, áliud, *another, other, one… another* (10)

    áliī…áliī…, *some…others…* (9)

álloquor, álloquī, allocútus sum, *to speak to, address* (54)

Álpēs, Álpium, f. pl., *the Alps* (39)

álter, áltera, álterum, *a/the second, one (of two), the other (of two), another* (1)

    álter…álter, *the one…the other* (16)

áltus, -a, -um, *tall, high, deep* (38)

    áltum, -ī, n., *the deep, the sea* (39)

ámbō, ámbae, ámbō, *both* (46)

ámbulō, -áre, -ávī, -ātúrus, *to walk* (2)

amíca, -ae, f., *friend* (2)

amícus, -ī, m., *friend* (3)

ámō, -áre, -ávī, -átus, *to like, love* (4)

ámor, amóris, m., *love* (34)

amphitheátrum, -ī, n., *amphitheater* (25)

ampléctor, ampléctī, ampléxus sum, *to embrace* (51)

an, conj., *or* (52)

    útrum…an…, conj., *whether…or…* (52)

ancílla, -ae, f., *slave-woman* (6)

Ándroclēs, Ándroclis, m., *Androcles* (49)

ánima, -ae, f., *soul, "heart"* (33)

animadvértō, animadvértere, animadvértī, animadvérsus, *to notice* (39)

ánimus, -ī, m., *mind* (16)

    ánimum recuperáre, *to regain one's senses, be fully awake* (21)

    Bónō ánimō es!/éste! *Be of good mind! Cheer up!* (32)

    in ánimō habére, *to intend* (16)

ánnus, -ī, m., *year* (38)

    múltīs post ánnīs, *many years afterward* (39)

ánte, prep. + acc., *before, in front of* (36, 39)

ánte, adv., *previously, before* (39)

ánteā, adv., *previously, before* (20)

ántequam, conj., *before* (39)

antíquus, -a, -um, *ancient* (26)

ánulus, -ī, m., *ring* (50)

apériō, aperíre, apéruī, apértus, *to open* (16, 26)

ápium, -ī, n., *parsley* (34)

apodytérium, -ī, n., *changing-room* (43)

appáreō, -ére, -uī, -itúrus, *to appear* (15, 18)

appáritor, appāritóris, m., *gatekeeper, public servant* (48, 54)

appéllō, -áre, -ávī, -átus, *to call, name* (21)

appropínquō, -áre, -ávī, -ātúrus + dat. or **ad** + acc., *to approach, come near (to)* (4, 22)

Aprílis, -is, -e, *April* (36)

áptō, -áre, -ávī, -átus, *to place, fit* (50)

ápud, prep. + acc., *with, at the house of, in front of, before* (16, 26)

áqua, -ae, f., *water* (6)

aquaedúctus, -ūs, m., *aqueduct* (23, 25)

áquilō, aquilónis, m., *north wind* (54)

ára, -ae, f., *altar* (53)

aránea, -ae, f., *cobweb* (34)

árbiter, árbitrī, m., *master* (34)

    árbiter bibéndī, *master of the drinking* (34)

árbor, árboris, f., *tree* (1)

arcéssō, arcéssere, arcessívī, arcessítus, *to summon, send for* (40, 54)

árcus, -ūs, m., *arch* (24, 25)

árdeō, ārdére, ársī, ārsúrus, *to burn, blaze* (53)

área, -ae, f., *open space, threshing-floor* (11)

aréna, -ae, f., *sand, arena* (48)

árma, -órum, n. pl., *arms, weapons* (39)

armátus, -a, -um, *armed* (42)

arrípiō, arrípere, arrípuī, arréptus, *to grab hold of, snatch, seize* (5, 19, 26)

ars, ártis, gen. pl., **ártium,** f., *skill* (14)

ascéndō, ascéndere, ascéndī, ascēnsúrus, *to climb, climb into (a carriage)* (4, 22)

Ásia, -ae, f., *Asia Minor* (21)

aspáragus, -ī, m., *asparagus* (33)

aspérgō, aspérgere, aspérsī, aspérsus, *to sprinkle, splash, spatter* (45)

   aspérsus, -a, -um, *sprinkled, spattered* (33)

at, conj. *but* (23)

Athénae, -árum, f. pl., *Athens* (39)

átque, conj., *and, also* (22)

átrium, -ī, n., *atrium, main room* (26)

atténtē, adv., *attentively, closely* (20)

attónitus, -a, -um, *astonished, astounded* (24)

audāx, audácis, *bold* (36)

aúdeō, audére, aúsus sum, semi-deponent + infin., *to dare (to)* (40)

aúdiō, -íre, -ívī, -ítus, *to hear, listen to* (4, 20)

aúferō, auférre, ábstulī, ablátus, irreg., *to carry away, take away* (29, 32)

aufúgiō, aufúgere, aufúgī, *to run away, escape* (29)

Augústus, -a, -um, *August* (36)

Augústus, -ī, m., *Augustus (first Roman emperor)* (39)

aúreus, -a, -um, *golden* (25)

auríga, -ae, m., *charioteer* (13)

aúrum, -ī, n., *gold* (21)

aúspex, aúspicis, m., *augur, officiating priest* (53)

aut, conj., *or* (26)

   aut...aut, conj., *either...or* (26)

aútem, conj., *however, but, moreover* (31)

auxílium, -ī, n., *help* (5, 15)

   Fer/Férte auxílium! *Bring help! Help!* (5)

Ávē!/Avéte! *Hail! Greetings!* (40, 48)

āvértō, āvértere, āvértī, āvérsus, *to turn away, divert* (54)

ávis, ávis, gen. pl., **ávium,** m./f., *bird* (50)

B

Bábylōn, Babylónis, f., *Babylon* (45)

báculum, -ī, n., *stick, staff* (10, 15)

bálneae, -árum, f. pl., *baths* (41)

bélliger, bellígera, bellígerum, *warlike* (48)

béllum, -ī, n., *war* (39)

béne, adv., *well* (22, 35)

benevoléntia, -ae, f., *kindness* (51)

béstia, -ae, f., *beast* (49)

bēstiárius, -a, -um, *involving wild beasts* (49)

bēstiárius, -ī, m., *a person who fights wild beasts in the arena* (49)

bíbō, bíbere, bíbī, *to drink* (31)

Bīthýnia, -ae, f., *Bithynia (province in Asia Minor)* (39)

blándē, adv., *in a coaxing/winning manner* (49)

bōlétus, -ī, m., *mushroom* (33)

bónus, -a, -um, *good* (12, 34)

   bóna, -órum, n. pl., *goods, possessions* (26)

   Bónō ánimō es!/éste! *Be of good mind! Cheer up!* (32)

bōs, bóvis, m./f., *ox, cow* (15)

brévis, -is, -e, *short* (2, 34)

   bréviter, *briefly* (35)

Británnī, -órum, m. pl., *Britons* (X)

Británnia, -ae, f., *Britain* (8)

Británnicus, -a, -um, *British* (3)

Brundísium, -ī, n., *Brundisium* (36)

   Brundísiī, *at Brundisium* (36)

   Brundísiō, *from Brundisium* (36)

   Brundísium, *to Brundisium* (36)

búlla, -ae, f., *luck-charm, locket* (51)

C

cachínnus, -ī, m., *laughter* (30)

cádō, cádere, cécidī, cāsúrus, *to fall* (3, 22)

caélum, -ī, n., *sky, heaven* (17)

Caésar, Caésaris, m., *Caesar, emperor* (27)

caldárium, -ī, n., *hot room (at baths)* (43)

cálidus, -a, -um, *warm* (5)

Calígula, -ae, m., *Caligula (emperor A.D. 37–41)* (27)

cálor, calóris, m., *heat* (43)

cálvus, -a, -um, *bald* (43)

cámpus, -ī, m., *plain, field* (43)

   Cámpus Mártius, -ī, m., *the Plain of Mars on the outskirts of Rome* (43)

candéla, -ae, f., *candle* (54)

candēlábrum, -ī, n., *candelabrum, lamp-stand* (32)

cándidus, -a, -um, *white, fair-skinned, beautiful* (34)

cánis, cánis, m./f., *dog, the lowest throw of the knucklebones* (12, 34)

cánō, cánere, cécinī, cántus, *to sing* (39)

cántō, -áre, -ávī, -átus, *to sing* (21)

capillátus, -a, -um, *with long hair* (43)

capíllī, -órum, m. pl., *hair* (54)

cápiō, cápere, cépī, cáptus, *to take, catch, capture, seize* (21)

   cōnsílium cápere, *to adopt a plan* (45)

captívus, -ī, m., *captive, prisoner* (26)

cáput, cápitis, n., *head* (25)

cáreō, carére, cáruī, caritúrus + abl., *to need, lack* (33)

cárō, cárnis, f., *meat, flesh* (31)

Carthágō, Cartháginis, f., *Carthage (city on the north coast of Africa)* (39)

cárus, -a, -um, *dear, beloved* (53)

cása, -ae, f., *hut, cottage* (42)

cássis, cássidis, f., *plumed metal helmet* (48)

castígō, -áre, -ávī, -átus, *to rebuke, reprimand* (37)

cástus, -a, -um, *virtuous, chaste* (53)

cásū, *by chance, accidentally* (32)

catérva, -ae, f., *crowd* (52)

caúda, -ae, f., *tail* (18)

caúpō, caupónis, m., *innkeeper* (17)

caupóna, -ae, f., *inn* (17, 20)

caúsa, -ae, f., *reason* (25)

   genitive + caúsā, *for the sake of, as* (52)

   honóris caúsā, *for the sake of an honor, as an honor* (52)

   quā dē caúsā, *for this reason* (32)

   Quam ob caúsam...? *For what reason...?* (28)

cávea, -ae, f., *cage* (49)

cáveō, cavére, cávī, caútus, *to be careful, watch out for, beware* (4, 13, 23)

céleber, célebris, célebre, *famous* (31)

céler, céleris, célere, *swift* (34)

   celériter, adv., *quickly* (8, 13, 35)

   celérius, adv., *more quickly* (35)

   celérrimē, adv., *very fast, very quickly* (14)

   celérrimus, -a, -um, *fastest, very fast* (29)

   quam celérrimē, adv., *as quickly as possible* (34)

celéritās, celeritátis, f., *speed* (29)

   súmmā celeritáte, *with the greatest speed, as fast as possible* (29)

célō, -áre, -ávī, -átus, *to hide, conceal* (11)

céna, -ae, f., *dinner* (19)

cénō, -áre, -ávī, -átus, *to dine, eat dinner* (19)

centésimus, -a, -um, *hundredth* (38)

céntum, *a hundred* (15, 38)

Cérberus, -ī, m., *Cerberus (three-headed dog guarding the underworld)* (32)

cértus, -a, -um, *certain* (35)

   cértē, adv., *certainly* (19, 35)

   prō cértō habére, *to be sure* (47)

céssō, -áre, -ávī, -ātúrus, *to be idle, do nothing, delay* (14)

céterī, -ae, -a, *the rest, the others* (33)

Chárōn, Charónis, m., *Charon (ferryman in the underworld)* (32)

Chrīstiánus, -a, -um, *Christian* (XII)

Chrīstiánī, -órum, m. pl., *the Christians* (XII)

cíbus, -ī, m., *food* (6)

cínis, cíneris, m., *ashes, dust (of the cremated body)* (54)

circénsis, -is, -e, *in the circus* (27)

   lúdī circénsēs, lūdórum circénsium, m. pl., *chariot-racing* (27)

círcum, prep. + acc., *around* (32)

circúmeō, circumíre, circúmiī or circumívī, circúmitus, irreg., *to go around* (24)

circumspíciō, circumspícere, circumspéxī, circumspéctus, *to look around* (48)

Círcus Máximus, -ī, m., *Circus Maximus (a stadium in Rome)* (23)

císium, -ī, n., *light two-wheeled carriage* (14, 15)

císta, -ae, f., *trunk, chest* (10)

cívis, cívis, gen. pl., cívium, m./f., *citizen* (13)

clam, adv., *secretly* (42)

clámō, -áre, -ávī, -ātúrus, *to shout* (3)

clámor, clāmóris, m., *shout, shouting* (5)

clárus, -a, -um, *bright* (53)

claúdō, claúdere, claúsī, claúsus, *to shut* (26)

   claúsus, -a, -um, *shut, closed* (24)

claúdus, -a, -um, *lame* (49)

clēménter, adv., *in a kindly manner* (49)

clíēns, cliéntis, m., *client, dependent* (25)

coépī, *I began* (38)

cógitō, -áre, -ávī, -átus, *to think* (21)

cognómen, cognóminis, n., *surname (third or fourth name of a Rome)* (IX, 52)

cognóscō, cognóscere, cognóvī, cógnitus, *to find out, learn* (43)

cógō, cógere, coégī, coáctus, *to compel, force* (49)

collábor, collábī, collápsus sum, *to collapse* (34, 37)

cóllis, cóllis, gen. pl., **cóllium**, m., *hill* (35)

collóquium, -ī, n., *conversation* (26)

cólloquor, cólloquī, collocútus sum, *to converse, speak together* (37)

cólō, cólere, cóluī, cúltus, *to cultivate* (23)

cómes, cómitis, m./f., *companion* (39)

cómiter, adv., *courteously, graciously, in a friendly way* (32)

cómitor, -árī, -átus sum, *to accompany* (51)

   comitátus, -a, -um, *accompanied* (54)

commémorō, -áre, -ávī, -átus, *to mention, comment on, recount* (54)

commissátiō, commissātiónis, f., *drinking party* (34)

commíttō, commíttere, commísī, commíssus, *to bring together, entrust* (48)

   púgnam commíttere, *to join battle* (48)

cómmodus, -a, -um, *pleasant* (54)

commóveō, commovére, commóvī, commótus, *to move, upset* (29, 30)

   commótus, -a, -um, *moved, excited* (14)

commúnis, -is, -e, *common* (45)

cómparō, -áre, -ávī, -átus, *to buy, obtain, get ready* (32)

cómpleō, complére, complévī, complétus, *to fill, complete* (33)

compléxus, -ūs, m., *embrace* (9, 25)

complúrēs, -ēs, -a, *several* (32)

compónō, compónere, compósuī, compósitus, *to compose* (53)

cóncidō, concídere, cóncidī, *to fall down* (14)

cóncinō, concínere, concínuī, *to sing together* (53)

cóncrepō, concrepáre, concrépuī, *to snap (the fingers)* (43)

concubínus, -ī, m., *bridegroom* (53)

concúrrō, concúrrere, concúrrī, concursúrus, *to run together, rush up* (35)

concúrsō, -áre, -ávī, -átus, *to run to and fro, run about* (29)

condémnō, -áre, -ávī, -átus, *to condemn* (49)

cóndō, cóndere, cóndidī, cónditus, *to found, establish* (36, 39)

condúcō, condúcere, condúxī, condúctus, *to hire* (23)

cónferō, cōnférre, cóntulī, collátus, irreg., *to confer, bestow* (54)

   mérita cōnférre, *to render services (to)* (54)

cōnfíciō, cōnfícere, cōnfécī, cōnféctus, *to accomplish, finish* (25, 32)

cōnfídō, cōnfídere, cōnfísus sum + dat., *to give trust (to), trust* (26)

cōnfúgiō, cōnfúgere, cōnfúgī, *to flee for refuge* (44)

congrédior, cóngredī, congréssus sum, *to come together* (47)

coníciō, conícere, coniécī, coniéctus, *to throw, throw together; to figure out, guess* (21, 48)

cóniūnx, cóniugis, m./f., *husband, wife* (26)

cónor, -árī, -átus sum, *to try* (36, 37)

cōnsecrō, -áre, -ávī, -átus, *to dedicate* (51)

cōnsénsus, -ūs, m., *agreement* (49)

cónsequor, cónsequī, cōnsecútus sum, *to catch up to, overtake* (35, 37)

cōnsídō, cōnsídere, cōnsédī, *to sit down* (23)

cōnsílium, -ī, n., *plan* (45)

   cōnsílium cápere, *to adopt a plan* (45)

cōnsístō, cōnsístere, cónstitī, *to halt, stop, stand* (48)

cōnspíciō, cōnspícere, cōnspéxī, cōnspéctus, *to catch sight of* (4, 21)

cónstat, *it is agreed* (47)

cōnstítuō, cōnstitúere, cōnstítuī, cōnstitútus, *to decide* (23)

cónsul, cónsulis, m., *consul* (36)

cōnsulō, cōnsúlere, cōnsúluī, cōnsúltus, *to consult* (7)

cōnsúltum, -ī, n., *decree* (52)

conticéscō, conticéscere, contícuī, *to become silent* (38, 39)

contíneō, continére, contínuī, conténtus, *to confine, hold* (47)

cóntrā, adv., *in return* (34)

cóntrā, prep. + acc., *against, opposite, in front of, facing* (43, 48)

convaléscō, convaléscere, convóluī, *to grow stronger, get well* (42)

convéniō, convenīre, convénī, conventúrus, *to come together, meet, assemble* (43)

convértō, convértere, convértī, convérsus, *to turn (around)* (48)

convérsus, -a, -um, *having turned, turning* (50)

convíva, -ae, m., *guest (at a banquet)* (31)

convívium, -ī, n., *feast, banquet* (34)

cónvocō, -áre, -ávī, -átus, *to call together* (12)

coórior, coorírī, coórtus sum, *to rise up, arise* (42)

cóquō, cóquere, cóxī, cóctus, *to cook* (6, 32)

cóquus, -ī, m., *cook* (33)

cor, córdis, n., *heart* (54)

Corneliánus, -a, -um, *belonging to Cornelius* (10)

Cornéliī, -órum, m. pl., *the members of the family of Cornelius* (22)

córnicen, cornícinis, m., *horn-player* (48)

coróna, -ae, f., *garland, crown* (34)

corónō, -áre, -ávī, -átus, *to crown* (34)

córpus, córporis, n., *body* (21)

corrípiō, corrípere, corrípuī, corréptus, *to seize, grab* (35)

cotídiē, adv., *daily, every day* (37)

cóxa, -ae, f., *hipbone* (54)

crās, adv., *tomorrow* (10, 13)

crédō, crédere, crédidī, créditus + dat., *to trust, believe* (35)

Cremóna, -ae, f., *Cremona (town in northern Italy)* (39)

créō, -áre, -ávī, -átus, *to appoint, create* (34, 54)

Créta, -ae, f., *Crete (large island southeast of Greece)* (39)

crínēs, crínium, m. pl., *hair* (28)

crótalum, -ī, n., *castanet* (21)

crūdélis, -is, -e, *cruel* (40)

crūdélitās, crūdēlitátis, f., *cruelty* (49)

cubículum, -ī, n., *room, bedroom* (8, 15)

cúbitum íre, *to go to bed* (19)

Cúius...? *Whose...?* (22)

culína, -ae, f., *kitchen* (21)

cúlpa, -ae, f., *fault, blame* (14)

cum, prep. + abl., *with* (12)

cum, conj., *when, since, whenever* (22, 40)

cum prímum, *as soon as* (40)

cúnctī, -ae, -a, *all* (14)

Cupídō, Cupídinis, m., *Cupid (the son of Venus)* (34)

cúpiō, cúpere, cupívī, cupítus, *to desire, want* (40)

Cūr...? *Why...?* (1)

cúra, -ae, f., *care* (34, 48)

cúrae ésse, *to be a cause of anxiety (to)* (50)

Cúria, -ae, f., *Senate House* (23)

cúrō, -áre, -ávī, -átus, *to look after, take care of* (6)

currículum, -ī, n., *race track* (27)

cúrrō, cúrrere, cucúrrī, cursúrus, *to run* (2, 23)

custódiō, -íre, -ívī, -ítus, *to guard* (17)

cústōs, custódis, m., *guard* (26, 44)

cýathus, -ī, m., *small ladle, measure (of wine)* (34)

D

dē, prep. + abl., *down from, from, concerning, about* (16, 53)

déa, -ae, f., *goddess* (X)

débeō, -ére, -uī, -itus, *to owe;* + infin., *ought* (26)

dēcédō, dēcédere, dēcéssī, dēcessúrus, *to die* (53)

décem, *ten* (15, 38)

Decémber, Decémbris, Decémbre, *December* (36)

décet, decére, décuit, *it is becoming, fitting; should* (50, 52)

Nōn décet patrem dēspondére fíliam, *That a father should betroth his daughter is not fitting, A father should not betroth his daughter* (50)

décimus, -a, -um, *tenth* (38)

dédicō, -áre, -ávī, -átus, *to dedicate* (33)

déditus, -a, -um, *devoted, dedicated* (50)

dēdúcō, dēdúcere, dēdúxī, dēdúctus, *to show into, bring, escort* (50)

dēféndō, dēféndere, dēféndī, dēfénsus, *to defend* (I, 35)

dēféssus, -a, -um, *tired* (2)

dēfrícō, dēfricáre, dēfrícuī, dēfríctus, *to rub down* (43)

dēíciō, dēícere, dēiécī, dēiéctus, *to throw down; pass., to fall* (32)

deínde, adv., *then, next* (8, 13)

dēléctō, -áre, -ávī, -átus, *to delight, amuse* (29)

déleō, dēlére, dēlévī, dēlétus, *to destroy* (38)

dēlíciae, -árum, f. pl., *delight* (48)

Délos, -ī, f., *Delos (small island off the eastern coast of Greece)* (39)

dēmíttō, dēmíttere, dēmísī, dēmíssus, *to let down, lower* (50)

dēmónstrō, -áre, -ávī, -átus, *to show* (24)

dēnárius, -ī, m., *denarius (silver coin)* (31)

dēpónō, dēpónere, dēpósuī, dēpósitus, *to lay down, put aside, set down* (31)

dērídeō, dērīdére, dērísī, dērísus, *to laugh at, get the last laugh* (33)

dēscéndō, dēscéndere, dēscéndī, dēscēnsúrus, *to come/go down, climb down* (4, 23)

dēsíderō, -áre, -ávī, -átus, *to long for, desire, miss* (26)

dēsíliō, dēsilíre, dēsíluī, *to leap down* (40)

désinō, dēsínere, désiī, désitus, *to stop* (53)

dēspóndeō, dēspondére, dēspóndī, dēspónsus, *to betroth, promise in marriage* (50)

déus, -ī, nom. pl., **dī**, dat., abl. pl., **dīs**, m., *god* (35, 39)

> **Dī immortálēs!** *Immortal Gods! Good heavens!* (33)

> **Prō dī immortálēs!** *Good heavens!* (42)

> **dī mánēs**, *the spirits of the dead* (54)

dēvértō, dēvértere, dēvértī, dēvérsus, *to turn aside* (14, 27)

dévorō, -áre, -ávī, -átus, *to devour* (20)

déxtra, -ae, f., *right hand* (53)

dī (nom. pl. of **déus**) (33, 39)

dícō, dícere, díxī, díctus, *to say, tell* (20, 21)

> **dícitur**, *(he/she/it) is said* (41)

> **salútem dícere**, *to send greetings* (36)

> **véra dícere**, *to tell the truth* (40)

Dídō, Dīdónis, f., *Dido (queen of Carthage)* (38)

díēs, diéī, m., *day* (5, 13, 25)

> **in díēs**, *every day, day by day* (34)

> **díēs nātális, diéī nātális**, m., *birthday* (46)

difficílis, -is, -e, *difficult* (34)

difficúltās, difficultátis, f., *difficulty* (35)

dígitus, -ī, m., *finger* (43)

> **dígitīs micáre**, *to play* morra (46)

díligēns, dīligéntis, *diligent, painstaking, thorough* (35)

> **dīligénter**, adv., *carefully* (19)

díligō, dīlígere, dīléxī, dīléctus, *to love, have special regard for* (54)

dīmíttō, dīmíttere, dīmísī, dīmíssus, *to send away* (51)

discédō, discédere, discéssī, discessúrus, *to go away, depart* (9, 22, 41)

discípulus, -ī, m., *pupil* (38)

díscō, díscere, dídicī, *to learn* (40)

dīs mánibus, *to the spirits of the dead* (54)

dissímilis, -is, -e, *dissimilar* (34)

díū, adv., *for a long time* (15, 35)

> **diūtíssimē**, adv., *longest* (35)

> **diútius**, adv., *longer* (35)

díves, dívitis, *rich* (42)

dīvítiae, -árum, f. pl., *wealth, riches* (48)

dívidō, dīvídere, dīvísī, dīvísus, *to divide* (IX)

dīvínus, -a, -um, *divine* (IX)

dō, dáre, dédī, dátus, *to give* (21)

> **dónō** (dat.) **dáre**, *to give as a gift* (44)

> **poénās dáre**, *to pay the penalty, be punished* (40)

> **sē quiétī dáre**, *to rest* (23)

dóceō, docére, dócuī, dóctus, *to teach* (6, 21)

dóleō, -ére, -uī, -itúrus, *to be sorry, be sad, be in pain, hurt* (18, 49)

dólor, dolóris, m., *grief* (38)

dómina, -ae, f., *mistress, lady of the house* (17)

dóminus, -ī, m., *master, owner* (11)

dómus, -ūs, f., *home* (23, 25, 39)

    dómī, *at home* (26, 39)

    dómō, *from home* (23, 39)

    dómum, *homeward, home* (23, 39)

dónec, conj., *until* (33)

dónō, -áre, -ávī, -átus, *to give; to present somebody* (acc.) *with something* (abl.) (34, 54)

dónum, -ī, n., *gift* (46)

    dónō (dat.) **dáre,** *to give as a gift* (46)

dórmiō, -íre, -ívī, -itúrus, *to sleep* (4)

dórmitō, -áre, -ávī, *to be sleepy* (39)

dúbium, -ī, n., *doubt* (30)

dúcō, dúcere, dúxī, dúctus, *to lead, take, bring* (7, 19, 20)

    exséquiās dúcere, *to carry out funeral rites* (53)

    in mātrimónium dúcere, *to marry* (50)

dum, conj., *while, as long as* (1)

dúo, dúae, dúo, *two* (15, 38)

duódecim, *twelve* (38)

duodécimus, -a, -um, *twelfth* (38)

duodēvīgíntī, *eighteen* (38)

duodēvīcésimus, -a, -um, *eighteenth* (38)

E

ē or **ex,** prep. + abl., *from, out of* (2, 5, 9)

ébrius, -a, -um, *drunk* (34)

Écce! *Look! Look at…!* (1)

édō, ésse, édī, ésus, irreg., *to eat* (33)

ēdúcō, ēdúcere, ēdúxī, ēdúctus, *to lead out* (46)

éfferō, efférre, éxtulī, ēlátus, irreg., *to carry out, bring out* (30)

effúgiō, effúgere, effúgī, *to flee, run away, escape* (11, 21, 29)

effúndō, effúndere, effúdī, effúsus, *to pour out;* pass., *to spill* (32)

égo, *I* (5, 27)

ēgrédior, ēgredī, ēgréssus sum, *to go out, leave, disembark* (37, 39)

Éheu! *Alas!* (7)

Ého! *Hey!* (25)

ēíciō, ēícere, ēiécī, ēiéctus, *to throw out, wash overboard* (30)

élegāns, ēlegántis, *elegant, tasteful* (29)

ēmíttō, ēmíttere, ēmísī, ēmíssus, *to send out* (30)

émō, émere, émī, émptus, *to buy* (21, 31)

énim, conj., *for* (20)

ēnúntiō, -áre, -ávī, -átus, *to reveal, divulge* (52)

éō, íre, iī or **ívī, itúrus,** irreg., *to go* (7, 17, 19, 20, 21)

    cúbitum íre, *to go to bed* (19)

éō, adv., *there, to that place* (23)

éō mágis, *all the more* (52)

epigrámma, epigrámmatis, n., *epigram* (47)

epístula, -ae, f., *letter* (7)

épulae, -árum, f. pl., *banquet, feast* (50)

équus, -ī, m., *horse* (10)

érgā, prep. + acc., *toward* (51)

ērípiō, ērípere, ērípuī, ēréptus, *to snatch from, rescue* (29)

érrō, -áre, -ávī, -atúrus, *to wander, be mistaken* (5, 18)

ērudítus, -a, -um, *learned, scholarly* (37)

ēruō, ērúere, ēruī, ērutus, *to dig up* (54)

ērúptiō, ēruptiónis, f., *eruption* (26)

ésse (see **sum** or **édō**)

Éstō! *All right! So be it!* (20)

ēsúriō, -íre, -ívī, -itúrus, *to be hungry* (19)

et, conj., *and, also* (1)

    et…et, conj., *both…and*

étiam, adv., *also, even* (1, 6, 13)

etiámsī, conj., *even if* (37)

Éuge! *Hurray!* (33)

Éugepae! *Hurray!* (7)

Eurýdicē, -ēs, f., *Eurydice (wife of Orpheus)* (VII)

ēvádō, ēvádere, ēvásī, ēvásus, *to escape* (42)

ēvértō, ēvértere, ēvértī, ēvérsus, *to overturn, upset* (32)

ex or **ē,** prep. + abl., *from, out of* (2, 5, 9)

exanimátus, -a, -um, *paralyzed* (49)

excédō, excédere, excéssī, excessúrus, *to go out, leave* (54)

    ē vítā excédere, *to die* (54)

excípiō, excípere, excépī, excéptus, *to welcome, receive, catch* (5, 16, 22)

excítō, -áre, -ávī, -átus, *to rouse, wake (someone) up* (8)

    excitátus, -a, -um, *wakened, aroused* (25)

exclámō, -áre, -ávī, -átus, *to exclaim, shout out* (10)

excúsō, -áre, -ávī, -átus, *to forgive, excuse* (33)

   sē excūsáre, *to apologize* (33)

éxeō, exíre, éxiī or **exívī, exitúrus,** irreg., *to go out* (5, 23, 44)

exérceō, -ére, -uī, -itus, *to exercise, train* (43)

exímius, -a, -um, *outstanding* (53)

éximō, exímere, exémī, exémptus, *to remove* (54)

expéllō, expéllere, éxpulī, expúlsus, *to drive out, expel* (39)

expergíscor, expergíscī, experréctus sum, *to wake up* (39)

expérior, experírī, expértus sum, *to test, try* (37)

éxplicō, -áre, -ávī, -átus, *to explain* (19)

   rem explicáre, *to explain the situation* (19)

éxprimō, exprímere, expréssī, expréssus, *to press out, express* (45)

exséquiae, -árum, f. pl., *funeral rites* (53)

   exséquiās dúcere, *to carry out funeral rites* (53)

exsíliō, exsilíre, exsíluī, *to leap out* (44)

exspéctō, -áre, -ávī, -átus, *to look out for, wait for* (15)

éxstāns, exstántis, *standing out, towering* (23)

exstínguō, exstínguere, exstínxī, exstínctus, *to put out, extinguish* (30)

éxstruō, exstrúere, exstrúxī, exstrúctus, *to build* (54)

éxta, -órum, n. pl., *the inner organs of sacrificial animals (heart, lungs, liver)* (53)

exténdō, exténdere, exténdī, exténtus, *to hold out* (18, 39)

éxtrā, prep. + acc., *outside* (23)

éxtrahō, extráhere, extráxī, extráctus, *to drag out, take out* (14, 21)

éxuō, exúere, éxuī, exútus, *to take off* (33)

F

fábula, -ae, f., *story* (20)

fácilis, -is, -e, *easy* (34)

   fácile, adv., *easily* (35)

fáciō, fácere, fécī, fáctus, *to make, do* (1, 23)

   íter fácere, *to travel* (13)

fáctiō, factiónis, f., *company (of charioteers), political faction* (27)

fáma, -ae, f., *fame* (X)

família, -ae, f., *family, household* (51)

familiáris, -is, -e, *belonging to the family/household* (51)

   familiárēs, familiárium, m. pl., *members of the household* (54)

fáscēs, fáscium, m. pl., *rods (symbols of office)* (54)

fátum, -ī, n., *fate* (39)

fátuus, -a, -um, *stupid* (13)

fáveō, favére, fávī, fautúrus + dat., *to give favor (to), favor, support* (27)

fax, fácis, f., *wedding-torch* (53)

fébris, fébris, gen. pl., **fébrium,** f., *fever* (54)

Februárius, -a, -um, *February* (36)

félēs, félis, gen. pl., **félium,** f., *cat* (21)

félīx, felícis, *lucky, happy, fortunate* (34)

   felíciter, adv., *well, happily, luckily* (35)

   Felíciter! adv., *Good luck!* (53)

fémina, -ae, f., *woman* (3)

fenéstra, -ae, f., *window* (30)

férculum, -ī, n., *dish, tray* (33)

férē, adv., *almost, approximately* (46)

fēriátus, -a, -um, *celebrating a holiday* (27)

fériō, -íre, -ívī, -ítus, *to hit, strike, kill* (16, 48)

férō, férre, túlī, látus, irreg., *to bring, carry, bear* (5, 12, 17, 21)

   Fer/Férte auxílium! *Bring help! Help!* (5)

férōx, ferócis, *fierce* (35)

   feróciter, adv., *fiercely* (13)

férula, -ae, f., *cane* (39)

festínō, -áre, -ávī, -átúrus, *to hurry* (9)

fidélis, -is, -e, *faithful* (31, 34)

fídēs, fídeī, f., *good faith, reliability, trust* (52)

fília, -ae, f., *daughter* (11)

fílius, -ī, m., *son* (11)

fíniō, -íre, -ívī, -ítus, *to finish* (21)

fínis, fínis, gen. pl., **fínium,** m., *end* (29)

fíō, fíerī, fáctus sum, irreg., *to become, be made, be done, happen* (34)

   Quid Séxtō fíet? *What will happen to Sextus?* (46)

flámma, -ae, f., *flame* (29)

flámmeum, -ī, n., *orange (bridal) veil* (53)

flámmeus, -a, -um, *flaming* (XII)

fléō, flére, flévī, flétus, *to weep, cry* (53)

flétus, -ūs, m., *weeping, tears* (54)

flōs, flóris, m., *flower* (34)

foédus, -a, -um, *filthy, disgusting* (34)

fóllis, fóllis, gen. pl., **fóllium,** m., *bag* (43)

fórās, adv., *outside* (41)

fórma, -ae, f., *form, shape,* (X)

fortásse, adv., *perhaps* (15)

fórte, adv., *by chance* (33)

fórtis, -is, -e, *brave* (18)

    fortíssimē, adv., *most/very bravely* (35)

    fórtiter, adv., *bravely* (35)

fortúna, -ae, f., *fortune (good or bad)* (54)

Fórum, -ī, n., *the Forum (town center of Rome)* (25)

fóssa, -ae, f., *ditch* (12)

frágor, fragóris, m., *crash, noise, din* (4)

frángō, frángere, frḗgī, fráctus, *to break* (54)

fráter, frátris, m., *brother* (11)

fratérnus, -a, -um, *brotherly* (54)

frīgidárium, -ī, n., *cold room (at baths)* (43)

frígidus, -a, -um, *cool, cold* (5)

fritíllus, -ī, m., *cylindrical box* (34)

frōns, fróntis, f., *forehead* (12)

frústrā, adv., *in vain* (14)

frústum, -ī, n., *scrap* (33)

fúgiō, fúgere, fū́gī, fugitū́rus, *to flee* (18, 25)

fúī (see **sum**)

fū́mus, -ī, m., *smoke* (29)

fúndus, -ī, m., *farm* (39)

fū́nebris, -is, -e, *funeral* (54)

fū́nus, fū́neris, n., *funeral* (53)

fūr, fū́ris, m., *thief* (44)

fúror, furóris, m., *frenzy* (48)

fúrtim, adv., *stealthily* (4, 13)

fū́stis, fū́stis, gen. pl., **fū́stium,** m., *club, cudgel* (35)

G

Gádēs, Gádium, f. pl., *Gades (Cadiz, a town in Spain)* (21)

Gállī, -órum, m. pl., *the Gauls* (X)

Gállia, -ae, f., *Gaul* (39)

gaúdeō, gaudére, gāvísus sum, *to be glad, rejoice* (14, 40)

gaúdium, -ī, n., *joy* (23)

gelátus, -a, -um, *chilled* (54)

gémō, gémere, gémuī, gémitus, *to groan* (3)

gēns, géntis, gen. pl., **géntium,** f., *family, clan;* pl., *peoples* (50, 54)

génus, géneris, n., *race, stock, nation* (39)

gérō, gérere, géssī, géstus, *to wear; carry on, perform, do* (10)

gladiátor, gladiātóris, m., *gladiator* (47)

gládius, -ī, m., *sword* (21, 26)

    gládium stríngere, *to draw a sword* (26)

glīs, glíris, m., *dormouse* (28)

glória, -ae, f., *fame, glory* (27)

grácilis, -is, -e, *slender* (34)

Graécia, -ae, f., *Greece* (21)

Graécus, -a, -um, *Greek* (17)

    Graécī, -órum, m. pl., *the Greeks* (I)

grammáticus, -ī, m., *secondary school teacher* (37)

grátia, -ae, f., *gratitude, thanks* (26)

    grátiās ágere + dat., *to thank* (26, 51)

grátis, adv., *free, for nothing* (31)

grátulor, -árī, -átus sum + dat., *to congratulate* (50)

grátus, -a, -um + dat., *loved (by), pleasing (to), dear (to)* (54)

grávis, -is, -e, *heavy, serious* (35)

grúnniō, -íre, *to grunt* (29)

gustátiō, gustātiónis, f., *hors d'oeuvre, first course* (33)

H

habénae, -árum, f. pl., *reins* (22)

hábeō, -ḗre, -uī, -itus, *to have, hold* (10, 20, 26)

    in ánimō habére, *to intend* (16)

    ōrātiónem habére, *to deliver a speech* (26)

    prō cértō habére, *to be sure* (47)

hábitō, -áre, -ávī, -átus, *to live, dwell* (1)

haéreō, haerére, haésī, haesúrus, *to stick* (14)

haréna, -ae, f., *sand* (54)

harpástum, -ī, n., *heavy hand ball* (43)

hásta, -ae, f., *spear* (48)

haud, adv., *not* (43, 54)

haúriō, hauríre, haúsī, haústus, *to drain* (34)

hédera, -ae, f., *ivy* (34)

Hércules, Hérculis, m., *Hercules (Greek hero)* (34)

héri, adv., *yesterday* (20)

Hespéria, -ae, f., *Hesperia (the land in the West, Italy)* (39)

Heu! = **Éheu!**

Héus! *Hey there!* (50)

hīc, adv., *here* (9, 13, 54)

hic, haec, hoc, *this, the latter* (18, 19, 20, 25, 26, 31)

híems, híemis, f., *winter* (39)

hílaris, -is, -e, *cheerful* (54)

hiláritās, hilaritátis, f., *good humor, merriment* (53)

Hispánia, -ae, f., *Spain* (39)

hódiē, adv., *today* (2, 13)

hólus, hóleris, n., *vegetable* (32)

hómō, hóminis, m., *man* (18)

hóminēs, hóminum, m. pl., *people* (15, 36)

hónor, honóris, m., *honor* (IX)

honóris caúsā, *for the sake of an honor, as an honor* (52)

hóra, -ae, f., *hour* (9)

Quóta hóra est? *What time is it?* (38)

Horátius, -ī, m., *Horace (Roman poet)* (39)

hórtor, -árī, -átus sum, *to encourage, urge* (51, 53)

hórtus, -ī, m., *garden* (3)

hórtulus, -ī, m., *small garden* (53)

hóspes, hóspitis, m., *guest, host, friend, a person related to one of another city by ties of hospitality* (16)

hūc, adv., *here, to here* (36)

hūc illúc, adv., *here and there, this way and that* (23)

hūmánus, -a, -um, *human* (48)

húmī, *on the ground* (27)

húmilis, -is, -e, *humble* (34)

hyacínthinus, -a, -um, *of hyacinth* (53)

Hýmēn! (Hýmēn! (an exclamation chanted at weddings; later thought of as the god of weddings) (53)

Hymenaée! = **Hýmēn!** (53)

I

iáceō, -ére, -uī, -itúrus, *to lie, be lying down* (26)

iáciō, iácere, iécī, iáctus, *to throw* (10, 20)

iáctō, -áre, -ávī, -átus, *to toss about, drive to and fro* (39)

iam, adv., *now, already* (1, 8, 13)

nōn iam, adv., *no longer* (2, 13)

iánitor, iānitóris, m., *doorkeeper* (9)

iánua, -ae, f., *door* (9)

Iānuárius, -a, -um, *January* (36)

íbi, adv., *there* (5, 13)

id (see **is**)

ídem, éadem, ídem, *the same* (3, 31)

ídem ac, *the same as* (39)

idéntidem, adv., *again and again, repeatedly* (13)

id quod, *that/a thing which* (50)

Ídūs, Íduum, f. pl., *the Ides* (36)

iēntáculum, -ī, n., *breakfast* (37)

ígitur, conj., *therefore* (4)

ignávus, -a, -um, *cowardly, lazy* (5)

ígnis, ígnis, gen. pl., **ígnium**, m., *fire* (32)

ignórō, -áre, -ávī, -átus, *to be ignorant, not to know* (40)

ílle, ílla, íllud, *that; he, she, it; the former; that famous* (11, 15, 16, 20, 22, 25, 26, 31)

illúc, adv., *there, to that place* (23)

hūc illúc, adv., *here and there, this way and that* (23)

imágō, imáginis, f., *likeness, mask* (54)

ímber, ímbris, gen. pl., **ímbrium**, m., *rain* (23)

immánis, -is, -e, *huge* (49)

ímmemor, immémoris + gen., *forgetful* (22)

immíttō, immíttere, immísī, immíssus, *to send in, release* (49)

ímmō, adv., *rather, on the contrary* (31)

ímmō vérō, adv., *on the contrary, in fact* (40)

immóbilis, -is, -e, *motionless* (12)

immortális, -is, -e, *immortal* (27)

Dī immortálēs! *Immortal gods! Good heavens!* (33)

Prō dī immortálēs! *Good heavens!* (42)

ímpar (see **pār**)

impédiō, -íre, -ívī, -ítus *to hinder, prevent* (11)

imperátor, imperātóris, m., *commander, emperor* (47)

ímperō, -áre, -ávī, -átus + dat., *to order* (51)

ímpetus, -ūs, m., *attack* (49)

impṓnō, impṓnere, impósuī, impósitus, *to place on, put* (54)

in, prep. + abl., *in, on, among* (1, 9, 28)
    in ánimō habḗre, *to intend* (16)
    in quíbus, *among whom* (28)

in, prep. + acc., *into, against* (3, 9)
    in díēs, *every day, day by day* (34)
    in mātrimṓnium dúcere, *to marry* (50)

incḗdō, incḗdere, incéssī, *to go in, march in* (48)

incéndium, -ī, n., *fire* (30)

incéndō, incéndere, incéndī, incénsus, *to burn, set on fire* (38)

incéssus, -ūs, m., *bearing, walk(ing)* (54)

íncidō, incídere, íncidī, incāsúrus, *to fall into/onto* (54)

incípiō, incípere, incḗpī, incéptus, *to begin* (49)

íncitō, -áre, -ávī, -átus, *to spur on, urge on, drive* (10)

íncola, -ae, m./f., *inhabitant, tenant* (30)

incólumis, -is, -e, *unhurt, safe and sound* (14)

incúrrō, incúrrere, incúrrī, incursúrus, *to run into*

índe, adv., *from there, then* (38, 40)

indígnē, adv., *undeservedly* (54)

índuō, indúere, índuī, indútus, *to put on* (8, 23)
    indútus, -a, -um, *clothed* (43)

íneō, iníre, íniī or **inívī, ínitus**, irreg., *to go into, enter* (28)

íners, inértis, *lazy* (53)

īnfándus, -a, -um, *unspeakable* (38)

īnfáns, īnfántis m./f., *infant, young child* (30)

ínferī, -ṓrum, m. pl., *the underworld* (32)

īnfériae, -árum, f. pl., *offerings and rites in honor of the dead at the tomb* (54)

ínferō, īnférre, íntulī, illátus, irreg., *to bring in* (39)

īnfírmus, -a, -um, *weak, shaky, frail* (4, 30)

ingénium, -ī, n., *intelligence, ingenuity* (52)

íngēns, ingéntis, *huge* (22)

ingravéscō, ingravéscere, *to grow worse* (54)

ingrédior, íngredī, ingréssus sum, *to go in, enter* (37)

iníciō, inícere, iniḗcī, iniéctus, *to throw into, thrust* (54)

innocéntia, -ae, f., *innocence* (21)

ínquit, *(he/she) says, said* (7)

ínscius, -a, -um, *not knowing* (45)

īnscrībō, īnscrībere, īnscrīpsī, īnscrīptus, *to write in, register* (51)

īnspíciō, īnspícere, īnspéxī, īnspéctus, *to examine* (21)

ínsula, -ae, f., *island, apartment building* (30)

intéllegō, intellégere, intelléxī, intelléctus, *to understand, realize* (49)

inténtus, -a, -um, *intent, eager* (38)

ínter, prep. + acc., *between, among* (33)

intérdiū, adv., *during the day, by day* (23)

intérdum, adv., *from time to time* (39)

ínterā, adv., *meanwhile* (10, 13)

ínterest, *it is important* (39)

interpéllō, -áre, -ávī, -átus, *to interrupt* (14)

intérrogō, -áre, -ávī, -átus, *to ask* (53)

íntrā, prep. + acc., *inside* (22)

íntrō, -áre, -ávī, -átus, *to enter, go into* (8, 19)

intrōdúcō, intrōdúcere, intrōdúxī, intrōdúctus, *to bring in* (49)

intróeō, introíre, intróiī or **introívī, introitúrus**, irreg., *to enter* (52)

inúrō, inúrere, inússī, inústus, *to brand* (12)

invéniō, inveníre, invḗnī, invéntus, *to come upon, find* (12, 21)

invítō, -áre, -ávī, -átus, *to invite* (28, 32, 51)

invítus, -a, -um, *unwilling* (21)

ínvocō, -áre, -ávī, -átus, *to invoke, call upon* (34)

Iō! (a ritual exclamation) (53)

iócus, -ī, m., *joke, funny story, prank* (16)
    per iócum, *as a prank/joke* (16)

ípse, ípsa, ípsum, *himself, herself, itself, themselves, very* (6, 10, 29, 31)

íra, -ae, f., *anger* (11)

īrācúndia, -ae, f., *irritability, bad temper* (40)

īrācúndus, -a, -um, *irritable, in a bad mood* (40)

īrátus, -a, -um, *angry* (3, 33)

íre (see **éō**) (7, 17)

irrúmpō, irrúmpere, irrúpī, irrúptus, *to burst in* (33)

is, éa, id, *he, she, it; this, that* (27, 31)

íta, adv., *thus, so, in this way, in such a way* (3, 13, 21, 50)
    Íta vḗrō! adv., *Yes! Indeed!* (3, 13)

Itália, -ae, f., *Italy* (1)

ítaque, adv., *and so, therefore* (16)

íter, itíneris, n., *journey, route* (10, 13, 15)

　íter fácere, *to travel* (13)

íterum, adv., *again, a second time* (8, 13)

Íthaca, -ae, f., *Ithaca (island home of Ulysses)* (39)

iúbeō, iubére, iússī, iússus, *to order, bid* (10, 19, 21)

iūcúndus, -a, -um, *pleasant, delightful* (54)

iúgulō, -áre, -ávī, -átus, *to kill, murder* (48)

Iúlius, -a, -um, *July* (36)

iúngō, iúngere, iúnxī, iúnctus, *to join* (53)

Iúnius, -a, -um, *June* (36)

Iúnō, Iūnónis, f., *Juno (queen of the gods)* (39)

iússa, -órum, n. pl., *commands, orders* (32)

iúvenis, iúvenis, m., *young man* (50)

K

Kaléndae, -árum, f. pl., *the Kalends (first day in the month)* (36)

L

lábor, lábī, lápsus sum, *to slip, fall, stumble* (44, 53)

lábor, labóris, m., *work, toil* (24, 48)

labórō, -áre, -ávī, -átus, *to work* (3)

lácrima, -ae, f., *tear* (45)

lácrimō, -áre, -ávī, -átus, *to weep, cry* (9)

laédō, laédere, laésī, laésus, *to harm* (46)

laétus, -a, -um, *happy, glad* (1)

　laétē, adv., *happily* (35)

lámbō, lámbere, lámbī, *to lick* (49)

lána, -ae, f., *wool* (6)

　lánam tráhere, *to spin wool* (6)

lángueō, -ére, *to be ill in bed* (54)

lánguidus, -a, -um, *drooping* (48)

lanísta, -ae, m., *trainer* (48)

lánius, -ī, m., *butcher* (31)

lantérna, -ae, f., *lantern* (37)

lapídeus, -a, -um, *of stone, stony* (33)

lápis, lápidis, m., *stone* (25)

larárium, -ī, n., *shrine of the household gods* (51)

Lárēs, Lárum, m. pl., *household gods* (51)

láteō, -ére, -uī, *to lie in hiding, hide* (49)

Latínus, -a, -um, *Latin* (39)

Látium, -ī, n., *Latium (the area of central Italy that included Rome)* (39)

lātrátus, -ūs, m., *a bark, barking* (25)

látrō, -áre, -ávī, -ātúrus, *to bark* (12)

latrúnculus, -ī, m., *robber;* pl., *pawns (a game like chess)* (46)

　lúdus latrunculórum, *game of bandits* (46)

laúdō, -áre, -ávī, -átus, *to praise* (18)

laúrus, -ī, f., *bay (tree), laurel* (53)

Lāvínius, -a, -um, *of Lavinium (name of the town where the Trojans first settled in Italy)* (39)

lávō, laváre, lávī, laútus, *to wash* (20, 54)

lectíca, -ae, f., *litter* (23)

lectīcárius, -ī, m., *litter-bearer* (23)

léctus, -ī, m., *bed, couch* (19)

lēgátus, -ī, m., *envoy* (18)

légō, légere, légī, léctus, *to read* (1, 24)

léntus, -a, -um, *slow* (35)

　léntē, adv., *slowly* (2, 13)

léō, leónis, m., *lion* (45)

lépidus, -a, -um, *charming* (54)

lépus, léporis, m., *hare* (31)

lévis, -is, -e, *light* (54)

lévis, -is, -e, *smooth* (54)

libénter, adv., *gladly* (36)

líber, líbrī, m., *book* (24)

Līberália, Līberálium, n. pl., *the Liberalia (Festival of Liber)* (51)

líberī, -órum, m. pl., *children* (10, 11)

líberō, -áre, -ávī, -átus, *to set free* (49)

libérta, -ae, f., *freedwoman* (54)

lībértās, lībertátis, f., *freedom* (21)

lībértus, -ī, m., *freedman* (29)

líbet, libére, líbuit or **libitum est**, *it is pleasing to someone* (dat.) *to do something* (infin.) (53)

lícet, licére, lícuit + dat., *it is allowed* (20, 24)

　lícet nóbīs, *we are allowed, we may* (20)

líctor, līctóris, m., *lictor, officer* (54)

lígō, -áre, -ávī, -átus, *to bind up* (35)

límen, líminis, n., *threshold, doorway* (51)

língua, -ae, f., *tongue, language* (39)

línquō, línquere, líquī, *to leave* (54)

línteum, -ī, n., *towel* (43)

liquámen, liquáminis, n., *garum (a sauce made from fish, used to season food)* (33)

líttera, -ae, f., *letter (of the alphabet)* (12)

    lítterae, -árum, f. pl., *letter, epistle, letters, literature* (39)

lítus, lítoris, n., *shore* (39)

locárius, -ī, m., *scalper* (48)

lócō, -áre, -ávī, -átus, *to place* (54)

lócus, -ī, m.; n. in pl., *place* (33)

lóngus, -a, -um, *long* (15)

    lóngē, adv., *far* (35)

lóquor, lóquī, locútus sum, *to speak, talk* (37)

lúbricus, -a, -um, *slippery* (54)

lucérna, -ae, f., *lamp* (54)

lúcet, lucére, lúxit, *it is light, it is day; (it) shines* (6, 50)

lúctor, -árī, -átus sum, *to wrestle* (43)

lúdia, -ae, f., *female slave attached to a gladiatorial school* (48)

lúdō, lúdere, lúsī, lūsúrus, *to play* (16)

    pílā lúdere, *to play ball* (16)

lúdus, -ī, m., *school, game* (26, 37, 46)

    lúdī, -órum, m. pl., *games* (24)

    lúdī circénsēs, lūdórum circénsium, m. pl., *chariot-racing* (27)

    lúdus latrunculórum, *game of bandits* (46)

lúna, -ae, f., *moon* (33)

lúpa, -ae, f., *she-wolf* (II)

lúpus, -ī, m., *wolf* (5)

lútum, -ī, n., *mud* (26)

lūx, lúcis, f., *light* (21)

    prímā lúce, *at dawn* (21)

M

mágis, adv., *more* (34, 35)

    éō mágis, adv., *all the more* (52)

magíster, magístrī, m., *schoolmaster, master, captain* (37, 42)

magístra, -ae, f., *female teacher, instructress* (X)

magníficus, -a, -um, *magnificent* (24)

magnópere, adv., *greatly* (31, 35)

mágnus, -a, -um, *big, great, large, loud (voice, laugh)* (4, 34)

máior, máior, máius, gen., **maióris**, *bigger* (34)

    maiórēs, maiórum, m. pl., *ancestors* (54)

Máius, -a, -um, *May* (36)

málō, m394lle, máluī, irreg., *to prefer* (47)

málum, -ī, n., *apple* (32)

málus, -a, -um, *bad, evil* (21, 34)

    áliquid málī, *some harm* (44)

    mále, adv., *badly* (35)

mandátum, -ī, n., *order, instruction* (22)

máne, adv., *early in the day, in the morning* (21)

máneō, manére, mánsī, mānsúrus, *to remain, stay, wait* (9, 20, 23)

mánēs, mánium, m. pl., *spirits of the dead* (54)

    dīs mánibus, *to the spirits of the dead* (54)

mánō, -áre, -ávī, *to flow* (54)

mānsuétus, -a, -um, *tame* (49)

Mántua, -ae, f., *Mantua (town in northern Italy)* (39)

mánus, -ūs, f., *hand, band (of men)* (18, 25)

máppa, -ae, f., *napkin* (27)

máre, máris, gen. pl., **márium**, n., *sea* (38)

marítus, -ī, m., *husband* (53)

Mārtiális, Marcus Valerius, m., *Martial (poet, ca. A.D. 40–104)* (47)

Mártius, -a, -um, *March; connected with Mars (the god of war and combat)* (36, 48)

máter, mátris, f., *mother* (6, 11)

mātrimónium, -ī, n., *marriage* (50)

    in mātrimónium dúcere, *to marry* (50)

mātróna, -ae, f., *married woman* (52)

mātúrē, adv., *early* (47)

máximus, -a, -um, *biggest, greatest, very great, very large* (23, 34)

    máximē, adv., *most, very much, very* (34, 35)

mē, *me* (4)

    mécum, *with me* (9)

médicus, -ī, m., *doctor* (33)

Mediolánum, -ī, n., *Milan* (39)

médius, -a, -um, *mid-, middle of* (20)

    média nox, médiae nóctis, f., *midnight* (20)

Mégara, -ae, f., *Megara (a city in Greece)* (21)

Mehércule! *By Hercules! Goodness me!* (18)

mélior, mélior, mélius, gen., **melióris,**
better (19, 34)

    mélius, adv., *better* (35)

mémor, mémoris, *remembering, mindful,*
unforgetting (39)

memorábilis, -is, -e, *memorable* (47)

memória, -ae, f., *memory* (30)

    memóriā tenére, *to remember* (37)

mendícus, -ī, m., *beggar* (29)

ménsa, -ae, f., *table* (29)

    secúndae ménsae, -árum, f. pl., *second course,*
dessert (33)

ménsis, ménsis, m., *month* (38)

mercátor, mercatóris, m., *merchant* (22)

Mercúrius, -ī, m., *Mercury (messenger god)* (32)

merīdiáni, -órum, m. pl., *midday fighters* (48)

merídiēs, -éī, m., *noon, midday* (44)

    merídiē, adv., *at noon* (33)

méritum, -ī, n., *good deed; pl., services* (54)

    mérita cōnférre, *to render services (to)* (54)

mérus, -a, -um, *pure* (34)

    mérum, -ī, n., *undiluted wine* (34)

méta, -ae, f., *mark, goal, turning post* (27)

métus, -ūs, m., *fear* (26)

    métū exanimátus, *paralyzed with fear* (47)

méus, -a, -um, *my, mine* (7)

mícō, micáre, mícuī, *to move quickly to and fro,*
flash (46)

    dígitīs micáre, *to play morra* (46)

mígrō, -áre, -ávī, -atúrus, *to move one's*
home (39)

míles, mílitis, m., *soldier* (20)

mílle, *a thousand* (15, 38)

    mília, mílium, n. pl., *thousands* (48)

millésimus, -a, -um, *thousandth* (38)

mímus, -ī, m., *actor of mime, buffoon* (54)

mínāx, minácis, *menacing* (48)

mínimus, -a, -um, *very small, smallest* (34)

    mínimē, adv., *least* (35)

    Mínimē (vérō)! adv., *No! Not at all!*
No indeed! (3,13)

mínor, mínor, mínus, gen., **minóris,** *smaller* (34)

    mínus, adv., *less* (35)

mínuō, minúere, mínuī, minútus, *to lessen, reduce,*
decrease (31)

mīrábilis, -is, -e, *wonderful* (49)

míror, -árī, -átus sum, *to wonder* (49)

mírus, -a, -um, *wonderful, marvelous, strange* (23)

mísceō, miscére, míscuī, míxtus, *to mix* (34)

míser, mísera, míserum, *unhappy, miserable,*
wretched (9)

miserábilis, -is, -e, *miserable, wretched* (30)

mítis, -is, -e, *gentle* (49)

míttō, míttere, mísī, míssus, *to send, let go* (9, 20,
31, 48)

módo, adv., *only* (18)

módus, -ī, m., *way, method, rhythmic/harmonious*
manner (34, 53)

moénia, moénium, n. pl., *walls* (39)

mólēs, mólis, gen. pl., **mólium,** f., *mass, huge*
bulk (24)

moléstus, -a, -um, *troublesome, annoying* (4)

    moléstus, -ī, m., *pest* (3)

móllis, -is, -e, *soft* (54)

móneō, -ére, -uī, -itus, *to advise, warn* (39, 51)

mōns, móntis, gen. pl., **móntium,** m., *mountain,*
hill (24)

    Mōns Vesúvius, Móntis Vesúviī, m., *Mount*
Vesuvius (a volcano in southern Italy) (26)

mónstrō, -áre, -ávī, -átus, *to show* (22)

monuméntum, -ī, n., *monument, tomb* (54)

mórbus, -ī, m., *illness* (54)

mórior, mórī, mórtuus sum, *to die* (39, 45)

móror, -árī, -átus sum, *to delay, remain, stay* (36, 37)

mors, mórtis, gen. pl., **mórtium,** f., *death* (21)

mortálēs, mortálium, m. pl., *mortals* (X)

mortíferē, adv., *mortally, critically* (53)

mórtuus, -a, -um, *dead* (16)

mōs, móris, m., *custom, pl., character* (52)

móveō, movére, móvī, mótus, *to move,*
shake (14, 24)

mox, adv., *soon, presently* (6, 13)

muliébris, -is, -e, *womanly, female, of a woman* (53)

múlier, mulíeris, f., *woman* (27)

múlsum, -ī, n., *wine sweetened with honey* (33)

multitúdō, multitúdinis, f., *crowd* (23)

múltus, -a, -um, *much* (31, 34)

   múltum, adv., *greatly, much* (31, 35)

   múltī, -ae, -a, *many* (3, 34)

   múltīs post ánnīs, *many years afterward* (39)

Mulviánus, -a, -um, *at the Mulvian Bridge* (XII)

múnus, múneris, n., *gift, service, gladiatorial show;*
   pl., *games* (47, 54)

múrmur, múrmuris, n., *murmur, rumble* (15)

múrus, -ī, m., *wall* (23)

mūs, múris, m., *mouse* (21)

Músa, -ae, f., *Muse (goddess of song and poetry)* (VII)

mússō, -áre, -ávī, -atúrus, *to mutter* (11)

mútus, -a, -um, *silent* (54)

mútuus, -a, -um, *mutual,* (49)

mýrtus, -ī, f., *myrtle* (53)

N

nam, conj., *for* (8)

nārrátor, nārrātóris, m., *narrator* (8)

nárrō, -áre, -ávī, -átus, *to tell (a story)* (20)

   nārrátus, -a, -um, *told* (20)

náscor, náscī, nátus sum, *to be born* (39)

násus, -ī, m., *nose* (33)

nātális, -is, -e, *of/belonging to birth* (46)

   díēs nātális, diḗī nātális, m., *birthday* (46)

nátiō, nātiónis, f., *nation* (XII)

nátō, -áre, -ávī, -atúrus, *to swim* (40)

nātúra, -ae, f., *nature* (XI)

nátus, -ī, m., *son* (54)

návigō, -áre, -ávī, -átus, *to sail* (38)

návis, návis, gen. pl, **návium,** f., *ship* (38)

-ne (indicates a question) (3)

nē, conj. + subjunctive, *not to, so that…not, to*
   prevent, to avoid (51, 53)

nē…quídem, adv., *not even* (34)

nē quis, *that no one* (52)

Neápolis, Neápolis, acc., **Neápolim,** f., *Naples* (15)

nec, conj., *and…not* (45)

   nec…nec…, *neither…nor*

necésse, adv. or indecl. adj., *necessary* (6, 13, 52)

nécō, -áre, -ávī, -átus, *to kill* (20)

néglegēns, neglegéntis, *careless* (28)

   neglegénter, adv., *carelessly* (28)

neglegéntia, -ae, f., *carelessness* (28)

néglegō, neglégere, negléxī, negléctus, *to neglect,*
   ignore (50)

negōtiósus, -a, -um, *busy* (47)

némō, néminis, m./f., *no one* (9)

nénia, -ae, f., *lament, dirge* (54)

néque, conj., *and…not* (6)

   néque…néque, conj., *neither…nor* (5)

   néque…néque…quídquam, *neither…*
    nor…anything (40)

nēquíquam, adv., *in vain* (54)

Nerōnéus, -a, -um, *of Nero* (43)

nésciō, -íre, -ívī, -ítus, *to be ignorant, not to know* (9)

níger, nígra, nígrum, *black* (33)

níhil, *nothing* (4)

   nīl, *nothing* (34)

nímis, adv., *too much* (34)

nísi, conj., *unless, if…not, except* (18, 26)

nóbilis, -is, -e, *noble* (50)

nóceō, -ére, -uī, -itúrus + dat., *to do harm (to),*
   harm (26)

nóctū, *at/by night* (45)

noctúrnus, -a, -um, *happening during the night* (22)

nólō, nólle, nóluī, irreg., *to be unwilling, not to*
   wish, refuse (5, 17, 21)

   Nólī/Nólíte + infin., *Don't…!* (9)

nómen, nóminis, n., *name* (1, 15)

nóminō, -áre, -ávī, -átus, *to name, call by name* (54)

nōn, adv., *not* (2, 13)

   nōn iam, adv., *no longer* (2, 13)

   nōn módo…sed étiam, *not only…but also* (X)

Nónae, -árum, f. pl., *Nones* (36)

nóndum, adv., *not yet* (6, 13)

Nónne…? (introduces a question that expects the
   answer "yes") (19)

nōnnúllī, -ae, -a, *some* (51)

nōnnúmquam, adv., *sometimes* (26)

nónus, -a, -um, *ninth* (16, 38)

nōs, *we, us* (8, 27)

nóster, nóstra, nóstrum, *our* (14, 27)

nótus, -a, -um, *known* (31)

nóvem, *nine* (15, 38)

Novémber, Novémbris, Novémbre, *November* (36)

nóvus, -a, -um, *new* (16)

nóva núpta, -ae, f., *bride* (53)

nox, nóctis, gen. pl., **nóctium**, f., *night* (11)

   média nōx, médiae nóctis, f., *midnight* (20)

núbēs, núbis, gen. pl., **núbium**, f., *cloud* (15)

núbō, núbere, núpsī, nūptúrus + dat., *to marry*

núllus, -a, -um, *no, none* (9)

Num…? adv., *Surely…not…?* (introduces a question that expects the answer "no") (46)

númerō, -áre, -ávī, -átus, *to count* (33)

númerus, -ī, m., *number* (11)

númquam, adv., *never* (20)

nunc, adv., *now* (6, 13)

núntius, -ī, m., *messenger* (7)

núper, adv., *recently* (50)

núpta, nóva, -ae, f., *bride* (53)

nūptiális, -is, -e, *of/for a wedding* (53)

núsquam, adv., *nowhere* (39)

nux, núcis, f., *nut* (53)

O

ō (used with vocative and in exclamations) (9)

ob, prep. + acc., *on account of* (39)

obdórmiō, -íre, -ívī, -ītúrus, *to go to sleep* (21)

obésus, -a, -um, *fat* (18)

obscúrō, -áre, -ávī, -átus, *to hide* (30)

óbsecrō, -áre, -ávī, -átus, *to beseech, beg* (40, 51)

obsérvō, -áre, -ávī, -átus, *to watch, pay attention to* (6, 50)

obsídeō, obsidére, obsédī, obséssus, *to besiege* (38)

obsígnō, -áre, -ávī, -átus, *to sign* (53)

obstupefáctus, -a, -um, *astounded* (48)

occídō, occídere, occídī, occísus, *to kill* (45)

occupátus, -a, -um, *busy* (7)

occúrrō, occúrrere, occúrrī, occursúrus + dat., *to meet* (24)

Ōcéanus, -ī, m., *Ocean* (53)

octávus, -a, -um, *eighth* (36, 38)

óctō, *eight* (15, 38)

Octóber, Octóbris, Octóbre, *October* (36)

óculus, -ī, m., *eye* (26)

officiósus, -a, -um + dat., *ready to serve, obliging* (54)

officium, -ī, n., *official ceremony, duty* (51)

óleum, -ī, n., *oil* (32)

olfáciō, olfácere, olfécī, olfáctus *to catch the scent of, smell, sniff* (12, 18)

ólim, adv., *once (upon a time)* (18)

olíva, -ae, f., *olive* (33)

olīvétum, -ī, n., *olive grove* (14, 15)

ómen, óminis, n., *omen* (53)

omíttō, omíttere, omísī, omíssus, *to leave out, omit* (39)

ómnis, -is, -e, *all, the whole, every, each* (6, 18)

ónerō, -áre, -ávī, -átus, *to load*

ónus, óneris, n., *load, burden* (15)

opériō, operíre, opéruī, opértus, *to hide, cover* (53)

opórtet, oportére, opórtuit, *it is fitting; ought* (50, 52)

   Festīnáre tē opórtet, *That you hurry is fitting, You ought to hurry* (50)

óppidum, -ī, n., *town* (39)

ópprimō, opprímere, oppréssī, oppréssus, *to overwhelm* (30)

   oppréssus, -a, -um, *crushed* (25)

óptimus, -a, -um, *best, very good, excellent* (20, 31, 34)

   óptimē, adv., *best, very well, excellently* (34, 35)

   vir óptime, *sir* (20)

óptō, -áre, -ávī, -átus, *to wish* (54)

óra, -ae, f., *shore* (39)

ōrátiō, ōrātiónis, f., *oration, speech* (26)

   ōrātiónem habére, *to deliver a speech* (26)

ōrátor, ōrātóris, m., *orator, speaker* (22)

órdior, ōrdírī, órsus sum, *to begin* (38)

órior, oríri, órtus sum, *to rise* (45)

ōrnāméntum, -ī, n., *decoration*; pl., *furnishings* (30)

órnō, -áre, -ávī, -átus, *to decorate, equip* (53)

   ōrnátus, -a, -um, *decorated* (32)

Órpheus, -ī, m., *Orpheus (legendary singer and husband of Eurydice)* (VII)

órō, -áre, -ávī, -átus, *to beg* (51)

ōs, ṓris, n., *mouth, face, expression* (38)

os, ossis, n., *bone* (54)

ṓsculum, -ī, n., *kiss* (45)

osténdō, osténdere, osténdī, osténtus, *to show, point out* (48)

ṓvum, -ī, n., *egg* (32)

P

paedagṓgus, -ī, m., *tutor* (37)

paéne, adv., *almost* (30)

palaéstra, -ae, f., *exercise ground* (43)

Palātínus, -a, -um, *on/belonging to the Palatine Hill* (24)

pálla, -ae, f., *palla* (10)

pállium, -ī, n., *cloak* (32)

pálus, -ī, m., *post* (43)

pánis, pánis, gen. pl., **pánium**, m., *bread* (32)

pār ímpār, *odds or evens (a game)* (46)

párcō, párcere, pepércī + dat., *to spare* (49)

párēns, paréntis, m./f., *parent* (11)

páreō, -ére, -uī + dat., *to obey* (39)

pária, párium, n. pl., *pairs* (48)

páriēs, paríetis, m., *wall (of a house or room)* (30)

párō, -áre, -ávī, -átus, *to prepare, get ready* (5, 20)

   parátus, -a, -um, *ready, prepared* (10)

   sē paráre, *to prepare oneself, get ready* (22)

pars, pártis, gen. pl., **pártium**, f., *part, direction, region* (13)

párvulus, -a, -um, *small, little* (26)

párvus, -a, -um, *small* (30, 34)

páscō, páscere, pávī, pástus, *to feed, pasture* (31)

pássum, -ī, n., *raisin-wine* (33)

páter, pátris, m., *father* (6, 11)

   pátrēs, pátrum, m. pl., *senators* (52)

pátior, pátī, pássus sum, *to suffer, endure* (38)

patrṓnus, -ī, m., *patron* (25)

pátruus, -ī, m., *uncle* (22)

paúcī, -ae, -a, *few* (34)

paulátim, adv., *gradually, little by little* (34)

paulísper, adv., *for a short time* (20)

paúlus, -a, -um, *little, small* (54)

   paúlum, adv., *little* (35)

   paúlum, -ī, n., *a small amount, a little* (37)

paúper, paúperis, *poor* (42)

pavīméntum, -ī, n., *tiled floor* (44)

péctō, péctere, péxī, péxus, *to comb* (28)

péctus, péctoris, n., *chest, breast* (54)

   péctus plángere, *to beat the breast* (54)

pecúnia, -ae, f., *money* (21)

pécus, pécoris, n., *livestock, sheep and cattle* (33)

péior, péior, péius, gen., **peiṓris**, *worse* (34)

   péius, adv., *worse* (35)

per, prep. + acc., *through, along* (6, 9)

   per iócum, *as a prank/joke* (16)

percútiō, percútere, percússī, percússus, *to strike* (35)

pérdō, pérdere, pérdidī, pérditus, *to destroy* (45)

pérferō, perférre, pértulī, perlátus, irreg., *to report* (52)

perīculṓsus, -a, -um, *dangerous* (17)

perículum, -ī, n., *danger* (14, 15)

peristýlium, -ī, n., *peristyle (courtyard surrounded with a colonnade)* (46)

pérlegō, perlégere, perlégī, perléctus, *to read through* (54)

pérna, -ae, f., *ham* (31)

pernóctō, -áre, -ávī, -ātúrus, *to spend the night* (17)

perpétuus, -a, -um, *lasting, permanent* (54)

   in perpétuum, *forever* (54)

persuádeō, persuādére, persuásī, persuásus, *to make something* (acc.) *agreeable to someone* (dat.), *to persuade someone of something; to persuade someone* (dat.) (36, 51)

pertérritus, -a, -um, *frightened, terrified* (5)

perturbátus, -a, -um, *confused* (50)

pervéniō, perveníre, pervénī, perventúrus + ad + acc., *to arrive (at), reach* (25)

pēs, pédis, m., *foot* (13)

péssimus, -a, -um, *worst* (34)

   péssimē, adv., *worst* (35)

pesténtia, -ae, f., *plague* (33)

pétō, pétere, petívī, petítus, *to look for, seek, head for, aim at, attack* (5, 21)

pictúra, -ae, f., *picture* (1)

píla, -ae, f., *ball* (16)

   pílā lúdere, *to play ball* (16)

pínguis, -is, -e, *fat, rich* (31)

pīráta, -ae, m., *pirate* (21)

pírum, -ī, n., *pear* (33)

piscína, -ae, f., *fishpond* (3)

pístor, pīstóris, m., *baker* (54)

pīstrínum, -ī, n., *bakery* (37)

pláceō, -ére, -uī + dat., *to please* (34, 52)

    plácuit, *it was decided* (52)

plácidē, adv., *gently, peacefully, quietly, tamely*
    (14, 49)

plángō, plángere, plánxī, plánctus, *to beat* (54)

    péctus plángere, *to beat the breast* (54)

plaústrum, -ī, n., *wagon, cart* (15)

plénus, -a, -um, *full* (11)

plórō, -áre, -ávī, -átus, *to lament, mourn* (54)

plúit, plúere, plúit, *it rains, is raining* (23)

plúrēs, plúrēs, plúra, gen., **plúrium**, *more* (34)

plúrimus, -a, -um, *most, very much* (34)

    plúrimī, -ae, -a, *most, very many* (34)

    plúrimum, adv., *most* (35)

plūs, plúris, n., *more* (34)

    plūs vínī, *more wine* (34)

plūs, adv., *more* (35)

Plútō, Plūtónis, m., *Pluto (king of the
    underworld)* (32)

póculum, -ī, n., *cup, goblet* (33)

poéna, -ae, f., *punishment, penalty* (40)

    poénās dáre, *to pay the penalty, be punished* (40)

poéta, -ae, f., *poet* (25)

pollíceor, pollicérī, pollícitus sum, *to promise* (45)

pómpa, -ae, f., *funeral procession* (54)

Pompéiī, -órum, m. pl., *Pompeii*

pónō, pónere, pósuī, pósitus, *to put, place* (10, 21)

pōns, póntis, gen. pl., **póntium**, m., *bridge* (23)

popína, -ae, f., *eating-house, bar* (33)

pópulus, -ī, m. *people* (47)

pórcus, -ī, m., *pig, pork* (28, 33)

pórta, -ae, f., *gate* (11)

pórtō, -áre, -ávī, -átus, *to carry* (6)

póscō, póscere, popóscī, *to demand, ask for* (34)

póssum, pósse, pótuī, irreg., *to be able; I
    can* (5, 14, 21)

post, prep. + acc., *after* (20)

post, adv., *after(ward), later* (39)

    múltīs post ánnīs, *many years afterward* (39)

pósteā, adv., *afterward* (33)

pósterus, -a, -um, *next, following* (52)

póstis, póstis, gen. pl., **póstium**, m., *door-post* (25)

póstquam, conj., *after* (20)

postrémus, -a, -um, *last* (53)

    postrémō, adv., *finally* (46)

postrídiē, adv., *on the following day* (26)

pótius quam, *rather than* (52)

praébeō, -ére, -uī, -itus, *to display, show,
    provide* (52)

praecédō, praecédere, praecéssī, praecessúrus,
    to go in front (53)

praecípiō, praecípere, praecépī, praecéptus +
    dat., *to instruct, order* (51)

praecípitō, -áre, -ávī, -átus, *to hurl* (18)

    sē praecipitáre, *to hurl oneself, rush* (18)

praeclárus, -a, -um, *distinguished, famous* (13)

**praecúrrō, praecúrrere, praecúrrī,
    praecursúrus**, *to run ahead* (18)

praédō, praedónis, m., *robber* (26)

praéferō, praeférre, praétulī, praelátus, irreg. +
    acc. and dat., *to carry X (acc.)
    in front of Y (dat.)* (37)

praéter, prep. + acc., *except* (21)

praetéreā, adv., *besides, too, moreover* (15)

praetéreō, praeteríre, praetériī or **praeterívī,
    praetéritus**, irreg., *to go past* (15)

praetéxta, tóga, -ae, f., *toga with purple border* (10)

praetextátus, -a, -um, *wearing the **toga
    praetexta*** (52)

prásinus, -a, -um, *green* (27)

prehéndō, prehéndere, prehéndī, prehénsus, *to
    seize* (44)

prétium, -ī, n., *price* (31)

prídiē, adv. + acc., *on the day before* (36)

prímus, -a, -um, *first* (21, 38)

    prímā lúce, *at dawn* (21)

    prímō, adv., *first, at first* (40)

    prímum, adv., *first, at first* (23)

    cum prímum, conj., *as soon as* (40)

    quam prímum, *as soon as possible* (40)

prínceps, príncipis, m., *emperor, leader, leading citizen* (7)

príor, príor, príus, gen., **prióris**, *first (of two), previous* (45)

  príus, adv., *earlier, previously* (33)

prīscus, -a, -um, *of olden times, ancient* (54)

procácitās, procācitátis, f., *insolence* (39)

prócāx, procácis, *insolent;* as slang, *pushy* (31)

prōcédō, prōcédere, prōcéssī, prōcessúrus, *to go forward* (33)

prō cértō habére, *to be sure* (47)

prócul, adv., *in the distance, far off, far* (15)

pródeō, prōdíre, pródiī, prōditúrus, irreg., *to come forth* (53)

Prō dī immortálēs! *Good heavens!* (42)

próferō, prōférre, prótulī, prōlátus, irreg., *to carry forward, continue* (52)

proficíscor, proficíscī, proféctus sum, *to set out, leave* (36, 37)

prófugus, -a, -um, *exiled, fugitive* (39)

prōgrédior, prōgredī, prōgréssus sum, *to go forward, advance* (45)

prōmíttō, prōmíttere, prōmísī, prōmíssus, *to promise* (9)

prónuba, -ae, f., *bride's attendant* (50)

prónus, -a, -um, *face down* (35)

própe, prep. + acc., *near* (5, 9)

própe, adv., *near, nearby, nearly* (45)

propínquus, -ī, m., *relative* (50)

prōpónō, prōpónere, prōpósuī, prōpósitus, *to propose* (X)

própter, prep. + acc., *on account of, because of* (26)

prōrúmpō, prōrúmpere, prōrúpī, prōrúptus, *to burst forth, burst out* (53)

prótinus, adv., *immediately* (54)

prōvíncia, -ae, f., *province* (XII)

próximus, -a, -um, *nearby* (33)

prūdēns, prūdéntis, *wise, sensible* (34)

  prūdénter, adv., *wisely, sensibly* (34, 35)

prūdéntia, -ae, f., *good sense, discretion, skill* (52)

públicus, -a, -um, *public* (51)

puélla, -ae, f., *girl* (1)

púer, púerī, m., *boy* (3)

puerílis, -is, -e, *childish, of childhood* (51)

púgiō, pūgiónis, m., *dagger* (42)

púgna, -ae, f., *fight, battle* (48)

  púgnam commíttere, *to join battle* (48)

púgnō, -áre, -ávī, -atúrus, *to fight* (48)

púlcher, púlchra, púlchrum, *beautiful, pretty, handsome* (28)

  pulchérrimus, -a, -um, *most/very beautiful* (32)

  púlchrē, adv., *finely, excellently* (35)

pulchritúdō, pulchritúdinis, f., *beauty* (53)

púllus, -ī, m., *chicken* (32)

pulvínar, pulvīnáris, n., *imperial seat (at games)* (48)

púlvis, púlveris, m., *dust* (15)

púniō, -íre, -ívī, -ítus, *to punish* (21)

púpa, -ae, f., *doll* (46)

púrgō, -áre, -ávī, -átus, to clean (6)

púrus, -a, -um, *spotless, clean, plain white* (51)

  tóga púra, -ae, f., *plain white toga* (51)

pútō, -áre, -ávī, -átus, *to think, consider* (46)

Pýramus, -ī, m., *Pyramus* (45)

Q

quā dē caúsā, *for this reason* (32)

quadrátus, -a, -um, *squared* (25)

quaérō, quaérere, quaesívī, quaesítus, *to seek, look for, ask (for)* (30)

Quális...? Quális...? Quále...? *What sort of...?* (4)

Quam...! adv., *How...! What a...!* (13, 29, 36)

Quam...? adv., *How...?* (36)

quam, adv., *than, as* (34, 36)

  pótius quam, *rather than* (51)

  quam, adv. + superlative adj. or adv., *as...as possible* (35, 36)

  quam celérrimē, adv., *as quickly as possible* (34)

  quam prímum, adv., *as soon as possible* (40)

Quam ob caúsam...? *For what reason...?* (28)

quámquam, conj., *although* (11)

Quándō...? adv., *When...?* (12, 21)

quandóquidem, adv., *since* (54)

Quántus, -a, -um...? *How big...? How much...?* (41)

  Quántī...? *How much (in price)...?* (31)

  Quántum...! adv., *How much...!* (41)

quártus, -a, -um, *fourth* (38)

quártus décimus, -a, -um, *fourteenth* (38)

quási, adv., *as if* (49)

quáttuor, *four* (15, 38)

quattuórdecim, *fourteen* (38)

-que, enclitic conj., *and* (36)

quī, quae, quod, *who, which, that* (1, 3, 14, 28, 29, 36)

Quī…? Quae…? Quod…? interrog. adj., *What…? Which…?* (29)

Quid ágis? *How are you?* (18, 53)

quídam, quaédam, quóddam, *a certain* (10, 29)

quídem, adv., *indeed* (31)

   nē…quídem, adv., *not even* (34)

quiḗs, quiḗtis, f., *rest* (23)

   sē quiḗtī dáre, *to rest* (23)

quiéscō, quiéscere, quiévī, quiētū́rus, *to rest, keep quiet* (13, 23)

quíndecim, *fifteen* (38)

quīngentḗsimus, -a, -um, *five-hundredth* (38)

quīngéntī, -ae, -a, *five hundred* (15, 38)

quīnquāgḗsimus, -a, -um, *fiftieth* (38)

quīnquāgíntā, *fifty* (15, 38)

quínque, *five* (15, 38)

quíntus, -a, -um, *fifth* (26, 38)

quíntus décimus, -a, -um, *fifteenth* (38)

Quirīnális, -is, -e, *Quirinal (Hill)* (35)

Quis…? Quid…? *Who…? What…?* (1, 4, 29)

   Quid ágis? *How are you?* (18, 53)

quis, sī (see **aliquis**) (51)

quis, nē (see **aliquis**) (52)

quō, adv., *there, to that place* (43)

   Quō cum, *When…there* (43)

Quō…? adv., *Where…to?* (4)

quō…eō…, *the (more)…the (more)…* (36, 47)

Quócum…? *With whom…?* (12, 26)

quod (see **quī, quae, quod**)

quod, conj., *because;* with verbs of feeling, *that* (1, 13, 29)

Quō īnstrūméntō…? *With what instrument…? By what means…? How…?* (12)

Quómodo…? adv., *In what way…? How…?* (12)

quóniam, conj., *since* (42)

quóque, adv., *also* (2, 13)

Quot…? *How many…?* (15, 38)

Quótus, -a, -um…? *What/Which (in numerical order)…?* (38)

   Quóta hóra est? *What time is it?* (38)

R

raéda, -ae, f., *carriage* (10)

raedárius, -ī, m., *coachman, driver* (10)

rámus, -ī, m., *branch* (4)

rápiō, rápere, rápuī, ráptus, *to snatch, seize* (40)

rebélliō, rebelliónis, f., *rebellion* (XI)

recípiō, recípere, recḗpī, recéptus, *to receive, recapture* (53)

récitō, -áre, -ávī, -átus, *to read aloud, recite* (29)

   recitándī, *of reciting* (39)

recognítiō, recognitiónis, f., *recognition* (49)

réctus, -a, -um, *right, proper* (35)

   réctē, adv., *rightly, properly* (31, 35)

recúmbō, recúmbere, recúbuī, *to recline, lie down* (29)

recúperō, -áre, -ávī, -átus, *to recover* (21)

   ánimum recuperáre, *to regain one's senses, be fully awake* (21)

réddō, réddere, réddidī, rédditus, *to give back, return* (29)

redémptor, redēmptóris, m., *contractor* (54)

rédeō, redíre, rédiī or **redívī, reditū́rus,** irreg., *to return, go back* (7, 23, 49)

   rédiēns, redeúntis, *returning* (39)

réditus, -ūs, m., *return* (25)

redúcō, redúcere, redúxī, redúctus, *to lead back, take back* (42)

réferō, reférre, réttulī, relátus, irreg., *to bring back, report, write down* (46)

refíciō, refícere, refḗcī, reféctus, *to remake, redo, restore* (32)

rēgína, -ae, f., *queen* (38)

régnum, -ī, n., *kingdom* (32)

regrédior, régredī, regréssus sum, *to go back, return* (36, 37)

relínquō, relínquere, relíquī, relíctus, *to leave behind* (16, 21)

remóveō, removére, remóvī, remótus, *to remove, move aside* (21)

rénovō, -áre, -ávī, -átus, *to renew, revive* (38)

repéllō, repéllere, réppulī, repúlsus, *to drive off, drive back* (5, 40)

répetō, repétere, repetívī, repetítus, *to pick up, recover* (43)

reprehéndō, reprehéndere, reprehéndī, reprehénsus, *to blame, scold* (6, 31)

requírō, requírere, requīsívī, requīsítus, *to ask, inquire* (54)

rēs, réī, f., *thing, matter, situation, affair* (19, 25)

   rem explicáre, *to explain the situation* (19)

   rēs urbánae, rérum urbānárum, f. pl., *affairs of the city/town* (33)

   rē vérā, adv., *really, actually* (49)

rescríbō, rescríbere, rescrípsī, rescríptus, *to write back, reply* (50)

resérvō, -áre, -ávī, -átus, *to reserve* (48)

resístō, resístere, réstitī + dat., *to resist* (42)

respóndeō, respondére, respóndī, respōnsúrus, *to reply* (5, 21)

respónsum, -ī, n., *reply* (38)

retíneō, retinére, retínuī, reténtus, *to hold back, keep* (31)

rē vérā, adv., *really, actually* (49)

révocō, -áre, -ávī, -átus, *to recall, call back* (7)

rēx, régis, m., *king*

rídeō, rīdére, rísī, rísus, *to laugh (at), smile* (3, 21)

rīdículus, -a, -um, *absurd, laughable* (43)

ríma, -ae, f., *crack* (45)

   rīmósus, -a, -um, *full of cracks, leaky* (23)

rísus, -ūs, m., *laugh, smile* (13, 25)

ríte, adv., *properly* (53)

rívus, -ī, m., *stream* (5)

ríxa, -ae, f., *quarrel* (29)

ríxor, -árī, -átus sum, *to quarrel* (45)

rogátiō, rogātiónis, f., *question* (40)

rógō, -áre, -ávī, -átus, *to ask* (12, 51)

   sē rogáre, *to ask oneself, wonder* (21)

rógus, -ī, m., *funeral pyre* (54)

Róma, -ae, f., *Rome* (7)

Rómā, *from Rome*

Rómae, *in Rome* (39)

Rómam, *to Rome* (7)

Rōmánus, -a, -um, *Roman* (1)

   Rōmánī, -órum, m. pl., *the Romans* (III)

rósa, -ae, f., *rose* (34)

róta, -ae, f., *wheel* (15)

ruína, -ae, f., *collapse, ruin* (38)

rúmpō, rúmpere, rúpī, rúptus, *to burst* (29)

rúrsus, adv., *again* (36)

rūs, rúris, n., *country, country estate* (39)

   rúre, *from the country* (39)

   rúrī, *in the country* (39)

   rūs, *to the country* (39)

russátus, -a, -um, *red* (27)

rústica, vílla, -ae, f., *country house and farm* (1)

rústicus, -ī, m., *peasant* (13)

S

sácculus, -ī, m., *small bag (used for holding money)* (34)

sácra, -órum, n. pl., *religious rites, sacrifice* (53)

sacríficō, -áre, -ávī, -átus, *to sacrifice* (53)

saéculum, -ī, n., *age, era* (48)

saépe, adv., *often* (2, 13, 35)

   saépius, adv., *more often* (35)

   saepíssimē, adv., *most often* (35)

saévus, -a, -um, *fierce, savage* (39)

sal, sális, m., *salt, wit* (34)

saltátrīx, saltātrícis, f., *dancer* (21)

sáltō, -áre, -ávī, -átúrus, *to dance* (21)

sálūs, salútis, f., *greetings* (36)

   salútem dícere, *to send greetings* (36)

   salútem plúrimam dícere, *to send fondest greetings* (36)

salútō, -áre, -ávī, -átus, *to greet, welcome* (7)

Sálvē!/Salvéte! *Greetings! Hello!* (7)

sálvus, -a, -um, *safe* (5)

sánē, adv., *certainly, of course* (36)

sanguíneus, -a, -um, *bloodstained* (45)

sánguis, sánguinis, m., *blood* (33)

sátis, adv., *enough* (23)

   sátis témporis, *enough time* (23)

scápha, -ae, f., *small boat, ship's boat* (40, 42)

sceléstus, -a, -um, *wicked* (10)

scélus, scéleris, n., *crime* (41)

scíndō, scíndere, scídī, scíssus, *to cut, split, carve, tear* (33, 54)

    scíssā véste, *with torn clothing* (54)

scíō, -íre, -ívī, -ítus, *to know* (16, 49)

scriblíta, -ae, f., *tart or pastry with cheese filling* (37)

scríbō, scríbere, scrípsī, scríptus, *to write* (1, 24)

sē, *himself, herself, oneself, itself, themselves* (11)

    sécum, *with him (her, it, them) (-self, -selves)*

sēcrétō, adv., *secretly* (45)

secúndus, -a, -um, *second* (9, 38)

    secúndae ménsae, -árum, f. pl., *second course, dessert* (33)

sēcúrus, -a, -um, *carefree, unconcerned* (35)

sed, conj., *but* (2)

sédecim, *sixteen* (38)

sédeō, sedére, sédī, sessúrus, *to sit* (1, 21)

sélla, -ae, f., *sedan chair, seat, chair* (28, 42, 44)

sēmisómnus, -a, -um, *half-asleep* (9)

sémper, adv., *always* (4, 13)

senátor, senātóris, m., *senator* (7)

senátus, -ūs, m., *Senate* (25)

sénex, sénis, m., *old man* (I, 43)

séniō, sēniónis, m., *the six (in throwing knucklebones)* (34)

séntiō, sentíre, sénsī, sénsus, *to feel, notice, realize* (45, 49)

sepéliō, sepelíre, sepelívī, sepúltus, *to bury* (39)

séptem, *seven* (15, 38)

Septémber, Septémbris, Septémbre, *September* (36)

septéndecim, *seventeen* (38)

septentriōnális, -is, -e, *northern* (39)

séptimus, -a, -um, *seventh* (13, 38)

séptimus décimus, -a, -um, *seventeenth* (38)

septuāgésimus, -a, -um, *seventieth* (IX)

sepúlcrum, -ī, n., *tomb* (22)

séquor, séquī, secútus sum, *to follow* (36, 37)

    séquēns, sequéntis, *following* (25)

serénus, -a, -um, *clear, bright* (50)

sérmō, sermónis, m., *conversation, talk* (54)

sérō, adv., *late* (21, 35)

    sérius, adv., *later* (35)

    séríssimē, adv., *latest* (35)

sérva, -ae, f., *slave-woman, slave-girl* (50)

sérviō, servíre, servívī, servītúrus + dat., *to serve* (53)

sérvitūs, servitútis, f., *slavery* (XI)

sérvō, -áre, -ávī, -átus, *to save* (26, 30)

sérvus, -ī, m., *slave* (3)

seu = síve, conj., *or if* (34)

sex, *six* (15, 38)

séxtus, -a, -um, *sixth* (37, 38)

séxtus décimus, -a, -um, *sixteenth* (38)

sī, conj., *if* (5)

    sī quis (= **áliquis**), *if anyone* (51)

    si vīs, *if you wish, please* (26)

sīc, adv., *thus, in this way* (38, 39, 50)

síccus, -a, -um, *dry* (53)

Sicília, -ae, f., *Sicily* (38)

sígnum, -ī, n., *signal, sign* (27)

siléntium, -ī, n., *silence* (15)

sílva, -ae, f., *woods, forest* (5)

símilis, -is, -e + dat., *similar (to), like* (34, 50)

símul, adv., *together, at the same time* (9, 13)

símulac, conj., *as soon as* (24)

símulō, -áre, -ávī, -átus, *to pretend* (21)

síne, prep. + abl., *without* (26)

siníster, sinístra, sinístrum, *left* (50)

sínō, sínere, sívī, sítus, *to allow* (34)

sīs = sī vīs, *if you wish, please* (36)

sítus, -a, -um, *located, situated, buried* (33, 54)

sōl, sólis, m., *sun* (50)

sólea, -ae, f., *sandal* (32)

sóleō, solére, sólitus sum + infin., *to be accustomed (to), be in the habit of* (10, 40)

sōlitúdō, sōlitúdinis, f., *solitude* (39)

sollícitus, -a, -um, *anxious, worried* (4)

sólus, -a, -um, *alone* (3)

sólvō, sólvere, sólvī, solútus, *to loosen, untie, dishevel* (54)

sómnium, -ī, n., *dream* (21)

sómnus, -ī, m., *sleep* (21)

sónitus, -ūs, m., *sound* (21, 25)

sórdidus, -a, -um, *dirty* (19)

sóror, soróris, f., *sister* (11)

S.P.D. = salútem plúrimam dícit (36)

spectáculum, -ī, n., *sight, spectacle* (30)

spectátor, spectātóris, m., *spectator* (27)

spéctō, -áre, -ávī, -átus, *to watch, look at* (7)

spéculum, -ī, n., *mirror* (28)

spēlúnca, -ae, f., *cave* (45)

spérō, -áre, -ávī, -átus, *to hope* (47)

spóndeō, spondére, spopóndī, spónsus, *to promise solemnly, pledge* (50)

spónsa, -ae, f., *betrothed woman, bride* (50)

spōnsália, spōnsálium, n. pl., *betrothal ceremony* (50)

spónsus, -ī, m., *betrothed man, bridegroom* (50)

státim, adv., *immediately* (5, 13)

státua, -ae, f., *statue* (3)

stéla, -ae, f., *tombstone* (33)

stércus, stércoris, n., *dung, manure* (21)

stértō, stértere, stértuī, *to snore* (25)

stílus, -ī, m., *pen* (25)

stírps, stírpis, gen. pl., **stírpium**, f., *thorn* (49)

stō, stáre, stétī, statúrus, *to stand* (10, 22)

stóla, -ae, f., *stola, a woman's outer-garment* (10)

strátum, -ī, n., *sheet, covering* (32)

strénuus, -a, -um, *active, energetic* (2)
  strénuē, adv., *strenuously, hard* (6, 13, 35)

strépitus, -ūs, m., *noise, clattering* (23, 25)

strígilis, strígilis, gen. pl., **strigílium**, f., *strigil, scraper* (43)

stríngō, stríngere, strínxī, stríctus, *to draw* (26)
  gládium stríngere, *to draw a sword* (26)

stúdeō, -ére, -uī + dat., *to study* (39)

stúdium, -ī, n., *enthusiasm, study* (41)

stúltus, -a, -um, *stupid, foolish* (23)

stúpeō, -ére, -uī, *to be amazed, gape* (23)

suávis, -is, -e, *sweet, delightful* (34)

sub, prep. + abl., *under, beneath* (1, 9)

súbitus, -a, -um, *sudden* (54)
  súbitō, adv., *suddenly* (3, 13)

submíssus, -a, -um, *quiet, subdued, soft* (50)

súbsequor, súbsequī, subsecútus sum, *to follow (up)* (44)

Subúra, -ae, f., *Subura (a section of Rome off the Forum, known for its night life)* (35)

súī (see **sē**)

sum, ésse, fúī, futúrus, irreg., *to be* (1, 14, 20, 21)

súmmus, -a, -um, *greatest, very great, the top of…* (35)
  súmmā celeritáte, *with the greatest speed, as fast as possible* (29)

súmō, súmere, súmpsī, súmptus, *to take, take up, pick out, assume (i.e., put on for the first time)* (22, 51)

súper, prep. + acc., *over, above* (53)

supérbus, -a, -um, *proud, arrogant* (48)

súperī, -órum, m. pl., *the gods above* (39)

súperō, -áre, -ávī, -átus, *to overcome, defeat* (42)

suppositícius, -ī, m., *substitute* (48)

súprā, prep. + acc., *above* (23)

súprā, adv., *above, on top* (21)

súrgō, súrgere, surréxī, surrēctúrus, *to get up, rise* (6, 21)

surrípiō, surrípere, surrípuī, surréptus, *to steal* (44)

súus, -a, -um, *his, her, its, their (own)* (9, 27, 54)

T

tabellárius, -ī, m., *courier* (13)

tabérna, -ae, f., *shop* (25)

tablínum, -ī, n., *study* (26)

tábulae, -árum, f. pl., *tablets, records* (51, 53)

Tabulárium, -ī, n., *Public Records Office* (51)

tabulátum, -ī, n., *story, floor* (30)

táceō, -ére, -uī, -itus, *to be quiet* (9)

tácitē, adv., *silently* (9, 13)

taéda, -ae, f., *torch* (53)

taédet, taedére, taésum est, *it bores, makes one (acc.) tired of something (gen.)* (16, 50, 52)
  mē taédet + gen., *it tires me of…, I am tired of/bored with…* (50)

Talássius, -ī, m., *Talassius (god of marriage)* (53)

tálī, -órum, m. pl., *knucklebones* (34)

tális, -is, -e, *such, like this, of this kind* (23, 50)
  tália, tálium, n. pl., *such things* (41)

tam, adv., *so* (30, 50)

támen, adv., *however, nevertheless* (6, 13)

támquam, conj., *just as if* (33)

tándem, adv., *at last, at length* (2, 13)

tángō, tángere, tétigī, táctus, *to touch* (54)

tántus, -a, -um, *so great, such a big* (24, 50)

  tántum, adv., *only; so much* (15, 50)

tárdus, -a, -um, *slow* (15)

tē (from **tū**) (4)

tégō, tégere, téxī, téctus, *to cover* (54)

téla, -ae, f., *web, fabric, loom* (41)

temerárius, -a, -um, *rash, reckless, bold* (5)

tempéstās, tempestátis, f., *storm* (38)

témplum, -ī, n., *temple* (40)

témptō, -áre, -ávī, -átus, *to try* (9)

témpus, témporis, n., *time* (2, 8, 12, 15)

  ad témpus, *on time* (37)

téneō, tenére, ténuī, téntus, *to hold* (9, 25)

  memóriā tenére, *to remember* (37)

tepidárium, -ī, n., *warm room (at baths)* (43)

ter, adv., *three times* (48)

térgeō, tergére, térsī, térsus, *to dry, wipe* (43)

térgum, -ī, n., *back, rear* (35)

térra, -ae, f., *earth, ground, land* (26, 38)

térreō, -ére, -uī, -itus, *to frighten, terrify* (4)

terríbilis, -is, -e, *frightening* (39)

térritus, -a, -um, *frightened* (39)

térror, terróris, m., *terror, fear* (22)

tértius, -a, -um, *third* (25, 36, 38)

tértius décimus, -a, -um, *thirteenth* (38)

téssera, -ae, f., *ticket* (48)

testāméntum, -ī, n., *will, testament* (IX)

téxō, téxere, téxuī, téxtus, *to weave* (41)

thérmae, -árum, f. pl., *public baths* (43)

Thérmae Nerōnéae, -árum, f. pl., *the Baths of Nero* (43)

Thísbē, Thísbēs, f., *Thisbe* (45)

Thrácia, -ae, f., *Thrace (country northeast of Greece)* (39)

tībícen, tībícinis, m., *piper* (54)

tígris, tígris, gen. pl., **tígrium**, m./f., *tiger* (49)

tímeō, -ére, -uī, *to fear, be afraid to/of* (5)

  timéndus, -a, um, *to be feared* (48)

tímidus, -a, -um, *afraid, fearful, timid* (21)

tímor, timóris, m., *fear* (35)

tóga, -ae, f., *toga* (8)

  tóga praetéxta, -ae, f., *toga with purple border* (10, 51)

  tóga púra, -ae, f., *plain white toga* (51)

  tóga virílis, tógae virílis, f., *toga of manhood, plain white toga* (10, 51)

tóllō, tóllere, sústulī, sublátus, irreg., *to lift, raise* (48)

tórus, -ī, m., *couch* (38)

tot, indecl. adj., *so many* (48, 50)

tótus, -a, -um, *all, the whole* (21)

trádō, trádere, trádidī, tráditus, *to hand over* (7, 22)

tráhō, tráhere, tráxī, tráctus, *to drag, pull* (6, 12, 25)

  lánam tráhere, *to spin wool* (6)

trāns, prep. + acc., *across* (39)

trānsgrédior, tránsgredī, trānsgréssus sum, *to cross* (X)

trédecim, *thirteenth* (38)

trémō, trémere, trémuī, *to tremble* (21)

trémor, tremóris, m., *cause of fright, terror* (48)

trépidāns, trepidántis, *in a panic* (52)

trēs, trēs, tría, *three* (13, 15, 38)

trīclínium, -ī, n., *dining room* (31)

trídēns, tridéntis, gen. pl., **tridéntium**, m., *trident* (48)

trígōn, trigónis, m., *ball game involving three people, ball (used in this game)* (43)

trístis, -is, -e, *sad* (36)

Tróia, -ae, f., *Troy* (I, 38)

Troiánus, -a, -um, *Trojan* (I)

  Troiánī, -órum, m. pl., *the Trojans* (I)

tū, *you* (sing.) (4, 27)

túbicen, tubícinis, m., *trumpet-player* (48)

túlī (see **férō**)

tum, adv., *at that moment, then* (4, 13)

tumúltus, -ūs, m., *uproar, commotion* (25)

túnica, -ae, f., *tunic* (8)

túrba, -ae, f., *crowd, mob; cause of confusion/turmoil* (23, 48)

túus, -a, -um, *your* (sing.) (9, 27)

U

Úbi...? adv., *Where...?* (10, 12)

úbi, adv., conj., *where, when* (1, 5, 13)

Ulíxēs, Ulíxis, m., *Ulysses, Odysseus (Greek hero of the Trojan War)* (38)

úlulō, -áre, -ávī, -átus, *to howl* (33)

úmbra, -ae, f., *shadow, shade (of the dead)* (31, 33)

úmquam, adv., *ever* (31)

únā, adv., *together* (33)

únda, -ae, f., *wave* (42)

Únde...? *From where...?* (12)

úndecim, *eleven* (38)

ūndécimus, -a, -um, *eleventh* (17, 38)

ūndēvīcésimus, -a, -um, *nineteenth* (38)

ūndēvīgíntī, *nineteen* (38)

úndique, adv., *on all sides, from all sides* (23)

unguéntum, -ī, n., *ointment, perfume, oil* (34, 43)

únguō, únguere, únxī, únctus, *to anoint, smear with oil* (43)

ūnivérsus, -a, -um, *the whole of, the entire* (48)

únus, -a, -um, *one* (15, 38)

   únā, adv., *together* (33)

urbánus, -a, -um, *of the city/town* (33)

   rēs urbánae, rérum urbānárum, f. pl., *affairs of the city/town* (33)

urbs, úrbis, gen. pl., **úrbium**, f., *city* (7)

úrgeō, urgére, úrsī, *to press, insist* (52)

ut, conj. + indicative, *as, when* (16, 54)

ut, conj. + subjunctive, *so that, that, to* (50, 53, 54)

utérque, útraque, utrúmque, *each (of two), both* (45)

útilis, -is, -e, *useful* (37)

útrum...an..., conj., *whether...or...* (52)

úva, -ae, f., *grape, bunch of grapes* (33)

úxor, uxóris, f., *wife* (11)

V

váldē, adv., *very, very much, exceedingly* (19)

váleō, -ére, -uī, -itúrus, *to be strong, be well* (40)

   Válē!/Valéte! *Goodbye!* (9)

valedícō, valedícere, valedíxī, valedictúrus, *to say goodbye* (45)

valētúdō, valētúdinis, f., *health (good or bad)* (39)

vápor, vapóris, m., *steam* (43)

várius, -a, -um, *different, various, varied, many-hued* (43, 53)

-ve, enclitic conj., *or* (34)

véhemēns, veheméntis, *violent* (35)

   veheménter, adv., *very much, violently, hard, insistently* (19)

vehículum, -ī, n., *vehicle* (13, 15)

véhō, véhere, véxī, véctus, *to carry;* pass., *to be carried, travel* (54)

   véctus, -a, -um, *having been carried, having traveled* (54)

vel, conj., *or* (37)

   vel...vel..., *either...or...*

vélámen, véláminis, n., *veil, shawl* (45)

vélle (see **vólō**)

véndō, véndere, véndidī, vénditus, *to sell* (28)

vénetus, -a, -um, *blue* (27)

véniō, veníre, vénī, ventúrus, *to come* (7, 20)

véntus, -ī, m., *wind* (42)

Vénus, Véneris, f., *Venus (the goddess of love); the highest throw of the knucklebones* (34)

venústus, -a, -um, *charming* (34)

vérberō, -áre, -ávī, -átus, *to beat, whip* (11)

verbósus, -a, -um, *talkative* (26)

vérbum, -ī, n., *word, verb* (39)

véreor, verérī, véritus sum, *to be afraid, fear* (37)

Vergílius, -ī, m., *Vergil (Roman poet)* (37)

versipéllis, versipéllis, gen. pl., **versipéllium**, m., *werewolf* (33)

vérsus, -ūs, m., *verse, line (of poetry)* (29)

vértō, vértere, vértī, vérsus, *to turn* (16)

vérus, -a, -um, *true* (40)

   ímmō vérō, adv., *on the contrary, in fact* (40)

   Íta vérō! *Yes! Indeed!* (3, 13)

   Mínimē vérō! *No indeed! Not at all!* (31)

   rē vérā, *really, actually* (49)

   véra dícere, *to tell the truth* (40)

   vérō, adv., *truly, really, indeed* (31)

véscor, véscī + abl., *to feed (on)* (49)

vésperī, *in the evening* (18)

véster, véstra, véstrum, *your* (pl.) (22, 27)

vestíbulum, -ī, n., *entrance passage* (43)

vēstígium, -ī, n., *track, footprint, trace* (12, 15)

vestīméntum, -ī, n., *clothing;* pl., *clothes* (33)

véstis, véstis, gen. pl., **véstium**, f., *clothing, garment* (29, 54)

   scíssā véste, *with torn clothing* (54)

vétō, vetáre, vétuī, vétitus, *to forbid, tell not to* (26)

vétus, véteris, *old* (34)

véxō, -áre, -ávī, -átus, *to annoy* (4)

   vexátus, -a, -um, *annoyed* (28)

vía, -ae, f., *road, street* (10)

   Vía Áppia, -ae, f., *Appian Way* (11)

   Vía Flāmínia, -ae, f., *the Via Flaminia (a road from Rome leading through the Campus Martius and north to Ariminum on the Adriatic Sea)* (54)

viátor, viātóris, m., *traveler* (18)

vīcésimus, -a, -um, *twentieth* (38)

vīcínus, -a, -um, *neighboring, adjacent* (1)

víctor, victóris, m., *conqueror, victor* (27)

victória, -ae, f., *victory* (XII)

vídeō, vidére, vídī, vísus, *to see* (4, 21, 49)

   vídeor, vidérī, vísus sum, *to seem, be seen* (21)

vígilō, -áre, -ávī, -ātúrus, *to stay awake* (19)

vīgíntī, *twenty* (36, 38)

vílicus, -ī, m., *overseer, farm manager* (11)

vílla, -ae, f., *country house* (1)

   vílla rústica, -ae, f., *country house and farm* (1)

víncō, víncere, vícī, víctus, *to conquer, win* (27)

vínea, -ae, f., *vineyard* (12)

vínum, -ī, n., *wine* (25)

vínō ábstinēns, *refraining from wine, abstemious* (34)

víolō, -áre, -ávī, -átus, *to do harm* (54)

vir, vírī, m., *man, husband* (3, 11)

   vir óptime, *sir* (20)

vírga, -ae, f., *stick, rod, switch* (13)

vírgō, vírginis, f., *maiden* (45)

virílis, -is, -e, *of manhood* (23)

   tóga virílis, tógae virílis, f., *toga of manhood, plain white toga* (10)

vīs, acc., **vim**, abl., **vī**, f., *force, amount;* pl. *strength* (30)

víscera, víscerum, n. pl., *vital organs* (53)

vísitō, -áre, -ávī, -átus, *to visit* (23)

vispíllō, vispillónis, m., *undertaker* (54)

víta, -ae, f., *life* (54)

   ē vítā excédere, *to die* (54)

vítō, -áre, -ávī, -átus, *to avoid* (13)

vítta, -ae, f., *ribbon, headband* (53)

vívō, vívere, víxī, victúrus, *to live* (39)

vix, adv., *scarcely, with difficulty, only just* (24)

vócō, -áre, -ávī, -átus, *to call, invite* (28)

vólō, vélle, vóluī, irreg., *to wish, want, be willing* (5, 17, 20, 21)

   sī vīs, *if you wish, please* (36)

volúptās, voluptátis, f., *pleasure, delight* (48)

vōs, *you* (pl.) (8, 27)

vōx, vócis, f., *voice* (4)

vúlnerō, -áre, -ávī, -átus, *to wound* (33)

vúlnus, vúlneris, n., *wound* (35)

vult (from **vólō**) (5, 17)

vúltus, -ūs, f., *face, expression* (45)

ENGLISH TO LATIN VOCABULARY

Verbs are usually cited in their infinitive form. For further information about the Latin words in this list, please consult the Latin to English Vocabulary list.

A

able, to be, **pósse**
about, **dē**
above, **súper, súprā**
absent, to be, **abésse**
abstemious, **vínō ábstinēns**
absurd, **rīdículus**
accidentally, **cásū**
accompanied, **comitátus**
accompany, to, **comitárī**
accomplish, to, **cōnfícere**
accuse, to, **accūsáre**
accustomed (to), to be, **solére**
across, **trāns**
active, **strénuus**
actor, **áctor**
actor of mime, **mímus**
actually, **rē vérā**
add, to, **áddere**
address, to, **álloquī**
adjacent, **vīcínus**
adopt, to, **adoptáre**
adopt a plan, to, **cōnsílium cápere**
advance, to, **prógredī**
advise, to, **monére**
Aeneas, **Aenéās**
Aeneid, the, **Aenéis**
affair, **rēs**
affairs of the city/town, **rēs urbánae**
affect, to, **afficere**
affected, **afféctus**
afraid, **tímidus**
afraid, to be, **verérī**

afraid (to/of), to be, **timére**
Africa, **África**
after, **póstquam**
after(ward), **post**
afterward, **pósteā**
again, **íterum, rúrsus**
again and again, **idéntidem**
against, **cóntrā, in**
age, **saéculum**
ago, **abhínc**
agreed, it is, **cónstat**
agreement, **cōnsénsus**
aim at, to, **pétere**
Alas!, **Éheu! Heu!**
Alba Longa, of, **Albánus**
all, **cúnctī, ómnis, tótus**
All right! **Éstō!**
allow, to, **sínere**
allowed, it is, **lícet**
allowed, we are, **lícet nóbīs**
almost, **férē, paéne**
alone, **sólus**
along, **per**
Alps, the, **Álpēs**
already, **iam**
also, **átque, et, étiam, quóque**
altar, **ára**
although, **quámquam**
always, **sémper**
amazed, to be, **stupére**
amazement, **admīrátiō**
amazement (to), to be a source of,
     admīrātiónī ésse
among, **in, ínter**
amount, **vīs**
amount, a small, **paúlum**
amphitheater, **amphitheátrum**
amuse, to, **dēlectáre**
ancestors, **maiórēs**

ancient, **antíquus, príscus**
and, **ac, átque, et, -que**
and…not, **nec, néque**
and so, **ítaque**
Androcles, **Ándroclēs**
anger, **íra**
angry, **īrátus**
anoint, to, **únguere**
annoy, to, **vexáre**
annoyed, **vexátus**
annoying, **moléstus**
another, **álius, álter**
another time, at, **áliās**
anxious, **sollícitus**
anyone, if, **sī quis**
apartment building, **ínsula**
apologize, to, **sē excūsáre**
appear, to, **appārére**
Appian Way, **Vía Áppia**
apple, **málum**
appoint, to, **creáre**
approach, to, **adíre, appropinquáre**
approximately, **férē**
April, **Aprílis**
aqueduct, **aquaedúctus**
arch, **árcus**
arena, **aréna**
arise, to, **coorírī**
armed, **armátus**
arms, **árma**
around, **círcum**
aroused, **excitátus**
arrive (at), to, **adveníre, perveníre**
arrogant, **supérbus**
as, gen. + **caúsā, quam, ut**
as an honor, **honóris caúsā**
as…as possible, **quam** + superl. adj. or adv.
as fast as possible, **súmmā celeritáte**
as if, **quási**
as long as, **dum**
as quickly as possible, **quam celérrimē**
as soon as, **cum prímum, símulac**
as soon as possible, **quam prímum**
as yet, **adhúc**

ashes, **cínis**
Asia Minor, **Ásia**
ask, to, **interrogáre, requírere, rogáre**
ask (for), to, **póscere, quaérere**
ask oneself, to, **sē rogáre**
asparagus, **aspáragus**
assemble, to, **conveníre**
assume, to, **súmere**
astonished, **attónitus**
astounded, **attónitus, obstupefáctus**
at, **ad**
at last, **tándem**
at length, **tándem**
at night, **nóctū**
at the house of, **ápud**
Athens, **Athénae**
atrium, **átrium**
attack, **ímpetus**
attack, to, **adoríri, pétere**
attendant, bride's, **prónuba**
attentively, **atténtē**
augur, **aúspex**
August, **Augústus**
Augustus, **Augústus**
avoid, to, **nē, vītáre**
awake, to be fully, **ánimum recuperáre**
away, to be, **abésse**

B

Babyon, **Bábylōn**
back, **térgum**
bad, **málus**
badly, **mále**
bag, **fóllis**
bag (used for holding money), small, **sácculus**
baker, **pístor**
bakery, **pīstrínum**
bald, **cálvus**
ball, **píla, trígōn**
ball game involving three people, **trígōn**
band (of men), **mánus**

banquet, **convívium, épulae**
bar, **popína**
bark, a, **lātrátus**
bark, to, **lātráre**
barking, **lātrátus**
baths, **bálneae**
baths, public, **thérmae**
Baths of Nero, the, **Thérmae Nerōnéae**
battle, **púgna**
battle, to join, **púgnam commítterre**
bay (tree), **laúrus**
be, to, **ésse**
be done, to, **fíerī**
be made, to, **fíerī**
Be of good mind! **Bónō ánimō es!/éste!**
bear, to, **férre**
bearing, **incéssus**
beast, **béstia**
beat, to, **plángere, verberáre**
beat the breast, to, **péctus plángere**
beautiful, **cándidus, púlcher**
beautiful, most/very, **pulchérrimus**
beauty, **pulchritúdō**
because, **quod**
because of, **própter**
become, to, **fíerī**
becoming, it is, **décet**
bed, **léctus**
bed, to go to, **cúbitum íre**
bedroom, **cubículum**
before, **ánte, ánteā, ántequam, ápud**
beg, to, **obsecráre, ōráre**
began, I, **coépī**
beggar, **mendícus**
begin, to, **incípere, ōrdírī**
believe, to, **crédere**
beloved, **cárus**
beneath, **sub**
beseech, to, **obsecráre**
besides, **praetéreā**
besiege, to, **obsidére**
best, **óptimē, óptimus**
bestow, to, **cōnférre**
betroth, to, **dēspondére**

betrothal ceremony, **spōnsália**
betrothed man, **spónsus**
betrothed woman, **spónsa**
better, **mélior, mélius**
between, **ínter**
beware, to, **cavére**
bid, to, **iubére**
big, **mágnus**
big, such a, **tántus**
bigger, **máior**
biggest, **máximus**
bind up, to, **ligáre**
bird, **ávis**
birth, of/belonging to, **nātális**
birthday, **díēs nātális**
Bithynia, **Bīthýnia**
black, **níger**
blame, **cúlpa**
blame, to, **reprehéndere**
blaze, to, **ārdére**
blood, **sánguis**
bloodstained, **sanguíneus**
blue, **vénetus**
boat, small/ship's, **scápha**
body, **córpus**
bold, **aúdāx, temerárius**
bone, **os**
book, **líber**
bored (with), I am, **mē taédet**
bores, it, **taédet**
born, to be, **náscī**
both, **ámbō, utérque**
both…and, **et…et**
box, cylindrical, **fritíllus**
boy, **púer**
branch, **rámus**
brand, to, **inúrere**
brave, **fórtis**
bravely, **fórtiter**
bravely, most/very, **fortíssimē**
bread, **pánis**
break, to, **frángere**
breakfast, **iēntáculum**
breast, **péctus**

bride, **nóva núpta, spónsa**
bridegroom, **concubínus, spónsus**
bridge, **pōns**
briefly, **bréviter**
bright, **clárus, serénus**
bring, to, **addúcere, afférre, dēdúcere, dúcere, férre**
bring back, to, **reférre**
Bring help! **Fer/Férte auxílium!**
bring in, to, **afférre, intrōdúcere, ínférre**
bring out, to, **efférre**
bring to, to, **afférre**
bring together, to, **commíttere**
Britain, **Británnia**
British, **Británnicus**
Britons, **Británnī**
brother, **fráter**
brotherly, **frātérnus**
Brundisium, **Brundísium**
Brundisium, at, **Brundísiī**
Brundisium, from, **Brundísiō**
Brundisium, to, **Brundísium**
buffoon, **mímus**
build, to, **aedificáre, exstrúere**
building, **aedifícium**
bulk, huge, **mólēs**
bunch of grapes, **úva**
burden, **ónus**
buried, **sítus**
burn, to, **ārdére, incéndere**
burst, to, **rúmpere**
burst forth, to, **prōrúmpere**
burst in, to, **irrúmpere**
burst out, to, **prōrúmpere**
bury, to, **sepelíre**
busy, **negōtiósus, occupátus**
but, at, **aútem, sed**
butcher, **lánius**
buy, to, **comparáre, émere**
by, **ā, ab**
By Hercules! **Mehércule!**
by night, **nóctū**
bystanders, **adstántēs**

C

Caesar, **Caésar**
cage, **cávea**
Caligula, **Calígula**
call, to, **appelláre, vocáre**
call back, to, **revocáre**
call by name, to, **nōmináre**
call together, to, **convocáre**
call upon, to, **invocáre**
can, I, **póssum**
candelabrum, **candēlábrum**
candle, **candéla**
cane, **férula**
captain, **magíster**
captive, **captívus**
capture, to, **cápere**
care, **cúra**
carefree, **sēcúrus**
careful, be, to, **cavére**
carefully, **dīligénter**
careless, **néglegēns**
carelessly, **neglegénter**
carelessness, **neglegéntia**
carriage, **raéda**
carriage, light two-wheeled, **císium**
carried, having been, **véctus**
carry, to, **férre, portáre, véhere**
carry away, to, **auférre**
carry forward, to, **prōférre**
carry on, to, **gérere**
carry out, to, **efférre**
carry out funeral rites, to, **exséquiās dúcere**
carry X in front of Y, to, **praeférre**
cart, **plaústrum**
Carthage, **Carthágō**
carve, to, **scíndere**
castanet, **crótalum**
cat, **félēs**
catch, to, **cápere, excípere**
catch sight of, to, **cōnspícere**
catch the scent of, to, **olfácere**
catch up to, to, **cónsequī**
cause of anxiety (to), to be a, **cúrae ésse**

cause of confusion/turmoil, **túrba**
cause of fright, **trémor**
cave, **spēlúnca**
Cerberus, **Cérberus**
ceremony, official, **offícium**
certain, **cértus**
certain, a, **quídam**
certainly, **cértē, sā́nē**
chair, **sélla**
chance, by, **cā́sū, fórte**
changing-room, **apodytérium**
character, **mṓrēs**
chariot-racing, **lū́dī circénsēs**
charioteer, **aurī́ga**
charming, **lépidus, venústus**
Charon, **Chárōn**
chaste, **cástus**
Cheer up! **Bónō ánimō es!/éste!**
cheerful, **hílaris**
chest, **císta, péctus**
chicken, **púllus**
child, young, **ínfāns**
childhood, of, **puerī́lis**
childish, **puerī́lis**
children, **líberī**
chilled, **gelátus**
Christian, **Chrīstiánus**
Christians, the, **Chrīstiā́nī**
circus, in the, **circénsis**
Circus Maximus, **Círcus Máximus**
citizen, **cívis**
city, **urbs**
city, of the, **urbā́nus**
clan, **gēns**
clattering, **strépitus**
clean, **pū́rus**
clean, to, **pūrgā́re**
clear, **serḗnus**
client, **clíēns**
climb, to, **ascéndere**
climb down, to, **dēscéndere**
climb into (a carriage), to, **ascéndere**
cloak, **pállium**
closed, **claúsus**

closely, **atténtē**
clothed, **indútus**
clothes, **vestīménta**
clothing, **vestīméntum, véstis**
clothing, with torn, **scíssā véste**
cloud, **nū́bēs**
club, **fū́stis**
coachman, **raedárius**
coaxing manner, in a, **blándē**
cobweb, **aránea**
cold, **frígidus**
cold room (at baths), **frīgidárium**
collapse, **ruína**
collapse, to, **collā́bī**
comb, to, **péctere**
come, to, **veníre**
come down, to, **dēscéndere**
come forth, to, **prōdíre**
come near (to), to, **appropinquā́re**
Come on! **Áge!/Ágite!**
come to, to, **adíre**
come together, to, **cóngredī, convenī́re**
come upon, to, **invenī́re**
commander, **imperā́tor**
commands, **iússa**
comment on, to, **commemorā́re**
common, **commū́nis**
commotion, **tumúltus**
companion, **cómes**
company (of charioteers), **fáctiō**
compel, to, **cṓgere**
complete, to, **complḗre**
compose, to, **compṓnere**
conceal, to, **cēlā́re**
concerning, **dē**
condemn, to, **condemnā́re**
confer, to, **cōnférre**
confine, to, **continḗre**
confused, **perturbā́tus**
confusion, cause of, **túrba**
congratulate, to, **grātulā́rī**
conquer, to, **víncere**
conqueror, **víctor**
consider, to, **putā́re**

consul, **cónsul**
consult, to, **cōnsúlere**
continue, to, **prōférre**
contractor, **redémptor**
contrary, on the, **ímmō vérō**
conversation, **collóquium, sérmō**
converse, to, **cólloquī**
cook, **cóquus**
cook, to, **cóquere**
cool, **frígidus**
Cornelius, belonging to,
    Cornēliánus
cottage, **cása**
couch, **léctus, tórus**
count, to, **numeráre**
country, **rūs**
country, from the, **rúre**
country, in the, **rúrī**
country, to the, **rūs**
country estate, **rūs**
country house, **vílla**
country house and farm, **vílla rústica**
courier, **tabellárius**
course, first, **gustátiō**
course, second, **secúndae ménsae**
courteously, **cómiter**
cover, to, **operíre, tégere**
covered, **aspérsus**
covering, **strátum**
cow, **bōs**
cowardly, **ignávus**
crack, **ríma**
cracks, full of, **rīmósus**
crash, **frágor**
create, to, **creáre**
Cremona, **Cremóna**
Crete, **Créta**
crime, **scélus**
critically, **mortíferē**
cross, to, **tránsgredī**
crowd, **catérva, multitúdō, túrba**
crown, **coróna**
crown, to, **corōnáre**
cruel, **crūdélis**

cruelty, **crūdélitās**
crushed, **oppréssus**
cry, to, **flére, lacrimáre**
cudgel, **fústis**
cultivate, to, **cólere**
cup, **póculum**
Cupid, **Cupídō**
custom, **mōs**
cut, to, **scíndere**
cylindrical box, **fritíllus**

D

dagger, **púgiō**
daily, **cotídiē**
dance, to, **saltáre**
dancer, **saltátrīx**
danger, **perículum**
dangerous, **perīculósus**
dare (to), to, **audére**
dark, it gets, **advesperáscit**
daughter, **fília**
dawn, at, **prímā lúce**
day, **díēs**
day, by, **intérdiū**
day, during the, **intérdiū**
day, early in the, **máne**
day, every, **in díēs**
day, it is, **lúcet**
day before, on the, **prídiē**
day by day, **in díēs**
dead, **mórtuus**
dear (to), **cárus, grátus**
death, **mors**
debate, to, **ágere**
December, **Decémber**
decide, to, **cōnstitúere**
decided, it was, **plácuit**
decorate, to, **ōrnáre**
decorated, **ōrnátus**
decoration, **ōrnāméntum**
decrease, to, **minúere**
decree, **cōnsúltum**
dedicate, to, **cōnsecráre, dēdicáre**

dedicated, **déditus**

deed, good, **méritum**

deep, **áltus**

deep, the, **áltum**

defeat, to, **superáre**

defend, to, **dēféndere**

delay, to, **cessáre, morárī**

delight, **dēlíciae, volúptās**

delight, to, **dēlectáre**

delightful, **iūcúndus, suávis**

deliver a speech, to, **ōrātiónem habére**

Delos, **Délos**

demand, to, **póscere**

denarius (silver coin), **dēnárius**

depart, to, **discédere**

dependent, **clíēns**

desire, to, **cúpere, dēsīderáre**

dessert, **secúndae ménsae**

destroy, to, **dēlére, pérdere**

detestable, **abōmindándus**

devoted, **déditus**

devour, to, **dēvoráre**

Dido, **Dídō**

die, to, **dēcédere, ē vítā excédere, mórī**

different, **várius**

difficult, **diffícilis**

difficulty, **difficúltās**

difficulty, with, **vix**

dig up, to, **ērúere**

diligent, **díligēns**

din, **frágor**

dine, to, **cēnáre**

dining room, **trīclínium**

dinner, **céna**

dinner, to eat, **cēnáre**

direction, **pars**

dirge, **nénia**

dirty, **sórdidus**

discretion, **prūdéntia**

discuss, to, **ágere**

disembark, to, **égredī**

disgusting, **foédus**

dish, **férculum**

dishevel, to, **sólvere**

display, to, **praebére**

dissimilar, **dissímilis**

distance, in the, **prócul**

distant, to be, **abésse**

distinguished, **praeclárus**

ditch, **fóssa**

divert, to, **āvértere**

divide, to, **dīvídere**

divine, **dīvínus**

divulge, to, **ēnūntiáre**

do, to, **ágere, fácere, gérere**

do harm (to), to, **nocére**

do nothing, to, **cessáre**

doctor, **médicus**

dog, **cánis**

doll, **púpa**

done, to be, **fíerī**

Don't…! **Nólī/Nōlíte** + infinitive

door, **iánua**

doorkeeper, **iánitor**

door-post, **póstis**

doorway, **límen**

dormouse, **glīs**

doubt, **dúbium**

down from, **dē**

drag, to, **tráhere**

drag out, to, **extráhere**

drain, to, **hauríre**

draw, to, **stríngere**

draw a sword, to, **gládium stríngere**

dream, **sómnium**

drink, to, **bíbere**

drinking party, **commissátiō**

drive, to, **ágere, incitáre**

drive back, to, **repéllere**

drive off, to, **repéllere**

drive out, to, **expéllere**

drive to and fro, to, **iactáre**

driver, **raedárius**

drooping, **lánguidus**

drunk, **ébrius**

dry, **síccus**

dry, to, **tergére**

dung, **stércus**

dust, **púlvis**
dust (of the cremated body), **cínis**
duty, **offícium**
dwell, to, **habitáre**

E

each, **ómnis**
each (of two), **utérque**
eager, **inténtus**
earlier, **príus**
early, **mātúrē**
early in the day, **máne**
earth, **térra**
easily, **fácile**
easy, **fácilis**
eat, to, **ésse**
eat dinner, to, **cēnáre**
eating-house, **popína**
egg, **óvum**
eight, **óctō**
eighteen, **duodēvīgíntī**
eighteenth, **duodēvīcésimus**
eighth, **octávus**
either…or, **aut…aut, vel…vel**
elegant, **élegāns**
eleven, **úndecim**
eleventh, **ūndécimus**
embrace, **compléxus**
embrace, to, **ampléctī**
emperor, **Caésar, imperátor, prínceps**
encourage, to, **hortárī**
end, **fínis**
endure, to, **pátī**
energetic, **strénuus**
enough, **sátis**
enough time, **sátis témporis**
enter, to, **íngredī, iníre, intráre, introíre**
enthusiasm, **stúdium**
entire, the, **ūnivérsus**
entrance passage, **vestíbulum**
entrust, to, **commíttere**
envoy, **lēgátus**
epigram, **epigrámma**

epistle, **lítterae**
equip, to, **ōrnáre**
era, **saéculum**
eruption, **ērúptiō**
escape, to, **aufúgere, effúgere, ēvádere**
escort, to, **dēdúcere**
establish, to, **cóndere**
Eurydice, **Eurýdicē**
even, **étiam**
even if, **etiámsī**
evening, in the, **vésperī**
ever, **úmquam**
every, **ómnis**
every day, **cotídiē, in díēs**
evil, **málus**
examine, to, **īnspícere**
exceedingly, **váldē**
excellent, **óptimus**
excellently, **óptimē, púlchrē**
except, **nísi, praéter**
excited, **commótus**
exclaim, to, **exclāmáre**
excuse, to, **excūsáre**
exercise, to, **exercére**
exercise ground, **palaéstra**
exiled, **prófugus**
expel, to, **expéllere**
explain, to, **explicáre**
explain the situation, to, **rem explicáre**
express, to, **exprímere**
expression, **ōs, vúltus**
extinguish, to, **exstínguere**
eye, **óculus**

F

fabric, **téla**
face, **ōs, vúltus**
face down, **prónus**
facing, **cóntrā**
in fact, **ímmō vérō**
fair-skinned, **cándidus**
faith, good, **fídēs**
faithful, **fidélis**

fall, to, **cádere, lábī**
fall down, to, **concídere**
fall into/onto, to, **incídere**
fame, **fáma, glória**
family, **família, gēns**
family, belonging to the, **familiáris**
famous, **céleber, praeclárus**
famous, that, **ílle**
far, **lónge, prócul**
far off, **prócul**
farm, **fúndus**
farm manager, **vílicus**
fast, very, **celérrimē, celérrimus**
fast as possible, as, **súmmā celeritáte**
fastest, **celérrimus**
fat, **obésus, pínguis**
fate, **fátum**
father, **páter**
fault, **cúlpa**
favor, to, **favére**
fear, **métus, térror, tímor**
fear, paralyzed with, **métū exanimátus**
fear, to, **timére, verérī**
feared, to be, **timéndus**
fearful, **tímidus**
feast, **convívium, épulae**
February, **Februárius**
feed (on), to, **páscere, véscī**
feel, to, **sentíre**
female, **mulíebris**
female slave attached to a gladiatorial school, **lúdia**
fever, **fébris**
few, **paúcī**
field, **áger, cámpus**
fierce, **férōx, saévus**
fiercely, **ácriter, feróciter**
fifteen, **quíndecim**
fifteenth, **quíntus décimus**
fifth, **quíntus**
fiftieth, **quīnquāgésimus**
fifty, **quīnquāgíntā**
fight, **púgna**
fight, to, **pugnáre**
figure out, to, **conícere**

fill, to, **complére**
filthy, **foédus**
finally, **postrémō**
find, to, **veníre**
find out, to, **cognóscere**
finely, **púlchrē**
finger, **dígitus**
finish, to, **cōnfícere, fīníre**
fire, **ígnis, incéndium**
first, **prímus**
first, (at), **prímō, prímum**
first (of two), **príor**
first course, **gustátiō**
first day in the month, **Kaléndae**
fishpond, **piscína**
fit, to, **aptáre**
fitting, it is, **décet, opórtet**
five, **quínque**
five hundred, **quīngéntī**
five-hundredth, **quīngentésimus**
flame, **flámma**
flaming, **flámmeus**
flash, to, **micáre**
flee, to, **effúgere, fúgere**
flee for refuge, to, **cōnfúgere**
flesh, **cárō**
floor, **tabulátum**
floor, tiled, **pavīméntum**
flow, to, **mānáre**
flower, **flōs**
follow, to, **séquī**
follow (up), to, **súbsequī**
following, **pósterus, séquēns**
following day, on the, **postrídiē**
food, **cíbus**
foolish, **stúltus**
foot, **pēs**
footprint, **vēstígium**
for, **énim, nam**
for a short time, **paulísper**
for the sake of, **caúsā**
for the sake of an honor, **honóris caúsā**
forbid, to, **vetáre**
force, **vīs**

force, to, **cṓgere**
forehead, **frōns**
forest, **sílva**
forever, **in perpétuum**
forgetful, **ímmemor**
forgive, to, **excūsā́re**
form, **fṓrma**
former, the, **ílle**
fortunate, **félīx**
fortune (good or bad), **fortū́na**
Forum, the, **Fórum**
found, to, **cóndere**
four, **quáttuor**
fourteen, **quattuórdecim**
fourteenth, **quártus décimus**
fourth, **quártus**
frail, **īnfírmus**
free, **grā́tīs**
freedman, **lībértus**
freedom, **lībértās**
freedwoman, **lībérta**
frenzy, **fúror**
friend, **amī́ca, amī́cus, hóspes**
friendly way, in a, **cṓmiter**
frighten, to, **terrḗre**
frightened, **pertérritus, térritus**
frightening, **terríbilis**
from, **ā́, ab, dē̄, ē̄, ex**
from time to time, **intérdum**
front of, in, **ánte, ápud, cóntrā**
full, **plḗnus**
funeral, **fū́nebris, fū́nus**
funeral pyre, **rógus**
funeral rites, **exséquiae**
funeral rites, to carry out, **exséquiās dū́cere**
furnishings, **ōrnāménta**

G

Gades, **Gā́dēs**
game, **lū́dus**
game of bandits, **lū́dus latrunculṓrum**
games (in the Circus), **lū́dī, mū́nera**
gape, to, **stupḗre**

garden, **hórtus**
garden, small, **hórtulus**
garland, **corṓna**
garment, **véstis**
garum, **liquā́men**
gate, **pórta**
gatekeeper, **appā́ritor**
Gaul, **Gállia**
Gauls, the, **Gállī**
gentle, **mī́tis**
gently, **plácidē**
get, to, **accípere**
get ready, to, **comparā́re, parā́re, sē parā́re**
get up, to, **súrgere**
get well, to, **convaléscere**
gift, **dṓnum, mū́nus**
girl, **puélla**
give, to, **dáre, dōnā́re**
give as a gift, to, **dṓnō dáre**
give back, to, **réddere**
give favor (to), to, **favḗre**
give trust (to), to, **cōnfī́dere**
glad, **laétus**
glad, to be, **gaudḗre**
gladiator, **gladiā́tor**
gladiatorial show, **mū́nus**
gladly, **libénter**
glory, **glṓria**
go, to, **íre**
go around, to, **circumī́re**
go away, to, **abī́re, discḗdere**
go back, to, **redī́re, régredī**
go down, to, **dēscéndere**
go forward, to, **prōcḗdere, prṓgredī**
go in, to, **incḗdere, íngredī**
go into, to, **inī́re, intrā́re**
go in front, to, **praecḗdere**
go out, to, **égredī, excḗdere, exī́re**
go past, to, **praeterī́re**
go to sleep, to, **obdormī́re**
goal, **mḗta**
goblet, **pṓculum**
god, **déus**
goddess, **déa**

gods above, the, **súperī**

gold, **aúrum**

golden, **aúreus**

good, **bónus**

good, very, **óptimus**

Good heavens! **Dī immortálēs! Prō dī immortálēs!**

Good luck! **Fēlíciter!**

good sense, **prūdéntia**

Goodbye! **Válē!/Valéte!**

Goodness me! **Mehércule!**

goods, **bóna**

grab, to, **corrípere**

grab hold of, to, **arrípere**

graciously, **cómiter**

gradually, **paulátim**

grape, **úva**

gratitude, **grátia**

great, **mágnus**

great, so, **tántus**

great, very, **máximus, súmmus**

greater, **máior**

greatest, **máximus, súmmus**

greatest speed, with the, **súmmā celeritáte**

greatly, **magnópere, múltum**

Greece, **Graécia**

Greek, **Graécus**

Greeks, the, **Graécī**

green, **prásinus**

greet, to, **salūtáre**

greetings, **sálūs**

Greetings! **Ávē!/Avéte! Sálvē!/Salvéte!**

greetings, to send, **salútem dícere**

grief, **dólor**

groan, to, **gémere**

ground, **térra**

ground, on the, **húmī**

grow worse, to, **ingravéscere**

grunt, to, **grunníre**

guard, **cústōs**

guard, to, **custōdíre**

guess, to, **conícere**

guest, **hóspes**

guest (at a banquet), **convíva**

H

habit of, to be in the, **solére**

Hail! **Ávē!/Avéte!**

hair, **capíllī, crínēs**

hair, with long, **capillátus**

half-asleep, **sēmisómnus**

halt, to, **cōnsístere**

ham, **pérna**

hand, **mánus**

hand ball, heavy, **harpástum**

hand over, to, **trádere**

handsome, **púlcher**

happen, to, **fíerī**

happen to Sextus?, What will, **Quid Séxtō fíet?**

happens, it, **áccidit**

happily, **fēlíciter, laëtē**

happy, **félīx, laétus**

hard, **strénuē**

hare, **lépus**

harm, some, **áliquid málī**

harm, to, **laédere, nocére**

harm (to), to do, **nocére, violáre**

harmonious manner, **módus**

have, to, **habére**

he, **is, ílle**

head, **cáput**

head for, to, **pétere**

headband, **vítta**

health (good or bad), **valētúdō**

hear, to, **audíre**

"heart," heart, **ánima, cor**

heat, **aéstus, cálor**

heaven, **caélum**

heavy, **grávis**

Hello! **Sálvē!/Salvéte!**

helmet, plumed metal, **cássis**

help, **auxílium**

Help! **Fer/Férte auxílium!**

help, to, **adiuváre**

her (own), **súus**

herself, **sē**

herself, with, **sécum**

Hercules, **Hércules**

here, **hīc, hūc**

here, to, **hūc**

here and there, **hūc illúc**

Hesperia, **Hespéria**

Hey! **Ého!**

Hey there! **Héus!**

hide, to, **cēláre, latére, obscūráre,
   operíre**

high, **áltus**

highest throw of the knucklebones, the, **Vénus**

hill, **cóllis, mōns**

himself, **ípse, sē**

himself, with, **sécum**

hinder, to, **impedíre**

hipbone, **cóxa**

hire, to, **condúcere**

his (own), **súus**

hit, to, **feríre**

hold, to, **continére, habére, tenére**

hold back, to, **retinére**

hold out, to, **exténdere**

holiday, celebrating a, **fēriátus**

home, **dómum, dómus**

home, at, **dómī**

home, from, **dómō**

homeward, **dómum**

honor, **hónor**

honor, as an, **honóris caúsā**

honor, for the sake of an, **honóris caúsā**

hope, to, **spēráre**

Horace, **Horátius**

horn-player, **córnicen**

horrible, **abōmindándus**

hors d'oeuvre, **gustátiō**

horse, **équus**

host, **hóspes**

hot room (at baths), **caldárium**

hour, **hóra**

house, **dómus**

house of, at the, **ápud**

household, **família**

household, belonging to the, **familiáris**

household, members of the, **familiárēs**

household gods, **Lárēs**

How…! **Quam…!**

How…? **Quam…? Quō īnstrūméntō…?
   Quómodo…?**

How are you! **Quid ágis?**

How big…? **Quántus**

How many…? **Quot…?**

How much…? **Quántus**

How much…! **Quántum…!**

How much (in price)…? **Quántī…?**

however, **aútem, támen**

howl, to, **ululáre**

huge, **immánis, íngēns**

human, **hūmánus**

humble, **húmilis**

humor, good, **hiláritās**

hundred, a, **céntum**

hundredth, **centésimus**

hungry, to be, **ēsuríre**

hurl, to, **praecipitáre**

hurl oneself, to, **sē praecipitáre**

Hurray! **Eúge! Eúgepae!**

hurry, to, **festīnáre**

hurt, to, **dolére**

husband, **cóniūnx, marítus, vir**

hut, **cása**

hyacinth, of, **hyacínthinus**

I

I, **égo**

Ides, the, **Ídūs**

idle, to be, **cessáre**

if, **sī**

if anyone, **sī quis**

if…not, **nísi**

ignorant, to be, **ignōráre, nescíre**

ignore, to, **neglégere**

ill, **aéger**

ill, to be, **aegrōtáre**

ill in bed, to be, **languére**

illness, **mórbus**

immediately, **prótinus, státim**

immortal, **immortális**

Immortal Gods! **Dī immortálēs!**
important, it is, **ínterest**
in, **in**
in fact, **ímmō vérō**
in front of, **ápud**
in return, **cóntrā**
in vain, **frústrā, nēquíquam**
Indeed! **Íta vérō!**
indeed, **quídem, vérō**
infant, **ínfāns**
ingenuity, **ingénium**
inhabitant, **íncola**
inn, **caupóna**
inner organs of sacrificial animals, the, **éxta**
innkeeper, **caúpō**
innocence, **innocéntia**
inquire, to, **requírere**
inside, **íntrā**
insist, to, **urgére**
insistently, **veheménter**
insolence, **procácitās**
insolent, **prócāx**
instruct, to, **praecípere**
instruction, **mandátum**
instrument…, With what, **Quō īnstrūméntō…?**
instructress, **magístra**
intelligence, **ingénium**
intend, to, **in ánimō habére**
intent, **inténtus**
interrupt, to, **interpelláre**
into, **in**
invite, to, **invītáre, vocáre**
invoke, to, **invocáre**
irritability, **īrācúndia**
irritable, **īrācúndus**
island, **ínsula**
it, **ílle, is**
Italy, **Itália**
Ithaca, **Íthaca**
its (own), **súus**
itself, **ípse, sē**
itself, with, **sécum**
ivy, **hédera**

J

January, **Iānuárius**
join, to, **iúngere**
join battle, to, **púgnam commíttere**
joke, **iócus**
joke, as a, **per iócum**
journey, **íter**
joy, **gaúdium**
July, **Iúlius**
June, **Iúnius**
Juno, **Iúnō**
just as if, **támquam**

K

Kalends, the, **Kaléndae**
keen, **ácer**
keep, to, **retinére**
kill, to, **feríre, iuguláre, necáre, occídere**
kind, of this, **tális**
kindness, **benevoléntia**
king, **rēx**
kingdom, **régnum**
kiss, **ósculum**
kitchen, **culína**
know, not to, **ignōráre, nescíre**
know, to, **scíre**
known, **nótus**
knucklebones, **tálī**

L

lack, to, **carére**
ladle, small, **cýathus**
lady of the house, **dómina**
lame, **claúdus**
lament, **nénia**
lament, to, **plōráre**
lamp, **lucérna**
lamp-stand, **candēlábrum**
land, **áger, térra**
language, **língua**
lantern, **lantérna**

large, **mágnus**
large, very, **máximus**
last, **postrémus**
last, at, **tándem**
last laugh, to get the, **dērīdére**
lasting, **perpétuus**
late, **sérō**
later, **post, sérius**
latest, **sēríssimē**
Latin, **Latínus**
Latium, **Látium**
latter, the, **hic**
laugh, **rísus**
laugh (at), to, **dērīdére, rīdére**
laughable, **rīdículus**
laughter, **cachínnus**
laurel, **laúrus**
Lavinium, of, **Lāvínius**
lay down, to, **dēpónere**
lazy, **ignávus, íners**
lead, to, **dúcere**
lead back, to, **redúcere**
lead on, to, **addúcere**
lead out, to, **ēdúcere**
leader, **prínceps**
leading citizen, **prínceps**
leaky, **rīmósus**
leap down, to, **dēsilíre**
leap out, to, **exsilíre**
learn, to, **cognóscere, díscere**
learned, **ērudítus**
least, **mínimē**
leave, to, **égredī, excédere, línquere, proficíscī**
leave behind, to, **relínquere**
leave out, to, **omíttere**
left, **siníster**
length, at, **tándem**
less, **mínus**
lessen, to, **minúere**
let down, to, **dēmíttere**
let go, to, **míttere**
letter, **epístula, lítterae**
letter (of the alphabet), **líttera**
letters, **lítterae**

Liberalia, the, **Līberália**
lick, to, **lámbere**
lictor, **líctor**
lie, to, **iacére**
lie down, to, **recúmbere**
lie in hiding, to, **latére**
life, **víta**
lift, to, **tóllere**
light, **lévis, lūx**
light, it is, **lúcet**
like, **símilis**
like, to, **amáre**
like this, **tális**
likeness, **imágō**
line (of poetry), **vérsus**
lion, **léō**
listen to, to, **audíre**
literature, **lítterae**
litter, **lectíca**
litter-bearer, **lectīcárius**
little, **paúlus, párvulus**
little, a, **paúlum**
little by little, **paulátim**
live, to, **habitáre, vívere**
livestock, **pécus**
load, **ónus**
load, to, **oneráre**
located, **sítus**
locket, **búlla**
long, **lóngus**
long for, to, **dēsīderáre**
long time, for a, **díū**
longer, **diútius**
longest, **diūtíssimē**
Look (at)...! **Écce...!**
look after, to, **cūráre**
look around, to, **circumspícere**
look around at, to, **respícere**
look at, to, **spectáre**
look for, to, **pétere, quaérere**
look out for, to, **exspectáre**
loom, **téla**
loosen, to, **sólvere**
loud (voice, laugh), **mágnus**

love, **ámor**
love, to, **amáre, dīlígere**
loved (by), **grátus**
lower, to, **dēmíttere**
luck-charm, **búlla**
luckily, **fēlíciter**
lucky, **félīx**
lying down, to be, **iacére**

M

made, to be, **fíerī**
magnificent, **magníficus**
maiden, **vírgō**
main room in a house, **átrium**
make, to, **fácere**
make something agreeable to someone, to,
    persuādére
man, **hómō, vir**
man, old, **sénex**
manhood, of, **virílis**
manner, in a kindly, **clēménter**
manner…?, In what, **Quómodo…?**
Mantua, **Mántua**
manure, **stércus**
many, **múltī**
many, very, **plúrimī**
many-hued, **várius**
many years afterward, **múltīs post ánnīs**
March, **Mártius**
march in, to, **incédere**
mark, **méta**
marriage, **mātrimónium**
marry, to, **in mātrimónium dúcere, núbere**
Martial, **Mārtiális, Márcus Valérius**
marvelous, **mírus**
mask, **imágō**
mass, **mólēs**
master, **árbiter, dóminus, magíster**
master of the drinking, **árbiter bibéndī**
matter, **rēs**
may, we, **lícet nóbīs**
me, **mē**
me, with, **mécum**

means…?, By what, **Quō īnstrūméntō…?**
meanwhile, **intéreā**
measure (of wine), **cýathus**
meat, **cárō**
meet, to, **conveníre, occúrrere**
Megara, **Mégara**
members of the family of Cornelius, the, **Cornéliī**
members of the household, **familiárēs**
memorable, **memorábilis**
memory, **memória**
menacing, **mínāx**
mention, to, **commemoráre**
merchant, **mercátor**
Mercury, **Mercúrius**
merriment, **hiláritās**
messenger, **núntius**
method, **módus**
mid-, **médius**
midday, **merídiēs**
midday fighters, **merīdiánī**
middle of, **médius**
midnight, **média nox**
Milan, **Mediolánum**
mind, **ánimus**
mindful, **mémor**
mine, **méus**
mirror, **spéculum**
miserable, **míser, miserábilis**
miss, to, **dēsīderáre**
mistaken, to be, **erráre**
mistress, **dómina**
mix, to, **miscére**
mob, **túrba**
moment, at that, **tum**
money, **pecúnia**
month, **ménsis**
monument, **monuméntum**
mood, in a bad, **īrācúndus**
moon, **lúna**
more, **mágis, plúrēs, plūs**
more, all the, **éō mágis**
moreover, **aútem, praetéreā**
morning, in the, **máne**
mortally, **mortífere**

mortals, **mortálēs**

most, **máximē, plúrimī, plúrimum, plúrimus**

mother, **máter**

motionless, **immóbilis**

Mount Vesuvius, **Mōns Vesúvius**

mountain, **mōns**

mourn, to, **plōráre**

mouse, **mūs**

mouth, **ōs**

move, to, **commovére, movére**

move aside, to, **removére**

move one's home, to, **migráre**

move quickly to and fro, to, **micáre**

move toward, to, **admovére**

moved, **commótus**

much, **múltum, múltus**

much, so, **tántum**

much, too, **nímis**

much, very, **máximē, plúrimus**

mud, **lútum**

Mulvian Bridge, at the, **Mulviánus**

murder, to, **iuguláre**

murmur, **múrmur**

Muse, **Músa**

mushroom, **bōlétus**

mutter, to, **mussáre**

mutual, **mútuus**

my, **méus**

myrtle, **mýrtus**

N

name, **nómen**

name, to, **appelláre, nōmináre**

napkin, **máppa**

Naples, **Neápolis**

narrator, **nārrátor**

nation, **génus, nátiō**

nature, **nātúra**

near, **ad, própe**

near, to be, **adésse**

nearby, **própe, próximus**

nearly, **própe**

necessary, **necésse**

need, to, **carére**

neglect, to, **neglégere**

neighboring, **vīcínus**

neither…nor, **nec…nec, néque…néque**

neither…nor…anything,
     néque…néque…quídquam

Nero, of, **Nerōnéus**

never, **númquam**

nevertheless, **támen**

new, **nóvus**

next, **deínde, pósterus**

night, **nox**

night, at/by, **nóctū**

night, happening during the, **noctúrnus**

nine, **nóvem**

nineteen, **ūndēvīgíntī**

nineteenth, **ūndēvīcésimus**

ninth, **nónus**

no, **núllus**

No! **Mínimē (vérō)**

No indeed! **Mínimē vérō!**

no longer, **nōn iam**

no one, **némō**

no one, that, **nē quis**

noble, **nóbilis**

noise, **frágor, strépitus**

none, **núllus**

Nones, **Nónae**

noon, **merídiēs**

noon, at, **merídiē**

northern, **septentriōnális**

north wind, **áquilō**

nose, **násus**

not, **haud, nōn**

Not at all! **Mínimē vérō!**

not even, **nē…quídem**

not knowing, **ínscius**

not only…but also, **nōn módō…sed étiam**

not to, **nē**

not yet, **nóndum**

nothing, **níhil, nīl**

nothing, for, **grátīs**

nothing, to do, **cessáre**

notice, to, **animadvértere, sentíre**

November, **Novémber**
now, **iam, nunc**
nowhere, **núsquam**
number, **númerus**
nut, **nux**

O

obey, to, **pārére**
obliging, **officiósus**
obtain, to, **comparáre**
Ocean, **Ōcéanus**
October, **Octóber**
odds or evens (a game), **pār ímpār**
Odysseus, **Ulíxēs**
of course, **sáne**
offerings and rites in honor of the dead at the
    tomb, **ínfériae**
officer, **líctor**
often, **saépe**
often, more, **saépius**
often, most, **saepíssimē**
oil, **óleum, unguéntum**
ointment, **unguéntum**
old, **vétus**
olden times, of, **príscus**
olive, **olíva**
olive grove, **olīvétum**
omen, **ómen**
omit, to, **omíttere**
on, **in**
on account of, **ob, própter**
on time, **ad témpus**
once (upon a time), **ólim**
one, **únus**
one (of two), the, **álter**
one...another, **álius...álius**
one...the other, the, **álter...álter**
oneself, **sē**
only, **módo, tántum**
only just, **vix**
open, to, **aperíre**
open space, **área**

opposite, **cóntrā**
or, **an, aut, -ve, vel**
or if, **seu**
oration, **ōrátiō**
orator, **ōrátor**
order, **mandátum**
orders, **iússa**
order, to, **imperáre, iubére, praecípere**
Orpheus, **Órpheus**
other, **álius**
other (of two), the, **álter**
others, the, **céterī**
otherwise, **áliter**
ought, **dēbére**
ought, one, **opórtet**
ought to hurry, You, **Festīnáre tē opórtet**
our, **nóster**
out of, **ē, ex**
outside, **éxtrā, fórās**
outstanding, **exímius**
over, **súper**
overcome, **afféctus**
overcome, to, **superáre**
overseer, **vílicus**
overtake, to, **cónsequī**
overturn, to, **ēvértere**
overwhelm, to, **opprímere**
owe, to, **dēbére**
owner, **dóminus**
ox, **bōs**

P

pain, to be in, **dolére**
painstaking, **díligēns**
pairs, **pária**
Palatine Hill, belonging to the, **Palātínus**
palla, **pálla**
panic, in a, **trépidāns**
paralyzed, **exanimátus**
parent, **párēns**
parsley, **ápium**
part, **párs**
pastry with cheese filling, **scriblíta**

pasture, to, **páscere**
patron, **patrónus**
pawns (a game like chess), **latrúnculī**
pay attention to, to, **observáre**
pay the penalty, to, **poénās dáre**
peacefully, **plácidē**
pear, **pírum**
peasant, **rústicus**
pen, **stílus**
penalty, **poéna**
people, **géntēs, hóminēs, pópulus**
perform, to, **gérere**
perfume, **unguéntum**
perhaps, **fortásse**
peristyle, **peristýlium**
permanent, **perpétuus**
person related to one of another city by ties of
    hospitality, **hóspes**
person who fights wild beasts in the arena,
    bēstiárius
persuade, to, **persuādére**
persuade someone of something, to, **persuādére**
pest, **moléstus**
pick out, to, **súmere**
pick up, to, **repétere**
picture, **pictúra**
pig, **pórcus**
piper, **tībícen**
pirate, **pīráta**
place, **lócus**
place, to, **aptáre, locáre, pónere**
place, to that, **éō, illúc, quō**
place on, to, **impónere**
plague, **pestiléntia**
plain, **cámpus**
Plain of Mars on the outskirts of Rome, the,
    Cámpus Mártius
plain white, **púrus**
plan, **cōnsílium**
plan, to adopt a, **cōnsílium cápere**
play, to, **lúdere**
play ball, to, **pílā lúdere**
play *morra*, to, **dígitīs micáre**
pleasant, **cómmodus, iūcúndus**

please, **sī vīs, sīs**
please, to, **placére**
pleasing (to), **grátus**
pleasing to someone to do something, it is, **líbet**
pleasure, **volúptās**
pledge, to, **spondére**
Pluto, **Plútō**
poet, **poéta**
point out, to, **osténdere**
political faction, **fáctiō**
Pompeii, **Pompéiī**
poor, **paúper**
pork, **pórcus**
possessions, **bóna**
post, **pálus**
pour out, to, **effúndere**
praise, to, **laudáre**
prank, **iócus**
prank, as a, **per iócum**
prefer, to, **málle**
prepare, to, **paráre**
prepare oneself, to, **sē paráre**
prepared, **parátus**
present, to be, **adésse**
present somebody with something, to, **dōnáre**
presently, **mox**
press, to, **urgére**
press out, to, **exprímere**
pretend, to, **simuláre**
pretty, **púlcher**
prevent, to, **impedíre, nē**
previous, **príor**
previously, **abhínc, ánte, ánteā, príus**
price, **prétium**
priest, officiating, **aúspex**
prisoner, **captívus**
procession, funeral, **pómpa**
promise, to, **pollicérī, prōmíttere**
promise in marriage, to, **dēspondére**
promise solemnly, to, **spondére**
proper, **réctus**
properly, **réctē, ríte**
propose, to, **prōpónere**
proud, **supérbus**

provide, to, **praebére**
province, **prōvíncia**
public, **públicus**
Public Records Office, **Tabulárium**
pull, to, **tráhere**
punish, to, **pūníre**
punished, to be, **poénās dáre**
punishment, **poéna**
pupil, **discípulus**
pure, **mérus**
pushy, **prócāx**
put, to, **impónere, pónere**
put aside, to, **dēpónere**
put on, to, **indúere**
put out, to, **exstínguere**
Pyramus, **Pýramus**

Q

quarrel, **ríxa**
quarrel, to, **rixárī**
queen, **rēgína**
question, **rogátiō**
quickly, **celériter**
quickly, more, **celérius**
quickly, very, **celérrimē**
quiet, **submíssus**
quiet, to be, **tacére**
quiet, to keep, **quiéscere**
quietly, **plácidē**
Quirinal (Hill), **Quirīnális**

R

race, **génus**
race track, **currículum**
rain, **ímber**
raining, it is, **plúit**
rains, it, **plúit**
raise, to, **tóllere**
raisin-wine, **pássum**
rash, **temerárius**
rather, **ímmō**

rather than, **pótius quam**
reach, to, **adveníre, perveníre**
read, to, **légere**
read aloud, to, **recitáre**
read through, to, **perlégere**
ready, **parátus**
ready, to get, **comparáre, sē paráre**
ready to serve, **officiósus**
realize, to, **intellégere, sentíre**
really, **rē vérā, vérō**
rear, **térgum**
reason, **caúsa**
reason, for this, **quā dē caúsā**
reason…?, For what, **Quam ob caúsam…?**
rebellion, **rebélliō**
rebuke, to, **castīgáre**
recall, to, **revocáre**
recapture, to, **recípere**
receive, to, **accípere, excípere, recípere**
recently, **núper**
recite, to, **recitáre**
reciting, of, **recitándī**
reckless, **temerárius**
recline, to, **recúmbere**
recline (at table), to, **accúmbere**
recognition, **recognítiō**
recognize, to, **agnóscere**
records, **tábulae**
recount, to, **commemoráre**
recover, to, **recuperáre, repétere**
red, **russátus**
redo, to, **refícere**
reduce, to, **minúere**
refraining from, **ábstinēns**
refraining from wine, **vínō ábstinēns**
refuse, to, **nólle**
regain one's senses, to, **ánimum recuperáre**
regard for, to have special, **dīlígere**
region, **pars**
register, to, **īnscríbere**
reins, **habénae**
rejoice, to, **gaudére**
relative, **propínquus**

release, to, **immíttere**
reliability, **fídēs**
religious rites, **sácra**
remain, to, **manére, morárī**
remake, to, **refícere**
remember, to, **memóriā tenére**
remembering, **mémor**
remove, to, **exímere, removére**
render services (to), to, **mérita cōnférre**
renew, to, **renováre**
repeatedly, **idéntidem**
reply, **respónsum**
reply, to, **rescríbere, respondére**
report, to, **perférre, reférre**
reprimand, to, **castīgáre**
rescue, to, **erípere**
reserve, to, **reserváre**
resist, to, **resístere**
rest, **quíēs**
rest, the, **céterī**
rest, to, **sē quiétī dáre, quiéscere**
restore, to, **refícere**
return, **réditus**
return, to, **réddere, redíre, régredī**
returning, **rédiēns**
reveal, to, **ēnūntiáre**
revive, to, **renováre**
rhythmic manner, **módus**
ribbon, **vítta**
rich, **díves, pínguis**
riches, **dīvítiae**
right, **réctus**
right hand, **déxtra**
rightly, **réctē**
ring, **ánulus**
rise, to, **orírī, súrgere**
rise up, to, **coorírī**
road, **vía**
robber, **latrúnculus, praédō**
rod, **vírga**
rods (symbols of office), **fáscēs**
Roman, **Rōmánus**
Romans, the, **Rōmánī**
Rome, **Rōma**

Rome, from, **Rōmā**
Rome, in, **Rōmae**
Rome, to, **Rōmam**
room, **cubículum**
room (at baths), warm, **tepidárium**
rose, **rósa**
rouse, to, **excitáre**
route, **íter**
rub down, to, **dēfricáre**
ruin, **ruína**
rumble, **múrmur**
run, to, **cúrrere**
run about, to, **concursáre**
run ahead, to, **praecúrrere**
run away, to, **aufúgere, effúgere**
run into, to, **incúrrere**
run to and fro, to, **concursáre**
run together, to, **concúrrere**
run toward/up to, to, **accúrrere**
rush, to, **sē praecipitáre**
rush up, to, **concúrrere**

S

sacrifice, **sácra**
sacrifice, to, **sacrificáre**
sad, **trístis**
sad, to be, **dolére**
safe, **sálvus**
safe and sound, **incólumis**
said, (he/she), **áit, ínquit**
said, (he/she/it) is, **dícitur**
sail, to, **nāvigáre**
salt, **sal**
same, the, **ídem**
same as, the, **ídem ac**
same time, at the, **símul**
sand, **aréna, haréna**
sandal, **sólea**
savage, **saévus**
save, to, **serváre**
say, to, **dícere**
say goodbye, to, **valedícere**
says, (he/she), **áit, ínquit**

scalper, **locárius**
scarcely, **vix**
scholarly, **ērudítus**
school, **lúdus**
schoolmaster, **magíster**
scold, to, **reprehéndere**
scrap, **frústum**
scraper, **strígilis**
sea, **aéquor, áltum, máre**
sea, of/belonging to the, **aequóreus**
seat, **sélla**
seat (at games), imperial, **pulvínar**
second, **secúndus**
second, a/the, **álter**
second time, a, **íterum**
secretly, **clam, sēcrétō**
sedan chair, **sélla**
see, to, **vidére**
seek, to, **pétere, quaérere**
seem, to, **vidérī**
seen, to be, **vidérī**
seize, to, **arrípere, cápere, corrípere, occupáre, prehéndere, rápere**
self, **ípse**
sell, to, **véndere**
Senate, **senátus**
Senate House, **Cúria**
senator, **senátor**
senators, **pátrēs**
send, to, **míttere**
send away, to, **dīmíttere**
send fondest greetings, to, **salútem plúrimam dícere**
send for, to, **arcéssere**
send greetings, to, **salútem dícere**
send in, to, **immíttere**
send out, to **ēmíttere**
sensible, **prúdēns**
sensibly, **prūdénter**
September, **Septémber**
serious, **grávis**
servant, public, **appáritor**
serve, to, **servíre**
service, **múnus**

services, **mérita**
set down, to, **dēpónere**
set free, to, **līberáre**
set on fire, to, **accéndere, incéndere**
set out, to, **proficíscī**
seven, **séptem**
seventeen, **septéndecim**
seventeenth, **séptimus décimus**
seventh, **séptimus**
seventieth, **septuāgésimus**
several, **complúrēs**
shade (of the dead), **úmbra**
shadow, **úmbra**
shake, to, **movére**
shaky, **īnfírmus**
shape, **fórma**
shawl, **vēlámen**
she, **éa, ílla**
she-wolf, **lúpa**
sheep and cattle, **pécus**
sheet, **strátum**
shines, (it), **lúcet**
ship, **návis**
ship's boat, **scápha**
shop, **tabérna**
shore, **lítus, óra**
short, **brévis**
short time, for a, **paulísper**
should, (someone), **décet**
shout, **clámor**
shout, to, **clāmáre**
shout out, to, **exclāmáre**
shouting, **clámor**
show, to, **dēmōnstráre, mōnstráre, osténdere, praebére**
show into, to, **dēdúcere**
shrine of household gods, **larárium**
shut, **claúsus**
shut, to, **claúdere**
Sicily, **Sicília**
sides, from/on all, **úndique**
sight, **spectáculum**
sign, **sígnum**
sign, to, **obsignáre**

signal, **sígnum**

silence, **siléntium**

silent, **mútus**

silent, to become, **conticéscere**

silently, **tácitē**

similar (to), **símilis**

since, **cum, quandóquidem, quóniam**

sing, to, **cánere, cantáre**

sing together, to, **concínere**

sir, **vir óptime**

sister, **sóror**

sit, to, **sedére**

sit down, to, **cōnsídere**

situated, **sítus**

situation, **rēs**

six, **sex**

six (in throwing knucklebones), the, **séniō**

sixteen, **sédecim**

sixteenth, **séxtus décimus**

sixth, **séxtus**

skill, **ars, prūdéntia**

sky, **caélum**

slave, **sérvus**

slave-girl, **sérva**

slave-woman, **ancílla, sérva**

slavery, **sérvitūs**

sleep, **sómnus**

sleep, to, **dormíre**

sleep, to go to, **obdormíre**

sleepy, to be, **dormitáre**

slender, **grácilis**

slip, to, **lábī**

slippery, **lúbricus**

slow, **léntus, tárdus**

slowly, **léntē**

small, **párvulus, párvus, paúlus**

small, very, **mínimus**

small amount, a, **paúlum**

small boat, **scápha**

smaller, **mínor**

smallest, **mínimus**

smear with oil, to, **únguere**

smell, to, **olfácere**

smile, **rísus**

smile, to, **rīdére**

smoke, **fúmus**

smooth, **lévis**

snap (the fingers), to, **concrepáre**

snatch, to, **arrípere, rápere**

snatch away, to, **abrípere**

snatch from, to, **ērípere**

sniff, to, **olfácere**

snore, to, **stértere**

so, **íta, tam**

So be it! **Éstō!**

so many, **tot**

so much, **ádeō**

so that, **ut**

soft, **móllis, submíssus**

soldier, **míles**

solitude, **sōlitúdō**

some, **áliquī, nōnnúllī**

some…others…, **áliī…áliī**

someone, **áliquis**

something, **áliquid**

sometimes, **nōnnúmquam**

son, **fílius, nátus**

soon, **mox**

sorry, to be, **dolére**

soul, **ánima**

sound, **sónitus**

space, open, **área**

Spain, **Hispánia**

spare, to, **párcere**

spatter, to, **aspérgere**

spattered, **aspérsus**

speak, to, **lóquī**

speak to, to, **álloquī**

speak together, to, **cólloquī**

speaker, **ōrátor**

spear, **hásta**

spectacle, **spectáculum**

spectator, **spectátor**

speech, **ōrátiō**

speed, **celéritās**

speed, with the greatest, **súmmā celeritáte**

spend the night, to, **pernoctáre**

spill, to, **effúndere**

spin wool, to, **lánam tráhere**
spirits of the dead, **dī mánēs, mánēs**
spirits of the dead, to the, **dīs mánibus**
splash, to, **aspérgere**
split, to, **scíndere**
spotless, **pŭrus**
sprinkle, to, **aspérgere**
sprinkled, **aspérsus**
spur on, to, **incitáre**
squared, **quadrátus**
staff, **báculum**
stand, to, **cōnsístere, stáre**
stand by/near, to, **adstáre**
standing out, **éxstāns**
statue, **státua**
stay, to, **manére, morárī**
stay awake, to, **vigiláre**
steal, to, **surrípere**
stealthily, **fŭrtim**
steam, **vápor**
stick, **báculum, vírga**
stick, to, **haerére**
still, **adhŭc**
stock, **génus**
stola, **stóla**
stone, **lápis**
stone, of, **lapídeus**
stony, **lapídeus**
stop, to, **cōnsístere, dēsínere**
storm, **tempéstās**
story, **fábula, tabulátum**
story, funny, **iócus**
strange, **mírus**
stream, **rívus**
street, **vía**
strength, **vírēs**
strenuously, **strénuē**
strigil, **strígilis**
strike, to, **feríre, percútere**
strong, to be, **valére**
stronger, to grow, **convaléscere**
study, **stúdium**
study, to, **studére**
study (room), **tablínum**

stumble, to, **lábī**
stupid, **fátuus, stúltus**
subdued, **submíssus**
substitute, **suppositícius**
Subura, **Subúra**
such, **tális**
such a big, **tántus**
such a way, in, **íta**
such an extent, to, **ádeō**
such things, **tália**
sudden, **súbitus**
suddenly, **súbitō**
suffer, to, **pátī**
summer, **aéstās**
summon, to, **arcéssere**
sun, **sōl**
support, to, **favére**
sure, to be, **prō cértō habére**
Surely…not…? **Num…?**
surname, **cognómen**
sweet, **suávis**
swift, **céler**
swim, to, **natáre**
switch, **vírga**
sword, **gládius**

T

table, **ménsa**
tablets, **tábulae**
tail, **caúda**
take, to, **cápere, dúcere, súmere**
take away (from), to, **adímere, auférre**
take back, to, **redúcere**
take care of, to, **cūráre**
take off, to, **exúere**
take out, to, **extráhere**
take up, to, **súmere**
Talassius, **Talássius**
talk, **sérmō**
talk, to, **lóquī**
talkative, **verbósus**
tall, **áltus**

tame, **mānsuḗtus**
tamely, **plácidē**
tart with cheese filling, **scriblíta**
tasteful, **élegāns**
teach, to, **docḗre**
teacher, female, **magístra**
teacher, secondary school, **grammáticus**
tear, **lácrima**
tear, to, **scíndere**
tears, **flḗtus**
tell, to, **dícere**
tell (a story), to, **nārrā́re**
tell not to, to, **vetā́re**
tell the truth, to, **vḗra dícere**
temper, bad, **īrācúndia**
temple, **témplum**
ten, **décem**
tenant, **íncola**
tenth, **décimus**
terrified, **pertérritus**
terrify, to, **terrḗre**
territory, **áger**
terror, **térror, trémor**
test, to, **experī́rī**
testament, **testāméntum**
than, **quam**
thank, to, **grátiās ágere**
Thank you! **Grátiās tíbi ágō!**
thanks, **grátia**
that, **is, ílle, quī, quod, ut**
that…not, **nē**
that famous, **ílle**
that no one, **nē quis**
that place, to, **éō**
that which, **id quod**
That you hurry is fitting, **Festīnā́re tē opórtet**
the (more)…the (more), **quō…éō…**
their (own), **súus**
themselves, **ípsī, sē**
themselves, with, **sḗcum**
then, **deínde, índe, tum**
there, **éō, íbi, illū́c, quō**
there, from, **índe**
therefore, **ígitur, ítaque**

thief, **fūr**
thing, **rēs**
thing which, a, **id quod**
think, to, **cōgitā́re, putā́re**
third, **tértius**
thirteen, **trédecim**
thirteenth, **tértius décimus**
this, **hic, is**
this way and that, **hūc illū́c**
Thisbe, **Thísbē**
thorn, **stirps**
thorough, **díligēns**
thousand, a, **mílle**
thousands, **mília**
thousandth, **mīllésimus**
Thrace, **Thrácia**
three, **trēs**
three times, **ter**
threshing-floor, **área**
threshold, **límen**
through, **per**
throw, to, **conícere, iácere**
throw down, to, **dēícere**
throw into, to, **inícere**
throw of the knucklebones, the highest, **Vénus**
throw of the knucklebones, the lowest, **cánis**
throw out, to, **ēícere**
throw together, to, **conícere**
thrust, to, **inícere**
thus, **íta, sīc**
ticket, **téssera**
tiger, **tígris**
time, **témpus**
time, on, **ad témpus**
time to time, from, **intérdum**
timid, **tímidus**
tired, **dēféssus**
tired (of), I am, **mē taédet**
tired of something, it makes one, **taédet**
tires, (it), **taédet**
to, **ad, ut**
to here, **hūc**
today, **hódiē**
toga, **tóga**

toga, plain white, **tóga púra, tóga virílis**
toga of manhood, **tóga virílis**
toga with purple border, **tóga praetéxta**
together, **símul, únā**
toil, **lábor**
told, **nārrátus**
tomb, **monuméntum, sepúlcrum**
tombstone, **stéla**
tomorrow, **crās**
tongue, **língua**
too, **praetéreā**
too much, **nímis**
top, on, **súprā**
top of…, the, **súmmus**
torch, **taéda**
toss about, to, **iactáre**
touch, to, **tángere**
toward, **ad, érgā**
towel, **línteum**
towering, **éxstāns**
town, **óppidum**
town, of the, **urbánus**
trace, **vēstígium**
track, **vēstígium**
train, to, **exercére**
trainer, **lanísta**
travel, to, **íter fácere**
traveled, having, **véctus**
traveler, **viátor**
tray, **férculum**
tree, **árbor**
tremble, to, **trémere**
trident, **trídēns**
Trojan, **Troiánus**
Trojans, the, **Troiánī**
troublesome, **moléstus**
Troy, **Tróia**
true, **vérus**
truly, **vérō**
trumpet-player, **túbicen**
trunk, **císta**
trust, **fídēs**
trust, to, **cōnfídere, crédere**
try, to, **cōnárī, experírī, temptáre**

tunic, **túnica**
turmoil, cause of, **túrba**
turn, to, **vértere**
turn (around), to, **convértere**
turn aside, to, **dēvértere**
turn away, to, **āvértere**
turned, having, **convérsus**
turning, **convérsus**
turning post, **méta**
tutor, **paedagógus**
twelfth, **duodécimus**
twelve, **duódecim**
twentieth, **vīcésimus**
twenty, **vīgíntī**
two, **dúo**
two-wheeled carriage, light,
    císium

U

Ulysses, **Ulíxēs**
uncle, **pátruus**
unconcerned, **sēcúrus**
under, **sub**
understand, to, **intellégere**
undertaker, **vispíllō**
underworld, the, **ínferī**
undeservedly, **indígnē**
unforgetting, **mémor**
unhappy, **míser**
unhurt, **incólumis**
unless, **nísi**
unspeakable, **īnfándus**
untie, to, **sólvere**
until, **dónec**
unwilling, **invítus**
unwilling, to be, **nólle**
uproar, **tumúltus**
upset, to, **commovére, ēvértere**
urge, to, **hortárī**
urge on, to, **incitáre**
us, **nōs**
useful, **útilis**

V

varied, **várius**
various, **várius**
vegetable, **hólus**
vehicle, **vehículum**
veil, **vēlámen**
veil, orange (bridal), **flámmeum**
Venus, **Vénus**
verb, **vérbum**
Vergil, **Vergílius**
verse, **vérsus**
very, **ípse, máximē, váldē**
very much, **váldē, veheménter**
Via Flaminia, the, **Vía Flāmínia**
victor, **víctor**
victory, **victória**
vineyard, **vínea**
violent, **véhemēns**
violently, **veheménter**
virtuous, **cástus**
visit, to, **vīsitáre**
vital organs, **víscera**
voice, **vōx**

W

wagon, **plaústrum**
wait, to, **manére**
wait for, to, **exspectáre**
wake (someone) up, to, **excitáre, expergíscī**
wakened, **excitátus**
walk, to, **ambuláre**
walk(ing), **incéssus**
wall, **múrus, páriēs**
walls, **moénia**
wander, to, **erráre**
want, to, **cúpere, vélle**
war, **béllum**
warlike, **bélliger**
warm, **cálidus**
warn, to, **monére**
wash, to, **laváre**
wash overboard, to, **ēícere**

watch, to, **observáre, spectáre**
watch out, to, **cavére**
water, **áqua**
wave, **únda**
way, **módus**
way, in this, **íta, sīc**
way...?, In what, **Quómodo...?**
way and that, this, **hūc illúc**
we, **nōs**
weak, **īnfírmus**
wealth, **dīvítiae**
weapons, **árma**
wear, to, **gérere**
wearing the **toga praetexta, praetextátus**
weave, to, **téxere**
web, **téla**
wedding, of/for a, **nūptiális**
wedding-torch, **fax**
weep, to, **flére, lacrimáre**
weeping, **flétus**
welcome, to, **accípere, excípere, salūtáre**
well, **béne, fēlíciter**
well, to be, **valére**
well, very, **óptimē**
werewolf, **versipéllis**
What...? **Quī...?, Quid...?**
What a...! **Quam...!**
What sort of...? **Quális...?**
What time is it? **Quóta hóra est?**
What/Which (in numerical order)...? **Quótus**
wheel, **róta**
when, **cum, úbi, ut**
When...? **Quándō...?**
When...there, **Quō cum**
whenever, **cum**
where, **úbi**
Where...? **Úbi...?**
where...?, From, **Únde...?**
Where...to? **Quō...?**
whether...or..., **útrum...an...**
which, **quī**
Which...? **Quī...?**
Which (in numerical order)...? **Quótus**
while, **dum**

whip, to, **verberáre**
white, **albátus**, **álbus**, **cándidus**
who, **quī**
Who…? **Quis…?**
whole, the, **ómnis**, **tótus**
whole of, the, **ūnivérsus**
whom…?, With, **Quócum…?**
Whose…? **Cúius…?**
Why…? **Cūr…?**
wicked, **sceléstus**
wife, **cóniūnx**, **úxor**
wild beasts, involving, **bēstiárius**
will, **testāméntum**
willing, to be, **vélle**
win, to, **víncere**
wind, **véntus**
window, **fenéstra**
wine, **vínum**
wine, undiluted, **mérum**
wine sweetened with honey, **múlsum**
winning manner, in a, **blándē**
winter, **híems**
wipe, to, **tergére**
wise, **prúdēns**
wisely, **prūdénter**
wish, if you, **sī vīs**, **sīs**
wish, not to, **nólle**
wish, to, **optáre**, **vélle**
wit, **sal**
with, **ápud**, **cum**
with difficulty, **vix**
without, **síne**
wolf, **lúpus**
woman, **fémina**, **múlier**

woman, married, **mātróna**
woman, of a, **mulíebris**
womanly, **mulíebris**
woman's outer-garment, **stóla**
wonder, to, **mīrárī**, **sē rogáre**
wonder (at), to, **admīrárī**
wonderful, **mīrábilis**, **mírus**
woods, **sílva**
wool, **lána**
word, **vérbum**
work, **lábor**
work, to, **labōráre**
worried, **sollícitus**
worse, **péior**, **péius**
worst, **péssimē**, **péssimus**
wound, **vúlnus**
wound, to, **vulneráre**
wrestle, to, **lūctárī**
wretched, **míser**, **miserábilis**
write, to, **scríbere**
write back, to, **rescríbere**
write down, to, **reférre**
write in, to, **īnscríbere**

Y

year, **ánnus**
Yes! **Íta vérō!**
yesterday, **héri**
you, (sing.) **tū**, (pl.) **vōs**
young child, **ínfāns**
young man, **aduléscēns**
your, (sing.) **túus**, (pl.) **véster**
youth, **aduléscēns**, **iúvenis**

INDEX OF GRAMMAR

INDEX OF CULTURAL INFORMATION